POULTRY PRODUCTION

POULTRY PRODUCTION

BY

DR. SUNIL KUMAR DAS

B.V.Sc. & A.H. (First Class)

M.V.Sc. (First Class First)

Veterinary Surgeon, Government of West Bengal

Additional Block Animal Health Centre, Manikpara,

Midnapore-721513, West-Bengal (India)

CBS

CBS Publishers & Distributors Pvt. Ltd.

New Delhi • Bengaluru • Chennai • Kochi • Kolkata • Mumbai

Hyderabad • Nagpur • Patna • Pune • Vijayawada

Dedicated to the memory of my revered father

ISBN: 81-239-0265-4

First Edition: 1994
Reprint: 2006, 2008, 2011, 2016

Published by:
Satish Kumar Jain for CBS Publishers & Distributors Pvt. Ltd.,
4819/XI Prahlad Street, 24 Ansari Road, Daryaganj, New Delhi - 110002
delhi@cbspd.com, cbspubs@airtelmail.in • www.cbspd.com
Ph.: 23289259, 23266861, 23266867 • Fax: 011-23243014

Corporate Office: 204 FIE, Industrial Area, Patparganj, Delhi - 110 092
Ph: 49344934 • Fax: 011-49344935
E-mail: publishing@cbspd.com • publicity@cbspd.com

Branches:
- ***Bengaluru:*** 2975, 17th Cross, K.R. Road, Bansankari 2nd Stage, Bengaluru - 70 • Ph: +91-80-26771678/79 • Fax: +91-80-26771680 E-mail: cbsbng@gmail.com, bangalore@cbspd.com
- ***Chennai:*** No. 7, Subbaraya Street, Shenoy Nagar, Chennai - 600030 Ph: +91-44-26681266, 26680620 • Fax: +91-44-42032115 E-mail: chennai@cbspd.com
- ***Kochi:*** Ashana House, 39/1904, A.M. Thomas Road, Valanjambalam, Ernakulum, Kochi • Ph: +91-484-4059061-65 Fax: +91-484-4059065 • E-mail: cochin@cbspd.com
- ***Kolkata:*** 6-B, Ground Floor, Rameshwar Shaw Road, Kolkata - 700014 Ph: +91-33-22891126/7/8 • E-mail: kolkata@cbspd.com
- ***Mumbai:*** 83-C, Dr. E. Moses Road, Worli, Mumbai - 400018 Ph: +91-9833017933, 022-24902340/41 • E-mail: mumbai@cbspd.com

Representatives:
- Hyderabad: 0-9885175004
- Patna: 0-9334159340
- Vijayawada: 0-9000660880
- Nagpur: 0-9021734563
- Pune: 0-9623451994

Printed at:
Neekunj Print Process, Delhi

PREFACE

Poultry is one of the most important disciplines of Animal Husbandry and Vetrinary Science. Poultry provides protective food in human nutrition in the form of egg and meat and employment opportunities at various level. Poultry farming has become increasingly populat both in rural and urban areas. It has made tremendous tride and has to an extent taken the shape of an industry. Poultry farming has become very encouraging enterprise in modern India for small farmers, landless labourers and educated unemployed as well as for big enterpeuners, keeping birds on industrial pattern. Person engaged in poultry production needs suffient knowledge of poultry rearing. Keeping this fact in mind 'Poultry Production' is published to help the under graduate and post graduate students of different agricultural and veterinary colleges and also for the extension workers, poultry farmers and those who are going to adopt the poultry farming. In this book, I do not claim credit for any original contribution on the subject. Rather it should be viewed as a concise collection of various topic from different books, bulletins, journals, scientific paper etc dealing with poultry production.

The author feels pround to express his deep sense of indebtedness and gratitude to his respected teacher Dr. R.K. ghosh, Professor, Dr. A.K. Chakraborty, Reader and Head and Dr. T.K. Mondal, Lecturer, Department of Pharmacology and Toxicology, Faculty of Vetrinary and Animal Sciences, Bidhan Chandra Krishi Viswa Vidayalya, Nadia, West Bengal for their guidance, kind help and constructive criticism during the preparation of this manuscript.

The author is also thankful to his senior Dr. A. Pal for reviewing the chapter on poultry diseases and class mate Dr. N. Ghosh, Veterinary Surgeon, Government of West Bengal for material help.

The author extends his thanks to Mr. R. Haldar for neat typing of the manusctipt.

Lastly, the author express his gratitude to Messrs CBS Publishers and Distributors for bringing out this book so efficiently and promptly.

'SUDHIR BHAWAN' **SUNIL KUMAR DAS**

Surekalna, Burdwan
Pin : 713408
January, 1, 1993

CONTENTS

INTRODUCTION

The Poultry refers to domesticated birds which are reared for their flesh, eggs and feathers and it includes a number of avain species such as chicken, duck, turkey, geese, swan, guinea - fowl, pea fowl, pigeons, phesants, quail etc. But it is very often used synonymously to chicken.

Chicken and ducks are kept for commercial production of both eggs and meat. Poultry keeping is a source of pleasure as well as income from selling of eggs and meats. Poultry farming has become increasingly popular both in urban and rural areas. Poultry farming has become very encouraging enterprise in modern India for small farmers, landless labourers and educated unemployed as well as for big enterpeuners keeping birds on industrial pattern. Poultry farming has made tremendous stride and has to an extend taken the shape of industry. The bayard poultry farming started fading out with the establishment of commercial enterprise. The per capita availability is hardly around 20 eggs, one of the lowest in the world as against per capita consumption of about 200 eggs per annum as recommended by the nutritional Advisory council. This would given an idea about the scope for increasing poultry production in the country.

IMPORTANCE OF POULTRY FARMING

(i) Poultry provides eggs and meats. Eggs are highly nutritive supplementary food.

(ii) Economic improvement of rural masses can be substantially achieved with introduction of scientific poultry farming.

(iii) Poultry farming as a tool of socio-economic transformation of rural poor has immenses potential in country like India where more than 50 percent of the people live below the proverty line.

(iv) Poultry farming requires less investment to start the enterprise.

(v) Eggs and table birds can be sold for cash as the pullet starts layining at about six months of age and broiler gets ready for marketing at the age between 6 to 8 weeks. As a result quick return can be expected from the investment. Poultry farming also provides continuous source of income.

(vi) Poultry farming in rural area has become a cottage industry.

(vii) Poultry and poultry products provide protein rich food at low cost.

(viii) Mixed famring with poultry provides opportunity for additional income during dull season of crop cultivation.

(ix) Poultry farming provides employment opportunity directly or indirectly.

Table : 1 Average composition of edible protein of Rice, cow milk, eggs and chicken meat.

Component (Percentage)	Rice	Cow Milk (Whole	Eggs		Chicken meat
			Hen	Duck	
Water	13.0	87.3	74.0	71.0	66.0
Protein	7.1	3.5	12.4	13.0	20.2
Fat	1.1	3.5	11.7	14.5	12.2
Carbohydrate	78.0	5.0	0.9	0.5	-
Fibre	0.7	-	-	-	-
Ash	0.8	0.7	1.0	1.0	1.0
Calories per 100 gms.	359	65.0	163.0	189.0	200.0

Source : Chatfield Charlotte, 1953 & 1954, Food composition Table, Minerals and Vitamins for International use, pp 25-28, F.A.O., Rome.

(x) Poultry manure is an extremely rich source of nitrogen and organic matter. Poultry manures contain 1.0 - 1.8% N, 1.4 - 1.8% P_2O_5 and 0.8 to 0.9 % K_2O. The built up litter is a balance organic manures. It contains 3% N, 2% P_2O_5 and 2% K_2O.

CHARACTERISTICS OF PULTRY BIRDS

(i) Poultry birds are warm blooded tetrapods.
(ii) Body is covered with epidermal feathers.
(iii) Neek flexible and long.
(iv) The forelimbs are modified as wings for flight. Feather provided with muscles at the base.
(v) The hind limbs are covered with scales and armed with claws.
(vi) The beak is horny and there is no teeth in the mouth.
(vii) Hind limbs are modified for walking or hopping in land and perching on trees and in aquatic or semiagualic birds for swiming.
(viii) The digestive system includes a crop and gizzard, the rectum opens into a cloaca, no urninary bladder. The ureters communicate with cloaca, the urine is semifluid.
(ix) The heart is four chambered with two atria and two verticles, a arotic arch persists. No sinus venosus.
(x) Eyes with sclerotic plates with eyelids and nictiating membrame.
(xi) Ear, the auditory aperture lies behind the eye sunk deep hidden by feathers.
(xii) The sexes are separate; the rightovary and oviduct are usually absent. The fertilization is internal.
(xiii) Eggs with large yolks is covered by a hard cell.

(xiv) The fertile egg undergoes metablastic segmentation. The incubation of egg is external.

(xv) There are twelve pair of cranial nerves

ORIGIN

India and nehbouring countries are the ancestral home of the present day domestic fowl. Jungle fowls *(Gallus gallus)* are believed to be the ancestors of modern domestic breed. The birds are domesticated for the production of meat and eggs. Poultry keeping in India was a predominantly a village occupation. The indigenous breeds are small in size and lay small number of small size egg. Scientific poultry keeping was first advocated by christian missoneries towards the beginning of the 20th century A.D. Their exotic breeds are supperior to those of the desi fowls in their performance. The poultry production gets preference in different five years plan. Organised effort to develop poultry in the country was started in 1957, when second Five year plan was launched.

ECONIMICS OF POULTRY PRODUCTION

Poultry birds provide food materials rich in animal protein comparatively at a low cost. We should have conditions that are necessary for poultry production. We should considered the followings for the economics of poultry production.

1. **Site Selection :** Open place having transport facitities should be selected for poultry farming. The place must be high enough to facilitate drainage.
2. **Capital :** Capital is prime need of starting poultry farm. Capital is needed according to size of the farm and their management practices. Capital invested by poultry farmer is good for running poultry farming profitability. The national Agricultural Bank and rural Development (NABARD) along with commercial and Cooperative banks financing a large number of Poultry Scheme all over the country for increasing production of eggs and broiler meats.
3. **Construction of houses :** Poultry house should be constructed most economically by using locally available materials. The poultry house should be constructed according to the system of poultry rearing.
4. **Collection of improved breeds :** Collection of improved breed is of prime need for starting poultry farm. Poultry breeding research centre have evolved the following layer and broiler stocks.

   Layers : H H -260, BH - 78, ILM - 90, ILR - 90, ILI - 80, Bhubaneswar Rhodo White, Arbor Aeres Leghorn cross, XL - Link, Starcross - 288 etc.

   Broilers : Ven Cobb, Bab cobb, IBL - 80, B-77, IBB - 83, CA-42, Starbro CA - 47 etc.
5. **Vaccine and medicine :** The healthy and disease free stock produces

THE POULTRY BIRDS ARE CLASSIFIED AS FOLLOWS :

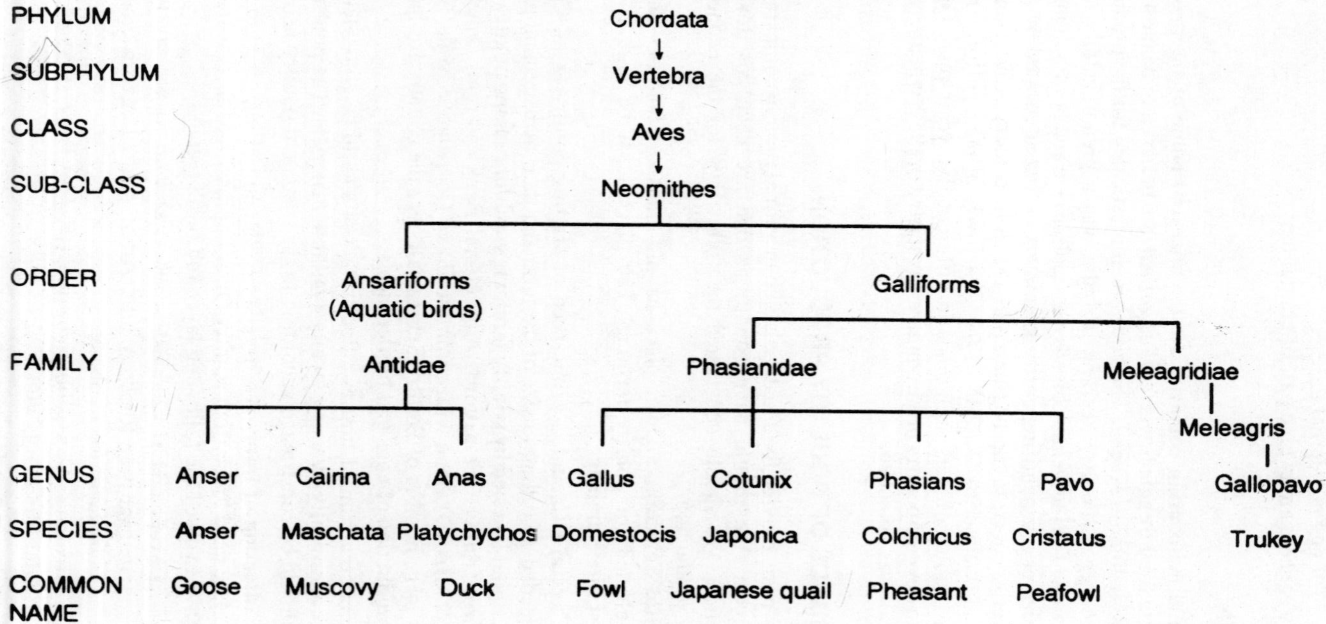

eggs and meats satisfactorily. Vaccine and medicine should be available as and when needed. Administration of proper vaccine and medicine is essential for prevention and treatment of diseases respectively.

6. **Feed :** Egg and meat production is closely related with sypply and consumption of balanced feed. The balanced food for the poultry is now available in the market. Major ingredients such as rice Polish, til oil cake etc. are available abundance at remunerative price. These can be used in poultry feed.
7. **Selection of birds :** Selection of birds is essential to cut down the expenditure and to prevents the disease. The weak, disease affected and unproductive birds should be culled or selled out if possible. The laying birds should be culled after completion of first year of laying.
8. **Marketing :** The present market demand as well as the remunerative price for poultry products should act as incentive for Poultry production. There should be regular marketing of eggs and meats.
9. **Skill and training :** Skill in Poultry production is helpful for becoming a successful poultry farmer. In most of the states and Union Territories, regular training is being given to the farmers in Poultry Production. All the states Poultry farms are in a position to cater necessary practical training to develop skill in Poultry Production. The agricultural universities through out the country and Tamil Naidu veterinary and animal Sciences University, Central Avian Research Institute (CARI) at Izatnagar offer undegraduate, postgraduate and doctorate degree in different areas of poultry production respectively. The college of veterinary science. Andhra Pradesh Agricultural University at Hydrabad offers Post graduate and Doctoral degree in Poultry sciences. The central Poultry training Institute at Hessarghata (Bangalore) Provides a series of short term course in various aspects of poultry production to trainees coming from different states of India as well as from foreign countries.

Table 2. Egg production of Poultry

Species	Age of Sexual maturity (month)	Production of Egg/year	Weight of eggs (Grams)
Chicken	5-6	240	57
Duck (Pekin)	7-8	110-175	80
Goose	24	15-50	215
Turkey	7	105	85
Quail (Bob white)	8-10	150-200	9
Guine fowl	10-12	40-60	9
Pheasant	8-10	40-60	32
Pigeon	6	12-15	17

Table 2 (a) Average Vitamin content of Rice, Cowmilk, Chicken eggs and Meat.

Vitamins	Amount (Per 100 grms)			
	Rice	Cowmilk	Chicken egg	Chicken meat
Vitamin-A (I.U.)*	-	140	1300	-
Vitamin-D (I.U.)	-	-	50	-
Vitamin-B1 (mg)	0.22	0.04	0.26	0.2
Vitamin-B2 (mg)	0.04	0.18	1.3	0.3
Vitamin-B4 (mg)	-	0.31	2.5	0.7

* I.U. = International Unit.

Table 2 (b) Nutrient content in the dropping of different animals (in percent)

Fresh manures	N	P_2O_5	K
Poultry manure	1.0-1.8	1.4-1.8	0.8-0.9
Dung :			
(i) Cattle	0.3-0.4	0.1-0.2	0.1-0.3
(ii) Sheep	0.5-0.7	0.4-0.6	0.3-1.0
(iii) Horse	0.4-0.5	0.3-0.4	0.3-0.4
Urine :			
(i) Cattle	0.9-1.2	tr.	0.5-1.0
(ii) Human	0.6-1.0	0.1-0.2	0.2-0.3
(iii) Sheep	1.5-1.7	tr.	1.8-2.0
Night Soil	1.0-1.6	0.8-1.2	0.2-0.6

Tr. = Trace

1

POULTRY BREEDING

Breeding is mating animals so at to secure in the progeny improvements of qualities such as vigour, habit, longivity, plumage, egg production, egg quality, meat quality, rapidity of growth etc. The genes that produce these qualities exist in minute cells of the body and are increased or decreased by selection and breeding. The genes are the basic units of inheritance and are arranged lineraly on the chromosomes. Genes are the carrier of heredity. Chromosomes occur in pairs in the living organism and passed from one generation to the next through gamets viz ovum and sperm. ovum and sperm contain half number of chromosomes. But the chromosomes number is restored in the Zygote due to union of sperm with ovum at the time of fertilization.

Gregor Johan Mendal (1822-1884), an Austrian monk, has been called the father of genetics. He established the fundamental laws of genetics. Genetics is the science which seeks to account for the likenesses and differences among organisms related by descent. It is because of heredity that these organism resembles each other.

HYBRID CROSSING AND ITS PRINCIPLE

Monohybrid Cross

A monohybrid cross is one which involves two parents differing in single trait or character. In one of this experiments, Mendel crossed homozygous tall pea plant with homozygous dwarf pea plant. In this cross one parent has the dominant gene for tall (TT) and the other the recessive genes for dwarf (tt). The members of the F_1 generation received a dominant gene (T) from one parent. They are all tall, and the gene for tall is dominent.

Parents :	O	TT	x	tt	O+
		(Tall)		(Dwarf)	

Tt . . . . F_1
(Tall)

F_2

Gements O	T	t
T	T T (Tall)	T t (Tall)
t	T t (Tall)	I t (Dwarf)

O+

The members of the F_1 generation were allowed to self pollinate; 75 percent of the progeny in F_1 generation had dominate character (i.e. tall) and 25 percent of them has recessive charactr (i.e. dwarf). The ration was 3 : 1.

Here the phenotype ratio is 3 tall, one dwarf (tt) and the genotype ratio is 1 TT (Tall), 2 Tt (tall) and 1 tt (dwarf)

Similarly dominance and recessive character was observed for several other traits in poultry like rose comb and single comb, normal plumage, silkly plumage etc.

Parents : O RR (Rose Comb) x rr O+ (Single Comb)

Rr . . . . F_1
(Rose Comb)

F_2

Gaments O	R	r
R	RR (Rose Comb)	Rr (Rose Comb)
r	Rr (Rose Comb)	rr (Single Comb)

O+

The frequent of occurance of rose Comb and single comb in F_2 generation is expected to be 3 : 1.

From the various monohybrid crosses made by Mendel, the following principles were formulated :

(i) **Principal of unit character :** The inheritance of vrious traits by an organism is controlled by factors (genes) and these factors occur in paris.

(ii) **Principle of dominant :** One gene in an allelic pair may 'hide' the expression of the other member of the pair.

(iii) **Principle of segregation (Mendel's First Law) :** In the formation of hapolid reproductive cells such as gametes and spores, only one gene of each allelic pair is received bỳ gamete or spore.

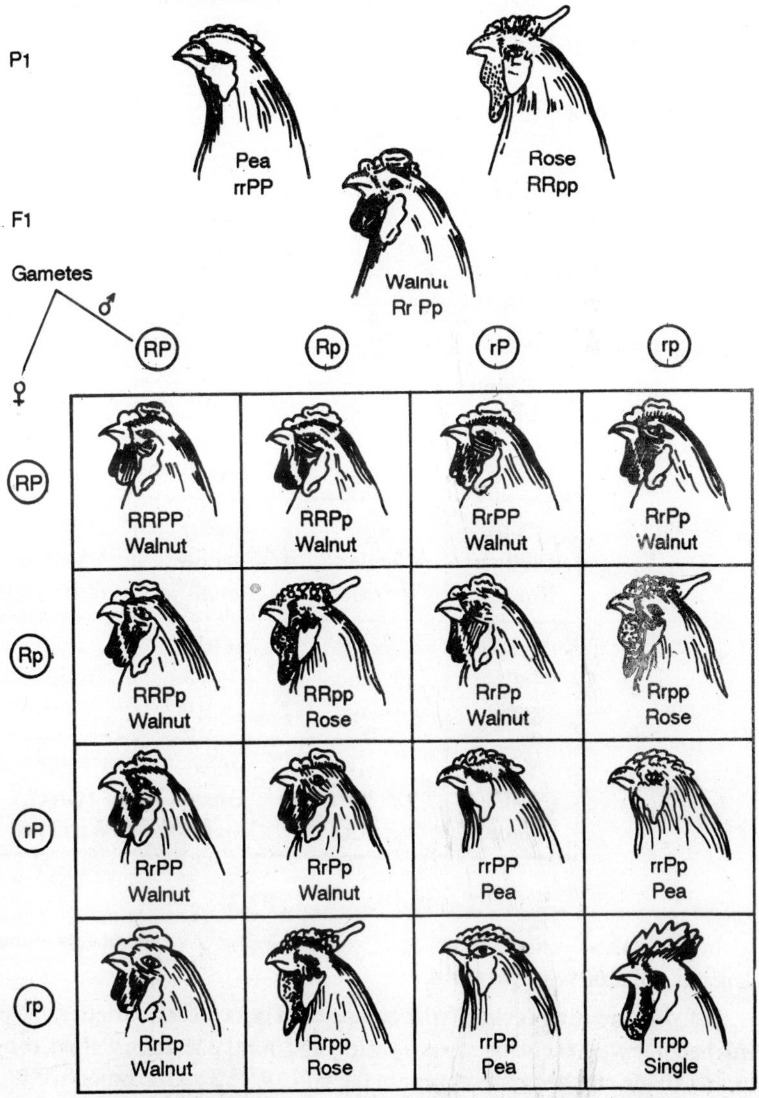

Fig. 1.1. Mating between pea combed and Rose combed fowl (dihybrid with interaction of factors).

Dihybride cross and the Mendeism Principles of Independent Assortment

A dihybrid cross is one which involves two parents differing in two traits. Mendel crossed two parent pea plant, one of which was homozygous for yellow round peas (YYRR) and the other homozygous for green wrinkled pea (yyrr).

YYRR (Yellow round) — yyrr (Green wrinkled)

(YR) (yr)

F_1 . . . . (Yr Rr)

F_2 Gametes → O	YR	Yr	yR	yyr
O^+ YR	YRR (Yellow Round)	YYRr (Yellow Round)	YyRR (Yellow Round)	YyRr (Yellow Round)
Yr	YYRr (Yellow Round)	YYrr (Yellow Wrinkled)	YyRr (Yellow Round)	Yyrr (Yellow Wrinkled)
yR	YyRR (Yellow Round)	YyRr (Yellow Round)	yyRR (Green Round)	yyRr (Green Round)
yr	YrRr (Yellow Round)	Yyrr (Yellow Wrinkled)	yyRr (Green Round)	yyrr (Green Wrinkled)

The ratio was 9 : 3 : 3 : 1.

In pea plants, yellow colour of seed is dominant over green and round shaped is dominat over wrinkled.

In fowls, crossing between rose combed and pea combed varieties, the F_1 birds become walnut combed, a new variety and in F_2 generation walnut, rose, pea and single combed birds appear in the ratio of 9 : 3 : 3 : 1 respectively as shown in Fig No. 1.

In fowls some breeds have feathered shank while some breeds have unfeathered shank. Crossing between feathered shank and unfeathered shank, the F_1 breeds become feathered and in F_2 generation feathered and unfeathered shank are found in the ratio of 15 : 1 as shown in cheeker board.

FFSS (Feathered) ffss (Unfeathered)

FS fs

F_1 . . . . FfSs

Feathered

F_2 Gametes → O	FS	Fs	fS	fs
O+ FS	FFSS Feathered	FFSs Feathered	FfSS Feathered	FfSs Feathered
Fs	FFSs Feathered	FFss Feathered	FfSs Feathered	Ffss Feathered
fS	FfSS Feathered	FfSs Feathered	ffSS Feathered	ffSs Feathered
fs	FfSs Feathered	Ffss Feathered	ffSs Feathered	ffss Un-feathered

This is modified dihybrid ratio in which two pairs of factors (i.e. F and S.) are responsiible for the expression of the character of shank.

SELECTION METHODS

Selection is the process of identifying and deciding the birds which will be allowed to breed for the next generation. The selection of sound breeding stock is essential for successful running of poultry firm. Followings are the two system of selection :

(i) **Individual selection or Mass selection :** Individual selection is very effective for improvement of highly heritable traits like body weight, and egg weight and is based on their phenotypic performance. Here the performance test is employed which is a measure of the phenotypic value of iindividual candidate for selection. Performance testing can usually be done on the farm under normal management condition. It is one of the most accurate test. The large birds on the average produce bigger eggs than small birds. So the body size must be maintained in order to maintain good eggs size. Good body size is essential in breeding stock.

(ii) **Family selection :** The economic traits like egg production, viability etc have low heritability and in this the phenotype is not a reliable indicator of genotype. Selection in such a cases is done on the basis of family averages, either dam family average or sire family average. This is called family selection. It has two phases :

(a) **Progenytesting :** Progeny testing attempts to evaluate the parents on the basis of phenotype performance of their progency. One of most advantages of progeny testing is high accuracy when many progency are obtained. But it is a time consuming process.

(b) **Shib testing :** The breeder birds are selected on the basis of appearance and performance of their brothers and sisters. This is called shibtesting. The traits like egg production is expressed in one sex (i.e. females) only and the coockerels are selecteed on the performance of their sisters.

However, the successful breeding programme should include a combination of individual selection and family selection.

SYSTEMS OF BREEDING :

1. **Inbreeding :** Inbreeding is the mating of related biird as brother to sister, son to dam and sire to daughter for some desirable quality or character.

Inbreeding can again be divided into following groups :

Inbreeding	*Line breeding*	Half brother and sister or mating of animals more distantly related e.g. cousin mating.
	Closs breeding	Sire to daughter, son to Dam, Full brother and sister.

(a) **Line breeding :** Line breeding involves the repetition of certain desiirable individuals and their offspring in successive generation for production of inbreed strains. It is systematic inbreeding and it promotes uniformity in character.

(b) **Close breeding :** Close breeding is mating of closely related birds such as borther to sister or sire to dauthter or son to dam. Continued inbreeding for several generation may results in lowered fertility, and hatchability, delayed maturity, slow growth, decrease in egg production, increased mortaility etc. Close breeding should be used only when both parents are outstanding invividuals.

2. **Out-crossing :** Out crossing is opposite of inbreeding i.e. mating together of individuals of two different srains or families of same breed or variety. The offspring of such a mating is known as the out cross. The main objective of outcrossing is to overcome the deleterious effect of inbreeding.
3. **Cross breeding :** Cross breeding is the breeding together of pure breed males of one breed with pure bred females of another breed. Cross breeding usually results in better hatchability, livability and growth rate of chicks. Hybrid vigour resulting from cross breed utilised extensively in broiler production. Cross breeding requires maintenance of two or more pure breed for the production of cross breed stocks.
4. **Grading :** Grading is the mating of pure breed males with non-decscript females and offspring for generation after generation. It is the method commonly followed to effect improvements. The offspring of such a mating is called grades.

METHODS OF MATING

Methods of mating used have marked influence on fertility and consequently on the offsprings obtained. Flock and pen mating are the two commonly used methods of mating. Stud mating and artificial insemination are also used for research work.

1. **Pen mating :** In pen mating, a number of hens are mated with a single male. Single sire pen mating permits maintenance of predigree by use of trapnests. Fertility is not as good as in case of flock mating. This is because certain hens may not like the particular cock and vice-versa.
2. **Flock mating :** In flock mating, number of males and females are bred together. It is also known as mass mating. Usually one male is sufficient for 10-15 females for egg type stock. Excellent fertility is usually obtained.
3. **Stud mating :** In stud mating, male is confined in a small coop or pen and females are brought individually to male for matting purpose. This method is employed when hens are kept in laying batteries and a valuable male is being used as breeder. But this method needs more labour involvement than flock mating.

4. **Artificial insemination :** Artificial insemination is employed in the birds which are housed in cages. This method has become more common in turkey breeding where poor fertility is often encountered. The turkey are not able to mate properly due to their large body size and wide breast.

2

EXTERNAL PARTS OF POULTRY

Fowls and ducks are collectively called Poultry. The external part of fowls and ducks are similar of Pigeon. They have also two pair of wings. But they can not fly like piegeon.

STUDY OF EXTERNAL PARTS OF A COCK.

The body of cockis divided into three parts; head, neck and fleshybody.

HEAD

Head is the anterior part of the body. The head terminates anteriorly in a pointed beak. The beak consists of the toothless jaw enclosed in hony coverings. Near the base of the upper beak are the slitlike nostril. The prominant laterally located eyes are provided with upper and lower lids and a nictiting membrrane. Behind the eye on either side is an external auditory aperature which is the entrance to the external meatus. This meatus or cana, leads to the tympanic membraane. There are two redlike pendulous muscles on either side of the eye or near the beak. They are called wattle. Earlobe is present on either side of ear. The colour of ear lobe in leghorn and minorca is white and other breeds have the ear lobe red in colour.

NECK

Neck connects the head and fleshy body. The long neck is flexible. There are some narrow feather on both sides on the neck, which is known as neck hackles.

FLESKY BODY

All parts of the body except eye, beak and some part of leg is covered with feathers. Cock have two wings and two legs. The fore limbs and hind limbs are converted into wings and legs respectively. The fore limbs are adapted for flying and hind limbs are adapted for walking and perching. The feathers in the wing meant for flight are called flight or Primary feathers. They are 10 in number. The feathers that are seen at the time of closing of wings of cock are called secondary feathers. Sickled hackles present on tail. The uper and lower portion of the leg is called thigh and shank respectively.

Most breeds of chicken have four toes, three extending forward and one backward. Spur develop in the adult cock.

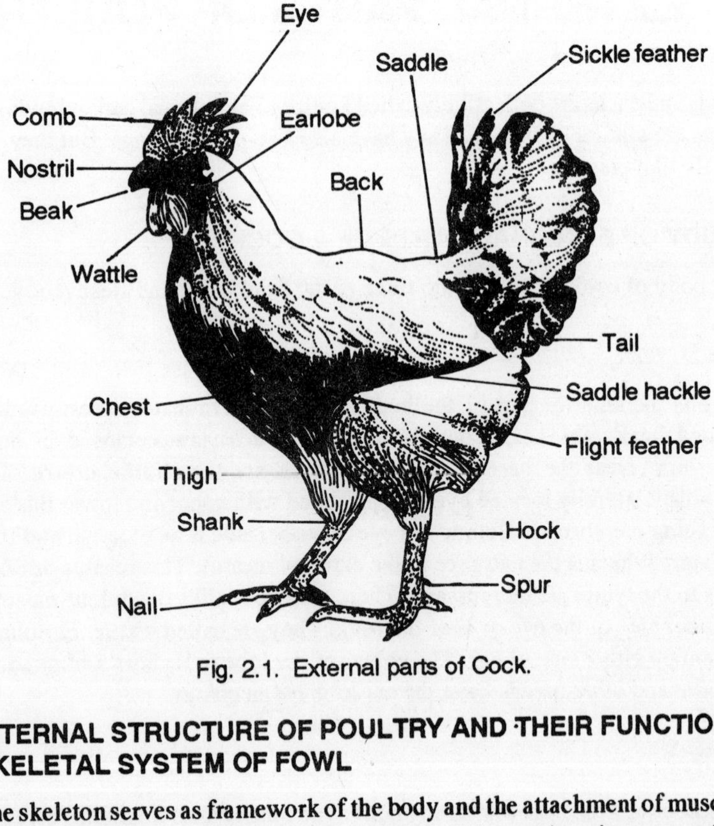

Fig. 2.1. External parts of Cock.

INTERNAL STRUCTURE OF POULTRY AND THEIR FUNCTIONS SKELETAL SYSTEM OF FOWL

The skeleton serves as framework of the body and the attachment of muscles, protects vital organs, holds the bone marrow and contains air spaces which aids in respiration and flight although domestic fowls are no longer prone to the skill of flying. The bone marrow produces the red blood cells and part of white blood cells. The skeleton is composed of an exoskeleton and endoskeleon. The exoskeleton consists of feathers, scales, claws and hony covering of the beak. The endoskeleton, made of bone and cartilage, is divided into axial and appendicular portion.

A. **Axial Skeleton :** The axial skeleton is composed of the skull, vertebral column, ribs and sternum. The skull is small in comprison with other parts of the body. Brain remains inside the skull. The vertebral column consists of cervical, thoracic, lumbar, sacral and caudal vertebrae. There are fourteen cervical vertebrae. Two beaks remains in the front side of the head. Nostril remains on the upper beak which is fixed and attached with the skull. The lower beak is free and there is great freedom of movement as and when needed. The neck is long and flexible. The cervical vertebrae fit upon each other in such a way that there is a great freedom of the head and neck for eating, care of plumage, defence and other purposes. The keel bone is long and thin. The breast bone or sternum is very large and projects back beyond the ribs, forming a part of abdominal floor. The ribs are attached above to the spinal column and below to the sternum.

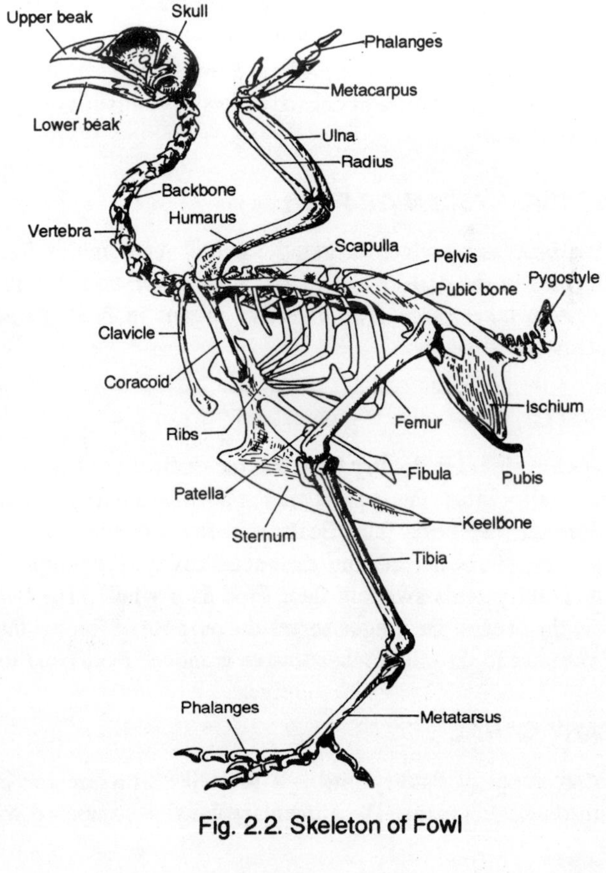

Fig. 2.2. Skeleton of Fowl

B. **Appendicular Skeleton :** The appendicular skeleton is composed of one pair of leg bones and wing bones, pectoral girdle and pelvic girdle.

(i) **Bones of wing :** The forelimb of the bird is converted into wing. The name of long bone of the wing is humerus. The radius and ulna form the bone of forearm. Carpus, metacarpus and phalanges bones are attached with radius and ulna respectively forming wing. The flight feathers and primary feathers are attached with ulna and metacarpus respectively.

(ii) **Bones of the legs :** There is a long bone in the thigh of the leg of the bird which is called femur. The femur is stout and cylinderical. The tibia or 'drumstick' is the largest bone of the limb. The poultry birds have four toes, three extending forward and one backyard. There are one metatarsus in the leg and phalanges in four toes. The phalanges are rudimentary. The hind limbs are adapted for walking and perching.

(iii) **Pectoral girdle :** The pectoral girdle consists of the scapula or shoulder blades, the coracoids and the claricle or 'wish bone'.

(iv) **Pelvic girdle :** The pelvic girdle is formed by the union of ileum, ischium and pubis or lay bones. It makes reproduction or egg laying less difficult.

THE DIGESTIVE SYSTEM OF FOWL.

Digestion is a process by which breaking down of the complex feeds into simple molecules in the digestive tract and their absorption into blood or lymphatic system takes place. The digestive organs in Poultry and their function are discussed below :

MOUTH PARTS

Teeth and lips are absent in Poultry bird. It is the distinctive character of the mouth of the poultry birds. These parts are replaced by a horny mandible on each jaw, forming the beak. The Beak, a horny structure, is the main prehensile organs. The beak leads into the buccal cavity. The tongue is large and pointed. Poultry birds swallow their food as a whole. The barb like Projections at the back of the tongue serves the purpose of forcing the grain toward the entrance to the gullet when tongue is moved from front to back.

ALIMENTARY CANAL

The alimentary canal of Poultry bird is a tube like structure and extents starting from mouth to cloaca. The alimentary canal is composed with the following parts :

(i) **Mouth** : The narrow opening in front of the head of poultry bird surrounded by two beak is called mouth. Teeth are absent in mouth of poultry bird.

(ii) **Buccal cavity** : The large chamber inside the mouth is called buccal cavity. Buccal cavity is surrounded by beak. The tongue is shaped like the barbed head of an arrow which lies on the floor of buccal cavity.

(iii) **Pharynx** : The last part of buccal cavity is called pharynx. This part in the poultry bird is not so prominent. The pharynx opens into esophagus.

(iv) **Oesophagus** : The oesophagus or gullet is distinguished by its enormous expansibility. Oesophagus leads to the crop. Food from the mouth directly passes to the crop through pharynx and oesophagus.

(v) **Crop** : The crop is an enlargement of the oesophagus. The crop acts as a reservoir of food and softening the ingested food. Food is generally sent to the stomach as needed by contraction of the wall of the Crop.

(vi) **Proventiculus** : Proventiculus, the glandular stomach in chicken is a fusiform organ. The proventiculus which is the anterior tube with thcik glandular wall secreting the gastric juice for digestion of food. The oesophagus terminates at the proventriculus which is relatively small. The food stays here for a short time.

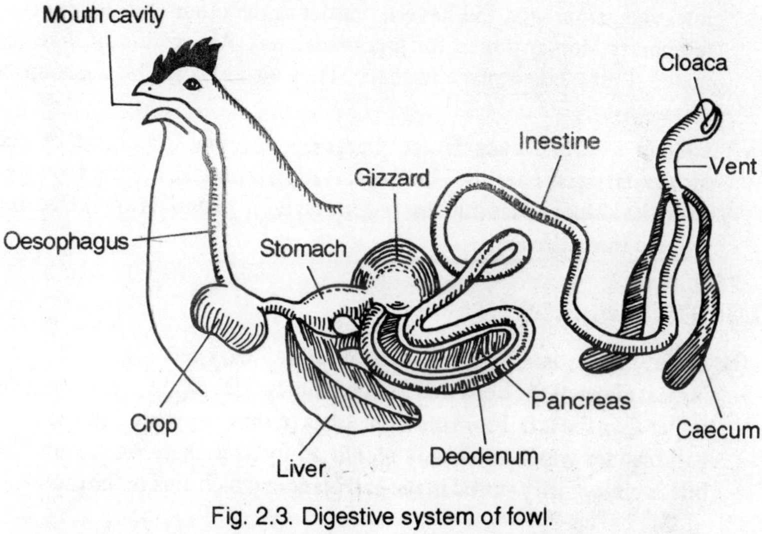

Fig. 2.3. Digestive system of fowl.

(vii) **Gizzard** : Gizzard, the muscular stomach of chickens, is the largest single organ of the body. It is discshaped and acts as the grinding organ. The Gizzard is highly muscular and its narrow lumen is lined by horny epithelium. It grinds the ingested feed into small particles with the help of strong muscles and grits present in it. The shell grits provided in the diets increase the efficiency of gizzard. The gizzard is reddish green colour and located just back of the proventriculus.

(viii) **Small intestine :** The small intestine begins at the exit from the gizzard and it is relatively of uniform caliber throughout its length. The small intestine cosists of three parts, namely duodenum, jejunum and ileum. The duodenum which form the distinct loop and the ileum which is thrown into numerous coil. Enclosed within the loop of the duodenum lies the pancreas which is the pink gland with three ducts.

The small intestine receives pancreatic juice from the pancreas and bile from liver. The small intestine in chicken shows both peristaltic and segmenting movements which aid in the expulsion of undigested food through caeca and rectrum. It is about 2½ feet long in mature bird.

(ix) **Large intestine :** The large intestine extends from caeca to cloaca. Colon and rectum are the two parts of large intestine which can not be differentiated in chicken as in mammals. The rectum opens into the cloaca. No digestion takes place in the rectum. But some amount of water is reabsorbed in the large intestine and rectum.

(x) **Caeca :** The junction of the ileum and the rectum is marked by a pair of very short blind tubes called the 'Caeca'. Caeca open into the intestine as one end but have no outlet at the other end. It serves as temporary storage organ for faecal material. Absorption of digested material may taked place in them. They also aids in the digesion of fibre.

(xi) **Cloaca :** The Cloaca is the Common opening for digestive and urogenital tracts of birds. The faecal material from the rectum and urine from the kidneys pass into this organ and these materials are mixed and excretd through vent.

DIGESTIVE GLANDS

(i) **Liver :** Liver is a large, several lobed and dark red organs. It is the largest gland of the body and divided into two lobes, the right being the larger than the left. From the right lobes of the liver is enlarged to form gall bladder which can easily identified by its dark green colour. The bile is temporarily stored in the gall bladder which aids in the digestion of fat.

(ii) **Pancreas :** The Pancreas lies between the limb of the duodenum. It is relatively long in birds than in mammals. Pancreas secreate a fluid which is known as pancreatic juice. It contains proteolytic, amylotytic and lypolytic enzyme. The Pancreatic juice empties into the duodenum.

(iii) **Spleen :** Spleen is found near the liver. it is a round reddish body and its diameter ranges from one forth to half inch. The spleen is concerned with the destruction of red blood corpuscles and construction of white blood corpuscles.

Table 2.1. Digestive Process in Poultry

Region	Secretion (Seereted by)	Enzyme	Enzyme acts on or Function	End product of Digestion
Mouth	Saliva (Salivary glands)	Amylase is seereted in some birds but most domestic birds lack this enzyme	Starch, dextrins lubricates the blood	Dextrins Glucose
Crop	Mucus		Lubricates and softens food	
Proventriculus	Gastric juice and acids (Chiefly HCl) walls of stomach Mucus	Pepsin Lipase (in carnivores) Amylase	Protein Fat	Proteoses, Poly- Peptides, Pep- tides, Higher fatty acids and glycerol Coating of Stomach lining of lubrication of food
Gizzard			Grit in the gizzard increases the motility and grinding action of the gizzard and the digestibility of coarse feed	Ground foods Reduced particle size

Contd.

Region	Secretion (Seereted by)	Enzyme	Enzyme acts on or Function	End product of Digestion
Duodenum (Small intestine)	Pancreatic juice (Pancreas)	Trypsin chymotry-psin	Proteins, Pro-teoses, pep-tones and peptides	Peptones, pep-tides Amino acids
		Amylopsin (Amy lase)	Starch, dextrine	Maltose, Dex-trins
		Steapsin (Lipase)	Fats	Higher fatty acids and glycerol
		Carboxy-peptidase	Peptides	Amino acids and peptides
		Collagenase	Collagen	Pepptides
		Cholesterol esterases	Cholestorol	Cholesterol esterified with falty acids
	Bile (Liver)		Fats	Emulsion of fats (soap Glycenl)
Small intestine	Intestinal juice (Screreted by intestinal wall)	Peptides (erepsin)	Paptides	Amino acids and dipeptides
		Sucrease (invertase)	Sucrose	Glucose and fructose
		Maltase	Maltose	Glucose
		Lactase	Lactose	Glucose and galactose
		Polynucleo-tidase	Nucleic Acid	Mono nucleotides
Caeca		A limited amount of microbial activity	Cellulose, poly saccha-rides, starches, sugars	Volatile fatty acids. Micro-bial protein, Vitamins-B Vitamin-K

Source : Poultry (1992), by G.C. Banerjee; Oxford & IBH Publishing Co. Pvt. Ltd.

REPRODUCTIVE SYSTEM OF FOWL

Poultry bird is an unisexnal animal. There is difference in male and female in Poultry bird. Male bird (Cock) have male reproductive system and female bird have female reproductivoe system. Male and Female birds are recognised by their body confirmation. Cock is big in size and they have sickle feather of big size. On the otherhand, the hen is small in size and they have no sickle feather. The comb of the cock is big in size in comparison to hen.

MALE REPRODUCTIVE SYSTEM

Male reproductive system produces male reproductive cells (Spermatoza), which when introduced into the oviduct of the female is being used for fertilization of eggs. Besideas, it produces also a hormone which influences sex character.

The male reproductive system consists of a pair of testes, Vas deferens, and papillae or rudimentary corpulatory organs.

TESTES

The testes are a pair of oval yellowish white bodies attached to the anterior ends of the kidneys in the dorsal body wall. The left testes is usually larger than right one. The testes are responsible for the production of spermatozoa and male sex hormone, testosterone. The testes consists of seminiferous tubles, rete tubules and vas efferentia. The spermatozoa are carried out of the testes by the seminal fluid which is also produced in the testes.

Each testes give rise to a relatively short epididymis, through which the spermatozoa pass to a long coiled duct, the dunctus deferens. Unlike the mammals, the testes never descend into an outer sac, called scrotum.

VAS DEFERENS

A narrow convoluted duct called the vas deferens (wolffian duct) arises from the inner border of each testes. This runs backwards parallel to the ureter to open independently into the middle compartment of the cloaca. The duct is dilated at the posterior end to form a seminal vesicle for storage of spermatozoa. The vas deferens convey the spermatozoa and seminal fluid from the testes to the cloaca.

PAPILLAE

The papillae is located on the median ventral portion of one of the transverse fold of the cloaca. The sperm are introduced by the papillae into the oviduct in the cloacal wall of the female at the time of mating with female.

CLOACA

The cloaca is the common opening for digestive and urogenital organ. It is the enlarged section of the alimentary canal which connects the large inestine and vent. The vent is the enlarged opening of the cloaca. The sperms from the testes pass through this organ and are eliminated through vent.

FEMALE REPRODUCTIVE SYSTEM

The female reproductive system includes ovary and oviduct.

OVARY

The female chick has two ovaries and two oviducts. The left ovary and its oviduct in adult birds are well developed and functional. But the right ovary and its oviduct remain present as a rudiment. The left ovary is situated at the cephalic end of the left kidney which is attached to the body wall through meso-ovarian ligament. The left ovary is covered with follicles containing at different stages of maturity which is large at the breeding season. The ova escape from the ovary into the body cavity or coelom from which they are caught by expanded funnel of the left oviduct. At the maturity, some of ova develop and ovulate to form egg. Each ova or yolk contains a germinal disc from whcih the embryo develops.

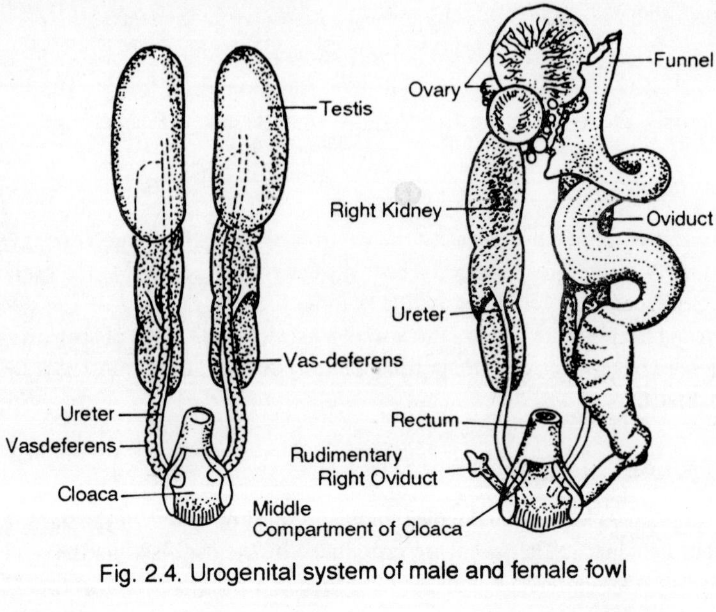

Fig. 2.4. Urogenital system of male and female fowl

OVIDUCT

The oviduct is a coiled tube that extends from the ovary to the cloaca and opens into the middle compartment of the cloaca. The oviduct is covered with blood vessels and moves about in the body as the eggs are developed and moves towards the uterus. The oviduct has the following five distinct parts.

(i) **Funnel or infundibulum :** It is the funnel shaped anterior portion of the oviduct which receives the ovum or yolk immediately after release from the graafian follicle. The ovum remains here for about 18 minutes before moving to the magnum. It measures about 9 cm in laying hens.

(ii) **Magnum :** It is the largest portion of the oviduct. It measures about 33 cm in laying bird and secretes the thick albumen or white portion of the egg. The ovum remains in magnum for about 174 minutes.

(iii) **Isthmus :** The ovum stays in isthmus for about 74 minutes. It is about 10 cm long in adults. The isthmus secretes the shell membrane.

(iv) **Uterus :** The uterus, known as shell gland, and is glandular in structure. But it secretes the shell membranes and calacareous shell which enclose the egg before it is laid. It measures 10 to 12 cm in laying birds. The ovum stays here for about 1240 minutes.

(v) **Vagina :** It is the terminal portion of the oviduct and measures about 12 cm in adults. It holds the egg until it is laid. The eggs as they pass down the left oviduct, first the albumen called the white of the egg which covers the yolk and then a double shell membrane and lastly the white calcareous shell are deposited around each egg on their way to the exterior.

The female reproductive cell, also known as gamete, ovum or egg is one of protein rich food. It is big in size and contains sufficient food materials for the development of the embryo.

FORMATION AND STRUCTURE OF THE EGGS

The formation of an egg is a complicated process and requires the formation of some specialized materials and their transport in the different parts of the female reproductive system which are sequential in steps and time dependent matter.

FORMATION OF YOLK

At the early stage of yolk formation, oocytes grow very slowly. The nutrients is supplied to the developing ovary by the blood supply in the follicle which are being produced in the liver. When the ovary become functional, few of the ova starts to increase their size. The onset of egg formation in hens is sudden. Each ovary contains thousands of ova or yolk.

The first yolk starts to develop before 10-11 days of first laying when the diameter of the first yolk reaches 4 mm, then few ova suddenly start to develop at an enormously increase rate. Each yolk is increasing about 4 mm in diameter every day until it reaches the full size of 40 mm in diameter. The suddenment of follicles takes about 6 to 9 days in chicken and 13 to 15 days in turkeys before ovulation.

OVULATION

When the developing ova reach its maturity is shedded from the follicles by its rupture along a definite line of the wall called stigma which contains normally no blood vesels. This process is called ovulation.

In most of the cases the shedded ova probably discharged into the body cavity and in the later stage it is engulfed by the infundibulum/funel of the oviduct by the continuous and repeated extended and decreased the edges of the infundibulum over the surface of the ova. When the shedded yolk is totally engulfed by the infundibulum then it is forcely back into the oviduct by the wave like contraction of the muscles to the oviduct. In rare cases the infundibulum fails to engulf the shedded yolk, then the yolk remain in the body cavity, which is later on ruptured and the liquid portion being absorbed and leaving abnormal deposite in the body cavity. In this condition the hen is known as internal layer.

FERTILIZATION

Fertilization is occured in the infundibulum of the oviduct. Formation of fertilised egg is only possible if the laying hen is mated with and the sperm cells have had sufficient time to reach to the infundibulum of the oviduct though cock's Sperm remain in oviduct for 2-3 weeks after mating but fresh sperm is only most suitable to fertilize the ova. If the laying hens are not mated then there is no hamper of laying but unfertilized egg will produced.

DEVELOPMENT OF EMBRYO

Fertilized eggs, immediately after fertilization start cell division and with this development of embryo occurs. Development of embryo occurs when the egg remains in the oviduct by 24 hours before laying and it continues after laying if the fertilized eggs unless stored below 82° F. The blastoderm increases in size and there is some changes in the consistency of yolk and white portion of the egg resulting damage of it. So, therefore if the egg is not used for hatching purpose then it is desirable to produce unfertilised eggs for longer storage.

SECRETION OF THICK WHITE

Soon after engulfed the sheded ovum by the infundibulum of the oviduct, the yolk is forced through the oviduct to the magnum region by the ciliary action or by peristaltic movement of the walls of the oviduct. Most of the white portion of the egg (albumen) are formed in the magnum and therefore it is known as albumen secreting region of the oviduct. Peristaltic movement of the magnum forced the ovum to the isthmus portion of the oviduct.

FORMATION OF SHELL MEMBRANE

Isthmus is a short section of the oviduct. In the isthmus, the inner and outer shell membranes of the developing egg are forrmed. Probably some amount of water is also added to albumin in the isthmus and the shape of the egg is determined in this region accordingly to the structural characteristic of the isthmus region of the oviduct.

ADDITION OF THIN WHITE AND SHELL

Developing eggs entered into uterus from isthmus and here it remains for about 24 hours. The thin white portion of the egg is formed in the uterus. Besides this the uterus is responsible for the formation of egg shell consisting of large amount calcium carbonate and it is carried to the uterus by the blood circulation. The calcium content of blood in laying hen is nearly double than non-layer. The calcium required for the formation of egg shell is mobilized from the long bones and feed. The shell pigments are formed in the uterus during the last five hours before laying the eggs.

Tabnle 2.2. Functions of the different parts of the oviduct.

Section	Length	Time spends by the developing egg.	Function
Infundibulum (funel)	9 cm	18 minutes	Engulf the shedded ova or yolk from the body cavity just after it released from the follicle. Fertilisation is also occured in this section of oviduct if live sperms are present.
Magnum	33 cm	3 hours (Approx) (2.54 hrs.)	Most of the egg protein (Albumen) is deposited around the yolk. The chalazae is also formed here.
Isthmus	10 cm	1.25 hours	The inner and outer shell membranes of the eggs are formed.

Contd.

Section	Length	Time spends by the developing egg.	Function
Uterus	10-12 cm	20 hours 40 minutes	The egg shell is formed in this region and the pigmentation of the egg shell is also occured here. Cuticles are also secreted.
Vagina	12 cm	Entire time from ovulation to laying is slightly more than 24 hours	The role of vagina in egg formation is not clearly known so far, some believe that it forms a protein to seal over the pores of the egg shell. Eggs passes through this section prior to laying.

3

STANDARD CLASSES, BREEDS AND VARIETIES OF FOWLS

The fowls are beneficial birds. They were wild birds in the past. They are then killed for meat and reared for cock fighting. Afterward, they are domesticated for the production of eggs and meat. Since the domestic birds decented from the red jungle fowl, they differ in some traits according to their place of existence. The birds having the same general body shape, weight and some common characteristics are denoted as breed. The groups of breeds which have developed in certain regions are called class. Such as Asiatic, English, Mediterrance etc. Varieties represent sub-division of breed.

CLASSIFICATION OF DIFFERENT BREEDS OF FOWL

Fowls are classified according to their utility

(i) **Egg type or laying birds :** The breed that lays big size egg and are not heavy in body weight are called egg type or laying birds. Leghorn and Minorca are egg type or laying bird.

(ii) **Dual purpose breed :** The breeds that lay more egg and are heavy in body weight are called dual purpose breeds. They are ideal breeds for the small farmers. Rhode Istand Red, Plymouth Rock, New Hampshire, Austalorp, Orpington, Wyandotte etc. are the dual purpose breeds.

(iii) **Table or meat type :** The breeds that lay less eggs and are heavy in body weight are called table or meat type breeds. They are mainly reared for meat production. Brahama, Cochin, Langshan, Aseel, Chitagong, broiler etc. are table or meat type breeds.

Table 3.1. Classes of Poultry

Birds Class	Description
• **CHICKENS**	
(i) Rock cornishgame hen or cornishgame hen.	A young immature chicken (usually 5-7 weeks of age) weighing not more than 2 lb. ready to cock weight, the progency of a cornish chicken or a cornish chicken crossed with another breed of chicken.
(ii) Broiler or fryer.	A young chicken (usually 8-12 weeks of age) or either Sex, that is tender meated with soft, pliable, Smooth-textured skin and flexible breast bone cartilage.
(iii) Roaster	A young chicken (usually 3-5 months of age), of either sex, that is tender meated with soft, pliable, smooth textured skin and breast bone cartilage that may be somewhat less flexible than that of a broiler or fryer.
(iv) Capon	A surgically unsexed male chicken (Usually under 8 months of age) that is tender-meated with soft, pliable and smooth-textured skin.
(v) Stag	A male chicken (usually under 10 months of age) with coarse skin, some what toughened and darkened flesh and considerable hardening of the breastbone cartilage. Stages show condition of fleshing and a degree of maturity intermediate between that of roaster and a cock or rooster.
(vi) Hen or stewing chicken or fowl	A mature female chicken (Usually more than 10 months of age) with meat less tender than that of a roaster and nonflexible breastbone tip.
(vii) Cock or rooster.	A mature male chicken with coarse skin, toughened and darkend meat and hardened breastbone tip.
• **TURKEY**	
(i) Fryer roaster turkey	A young, immature turkey (usually under 16 weeks of age) of either sex that is tender meated with soft, pliable, smooth textured skin and flexible breast bone cartilage.

Contd.

	Birds Class	Description
(ii)	Young hen turkey	A young female turkey (Usually 5-7 months of age) that is tender meated with soft, pliable smooth textured skin and breast bone cartilage that is somewhat less flexible than in a fryer-roaster turkey.
(iii)	Young tom Turkey	A young male turkey (usually 5-7 months of age) that is tender meated with soft, Pliable, smooth textured skin and breastbone cartilage that is somewhat less flexible than in a fryer roaster turkey.
(iv)	Yearling hen turkey	A fully matured female turkey (usually under 15 months of age) that is reasonably is reasonably tender meated and with reasonably smooth textured skin.
(v)	Yearling tom turkey	A fully matured male turkey (Usually under 15 months of age) that is reasonably tender meated and with reasonably smooth textured skin
(vi)	Mature turkey or old turkey (hen or tom)	An old turkey of either sex (Usually in excess of 15 months of age) with coarse skin and toughened flesh.
• **DUCKS**		
(i)	Broiler duckling or fryer duckling	A young duck (usually under 8 weeks of age) of either sex that is tender meated and has a soft bill and soft wind pipe.
(ii)	Roaster duckling	A young duck (Usually under 16 weeks of age) of either sex that is tender meated and has a bill that is not completely hardened and a wind pipe easiily dented.
(iii)	Mature duck or old duck.	A duck (Usually over 8 months of age) of either sex with toughened flesh, hardened bill and hardened wind pipe.
• **GUINEAS**		
(i)	Young guinea	Can be of either sex, is tender meated and has a flexible breastbone cartilage.
(ii)	Mature guinea or old guinea	Can be of either sex, has toughened flesh and a hardened breastbone.

Contd.

Birds Class	Description
• **GEESE**	
(i) Young goose	Can be of either sex, is tender meated and has a windpipe that is easily dented.
(ii) Mature goose or old goose	Can be of either sex, has toughened flesh and hardened windpipe.
• **PIGEONS**	
(i) squab	Young immature pigeon of either sex and extra tender meated.
(ii) Piegon	Mature pigeon of either sex, with coarse skin and toughened flesh.

Source : Poultry grading Manual, Ag. Hdbk No. 31 USDA, 1971.

Table 3.2. Standard classes, breeds and varieties of Fowls.

Class	Breed	Variety
1. American	Rhode island Red.	Single comb, Rose Comb etc.
	Rhode Island White	—
	Plymouth Rock	Barred, White, Buff, Silver Pencilled, Blue partridge, columbian etc.
2. American	Wyandolte	Silver-laced, Golden laced, White etc.
	New Hamshire	
3. Asiatic	Brahma	Buff, Black, Patridge, Light Dark etc.
	Cochin	Buff, white Black etc.
	Langshan	Black, white etc.
4. Mediterra-nean	Leghorn	Single comb, Rose comb, Darkbrown, Black light, Brown, Buff white, white etc.
	Minorca	Black-brown
5. English	Sussex	Speckled, Light, Red etc.
	Australorp	
	Orpington	Buff, Black, White Blue etc.
6. Indian	Aseel, Chittagong, Black Haringhta, Ghagus.	

CHARACTERISTICS OF SOME BREEDS OF POULTRY

(i) **American Breeds :** A number of breeds have been developed in America to meet the market demand for a bird with a yellow skin, clean shanks free from feathers and adapted to the conditions of the country. Out of 12 breeds, Rhode Island Red, Plymouth Rock, Wynadotte, New Hampshire etc. are popular breed. The birds belonging to this breed are of medium size, good sitter and grow very rapidly. All have red ear lobes and except Lamona, Lay brown shelled eggs and are classed as broody. They are reared both for meat and egg production.

(a) **Rhode Island Red :** Rhode Island Red is orginated from Rhode Island in England. It was developed after crossing with the red Malay game, Leghorn and Asiatic native stock in 1857.

The Rhode Island Red has a long rectangular body, broad and deep breast carried well forward, flat buck with red eyes and red earlobes. The most common colour is red buff, but white and brown varieties are also found. The plumage colour of this breed is rich dark or brownish red in colour, evenly distributed over the entire surface and is well glossed. The wing when open shows black in both primary and Secondary feathers. But the tail covers, sickle feathers and main tail feathers are black. Neck hackle shows little black marking. Legs and feet are deep yellow but may show brown colour. There are two varieties of this breed :

I. Single Comb

II. Rose Comb

Fig. 3.1. Rhode Island Red (a) Cock, (b) Hen

They are identical in character. But only difference among varieties is the type of comb. The single comb Rhode Island Red strain is still very popular for commercial production of brown shelled eggs. The hen lays 150-200 egg per year having weight 40-60 gm each. The hen starts laying from 180-210 days of age.

Rhode island Red is a dual purpose breed having both meat production and egg laying qualities. Hen are prolific layers of large brown shelled eggs and very hardy and stand cold and damp well. The chicken of this breed are fairly easy to rear. It is a heavy type of bread and good sitters. The standard body weight of this breed is as follows :

Cock	:	3.8 Kg.
Hen	:	3.0 Kg.
Cockerel	:	3.4 Kg.
Pullet	:	2.5 Kg.

Rhode Island Red is most suitable for upgrading of indignenous stock. Rhode island white is one of the variety of Rhodeisland Red. But this is not so popular breed.

PLYMOUTTH ROCK

The plymouth rock is one of the most popular breeds in America, because it is a bird of good size with excellend fleshing properties and good egg laying abiliies. It is orginated as early as 1865 from the crosses of Dominique and Black cochin. The birds belonging to this breed have long body fairly broad with fairly prominet brest and good depth of body and have a single comb. The birds of this breed possesses excellent fleshing properties and good laying abilities., The plumage colour is a greyish white, each feather crossed by almost black bars which should be even in the width, straight and should extend down to the skin.

Each feather should end with a narrow, dark tip which with alternate dark and light bars, gives a bluish cast or shade to the surface colour. Solid black or partly black feathers may occur in some birds of practically all strains in this variety. Black spots on the shanks are also common particularly in females. The colour of comb, ear lobes and wattle is red. The hen lays 150 eggs per year and they are good Sitter. Barred and white Plymouth Rock are two most popular varieties of this breed.

BARRED PLYMOUTH ROCK

Barred Plymouth Rock havegreyish white plumage. The male birds have black and white bars of equal width, whereas in female the white bars should be as wide as the black bars. Each feather ends in a narrow dark tips. Alternate dark and light bars gives a bluish cast to the surface colour. The cocks of this variety are good for grading up the ordinary village fowls.

WHITE PLYMOUTH ROCK

The white variety is popular due to white or light coloured plumage desired in broiler birds. The plumage of this variety is white throughout and usually free from black ticking, brassiness and creaminess.

The other vrieties of plymouth Rock are white, Buff silver pencilled, partridge, columbian and blue. The standard body weight of this variety is as follows :

Chick	:	3.5 - 4.0 Kg.
Hen	:	2.5 - 3.0 Kg.
Cockrel	:	3.0 - 3.5 Kg.
Pullet	:	2.0 - 2.5 Kg.

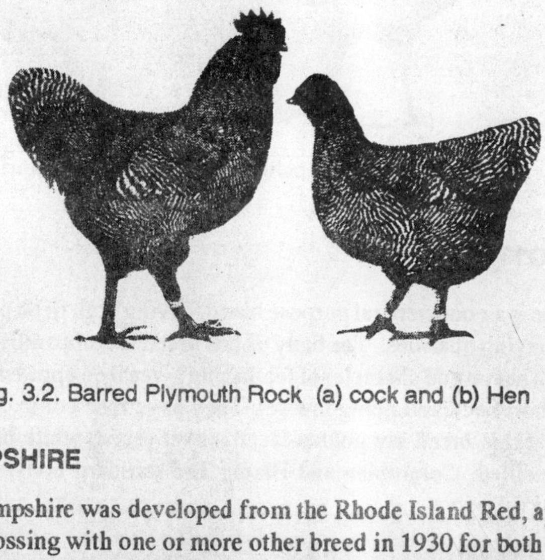

Fig. 3.2. Barred Plymouth Rock (a) cock and (b) Hen

NEW HAMPSHIRE

The New Hampshire was developed from the Rhode Island Red, apparently with some crossing with one or more other breed in 1930 for both meat and egg production. It is a popular breed, having less rectangular body than that of Rhode Island Red. The characteristics feattures of this breed are Single comb, Chestnut-red plumage, early maturity, rapid feathering, etc. They are good producer of large brown shell eggs and good quality meat. The lower neck feathers of females are distinctly tipped with black and the main tail feathers are black, edge with chestnut red. The under colour of both the sexes is light salmon. The stadard weight of this breed is as follows :

Cock	:	3.8 Kg.
Hen	:	2.9 kg.
Cockerel	:	3.4 Kg.
Pullet	:	2.5 Kg.

Some strains of this breed are used for boriler production and others for commercial production of eggs.

Fig. 3.3. New Hampshires (a) Cock and (b) Hen

WYNADOTTE

Wynadotte is a good general purpose breed, having both flesh production and good egg laying qualities. The body of this breed is comparatively round and the general shape and character of feathering gives it an appearance of having a rather short back and being low set. They have rose comb. The important varieties of this breed are golden-laced, silver-laced, white buff, Partridge, Silver-pencilled, Columbian and Black. The standard body weight of this breed is as follows :

Cock	: 3.8 Kg.
Hen	: 3.0 Kg.
Cockerel	: 3.4 Kg.
Pullet	: 2.5 Kg.

ASIATIC BREEDS

Brahma, Cochin and Langshan are the important Asiatic breed. They have large bodies, feathered shanks and they are good for meat production. They have yellow skin, except the Black Langshan in which the skin is a pinkish white and red ear lobes. The hens lays brown shelled eggs and are classed as broody. They are naturally poor layers.

BRAHMA

The Brahmas originated in the Brahmaputra district of India, where fowls of their ancestral type, known as "Grey Chittagongs", are still to be found. This breed was exported to America in 1846 and to England in 1853. The breed is well known for its massive, well feathered and proportioned body. Pea comb, feathered fleshy yellow shank, red ear lobes, yellow toes, beak and skins are the breed characteristics. The hen lays brown shelled eggs and are classed as broody. They are not good layers. They are primarily reared for meat production. The most common varieties of this breed are Light, Dark and Buff. The standard body weight of this breed is as follows :

	Dark Brahama	Light Brahma
Cock	: 4.9 Kg.	5.4 Kg.
Hen	: 3.6 Kg.	4.3 Kg.
Cockerel	: 4.0 Kg.	4.5 Kg.
Pullet	: 3.1 Kg.	3.6 Kg.

COCHIN

This breed originated in the Shanghai district of China. They are also known as "Sanghai fowl" and they were first imported into England in 1845 and a little later into America. The outstanding characteristics of this breed are its massive appearance, thickly feathered shanks, single comb and cushion like structure at the base of the tail. The breast of the Cochin is Carried low and the feathering is extremely long and profuse. The popular varieties of this breed are Buff, Patridge, White and Black. The standard body weight of this breed is as follows :

Cock	: 4.9 Kg.
Hen	: 3.8 Kg.
Cockerel	: 3.6 Kg.
Pullet	: 3.1 Kg.

LANGSHAN

The Langshan originated in Langhsan region of china. They were imported into England in 1872 and a little latter into America. The principal breed characteristic are shorted and deeper body than Brahma or cochin, longer tail feathers, tail carried high, long legs and single comb. Langshan is graceful bird with proportioned body. Followings are the two important varieties of this breed :

Black Langshan : It has dark brown beak, bluish black shanks and toes and

Pinkish white bottom of the feet. The plumage colour of this breed is black.

White Langshan : It has greyish white plumage, slaty blue to pinkish white beak, slaty blue shanks and toes with pink between the scales.

The standard body weight of this breed is as follows :

Cock	: 3.8 Kg.
Hen	: 3.4 Kg.
Cockerel	: 3.6 Kg.
Pullet	: 2.9 Kg.

MEDITERRANEAN BREEDS

The Mediteraneanbreeds of Italian origin include Leghorn, Minorea, Ancona, Andalusians and Spanish. Out of these varieties, Leghorn is by far the most Popular. The mediterranean breeds are really good layer and are lighter in body weight than those of Asiatic breeds. The outstanding characteristics of this breed are white ear lobes, relatively large combs, non-broodiness, early maturity and large whitte shelled eggs producer.

LEGHORN

Leghorn originated in Italy and was introduced by Christian missionaries and fanciers in U.P., Travancore Cochin and a few other states. Now-a-days Leghorn is one of the most popular breed throughout the plains of india. The cocks of Leghorn breed are used for grading up the non-descript fowls in the villages. Leghorns are known for their stylish carriage.

The leghorn is famous for its compact and light body, uniform blending, pretty carriage, small head with well set rose or single comb early maturity and large white egg production. It is popular for egg producing farms, because of its small body size and hence less feed requirement for their maintenance. It has a relatively long back, prominent breast and comparatively long shanks. The popular varieties of this breed are white, Brown and Black. Out of these varieties, white Leghorn is the most popular for its excellent laying qualities. Now-a-days, brown Leghorn is gaining popularity slowly. Leghorn breed grow first during the early stages and give a good type of tender meat. In India, white Leghorn has given good result especially in the drier parts of the country, but is not regarded as suited for heavy or wet soils or for hills. The single comb of the male should be of medium size and it should stand erect with five deeply serrated points. In females, the first point of comb should stand erect but the remainder of the comb may drop to one side. The colour of beaks, skin, shanks (Legs) and toes of all the varieties is yellow. The sickle hackle of the male is some what big and long. The ear lobe is big and yellow in colour. The wattle is somewhat long and dropping. They are light type of breed. The hen starts laying from five to six and half months of age. They lay 200-250 eggs per year, each weighing about 50-60 gm. The hen of this breed are not good sitter. The standard body weight of this breed is as follows :

Cock	: 3.5 kg.
Hen	: 3.0 Kg.
Cockerel	: 3.0 Kg.
Pullet	: 2.5 Kg.

Fig. 3.4. White Leghorns (a) Cock and (b) Hen.

MINORCA

The Minorca is originally called Red faced spanish and is the nearest in shape and appearance to Black spanish. The original home of this breed is Minorca Island of Spain. Minorca is the largest and haeaviest of Mediterranean breeds of Poultry. The outstanding characteristics of this breed are long strong body, long wattle, large white ear lobes, firm muscular legs set squarely under powerful looking body and large and full tail moderately elevated. The comb is erect with six evenly and deeply serrated points. The back, shank and toes are black. But the colour of skin is white. The minorca is the best layers and they are excellent producer of large white egg. They are good foragers and small eaters, The chicken of this breed grow quickly. The minorca was at one time even more popular than that of Leghorn due to their superior size of white egg. But they are lossing their popularity due to decline of its production. The important varieties of this breed are single comb Black, Single comb white, Rose comb white, Rose comb Black and single comb

Buff. The standard body weight of this breed is as follows :

Cock	: 3.5 kg.
Hen	: 2.9 Kg.
Cockerel	: 2.9 Kg.
Pullet	: 2.5 Kg.

ANCONA

Ancona originated in the vicinity of Ancona in Italy. The breed was imported into England and from there into America. The Single comb Ancona and Rose comb Ancona are the two varieties of this breed. The two varieties are identical in the shape of the comb. The Ancona has a plumage colour of lustrous black with certain of the feathers typped with a V-Shaped pretty looking white tip. The beak is yellow with upper mandible shaped with black. The shanks and toes are yellow or yellow mottled with black.

The standard body weight of this breed is as follows :

Cock	: 2.5 kg.
Hen	: 2.9 Kg.
Cockerel	: 2.9 Kg.
Pullet	: 2.5 Kg.

ENGLISH BREED

The breed of English origin are mostly utility breed noted for their excellent fleshing properties. All the English breeds have white skin and red ear lobes except Cornish and lay brown shelled eggs, except Drorkin and Red cap. All the English breeds are classed as broody. But this character can be gradually eliminated by selective breeding. Out of six English breeds, Sussex, Australorp and Orpington are most popularr breed. They are favoured for flesh production. They have white skin and red ear lobes and they lay brown shelled eggs.

AUSTRALORP

This breed was developed in Australia and originated from Black orpington. It is more outstanding and less massive in appearance than black orpington. The breed is suitable for flesh and egg production. They are called dual purpose breed due to their aforesaid qualities. The back is somewhat long and the body gradually slopes towards the tail. The body has good depth and more closely feathered than the orpington. The plumage is lustrous black in all section and the under colouring is dull black. Single comb, black beak and black or lead black shanks and toes are the characteristic features of this breed. The bottom of feet and toes are pinkish white.

The "Austro white", a hybrid cross is produced by crossing between the Australop male and the white leghorn female. They are good layer and are maintained in large flocks in commercial egg production farms of India. The standard body weight of this breed is as follows :

Cock	: 4.0 kg.
Hen	: 3.0 Kg.
Cockerel	: 3.5 Kg.
Pullet	: 2.5 Kg.

Fig. 3.5. Australorp (a) Cock and (b) Hen.

SUSSEX

Sussex was developed in England in the 18th century primarily as table bird. It was developed from birds with four toes. The sussex has a long body, broad at the shoulder and with good depth from front to rear. The breast is well developed and the bird has excellent fleshing qualities. They have single combs, and horn-coloured beaks, shanks and toes. There are three varieties of this breed :

(i) **Light sussex :** It was first admitted to the standard of perfection in 1929. The colour of the plumage of this variety is quite similar to that of the columbian plymouth Rock and columbian wyandotte. This variety lays well in the wormer months in India.

(ii) **Red Sussex :** The plumage of this variety is deep rich red with the exception in the primaries where the lower web are black with the narrow edging of red, in the secondaries, where the upper webs are black and the tail which is black. The under colour of all sections are red with a slight bar of both sexes.

Fig. 3.6. Light Sussex (a) Cock and (b) Hen.

(iii) **Speckled sussex :** It is reddish bay in colour, each feather being tipped with white. In the male, the neck is lustrous reddish bay, each feather having a black strip extending length wise. The under colour of all the sections in both the sexes is slate shading to Salmon. The standard body weight of this breed is as follows :

Cock	:	4.5 kg.
Hen	:	3.5 Kg.
Cockerel	:	3.5 Kg.
Pullet	:	3.0 Kg.

ORPRINGTON

Orprington was developed in kent in England. They have long, deep and well rounded body with a full breast and a broad back and they are more loosely feathered than the breeds of American class. They have single comb. There are four varieties of orprington

(i) **Buff orprington :** It was devolved from Buff cochin, Dark dorkings and Golden Spangled Hamburgs. The plumage is same as in other Buff breeds, such as Buff Plymouth Rock. The Shanks and toes are white.

(ii) **Black orprington :** It was developed in about 1886 from mating involving the Black Minorca, clean-legged Black Deghshans and black coloured specimens with plymouth Rock blood. The shanks and toes are black and the bottom of the feet is white.

(iii) **Blue orprington :** It is of very recent origin. It has the same general colour as the Blue plymouth Rock. But the shanks and toes are leaden blue.

(iv) **White Orprington :** It is, in all possibility, originated as a sport bird from the black variety. The colour is same as in white plymouth Rock. But only exception is that the shanks and toes are white.

CORNISH

Cornish orginally known as the Cornish Indian Game, appears to have been developed in England about the middle of the nineteenth century from crossing involving the Aseel, the Malay and English game breeds. The breed have good fleshing qualities having broad and deep breast. It has close and compact feathering, yellow skin and pea comb. The common varieties of this breed are Dark, white and white laced red. Out of these three varieties, white variety is most popular as meat type breed. Males of white cornish is extensively used in different crosses for broiler production. The standard body weight of this variety is as follows :

		Dark and white variety	**White-laced red variety**
Cock	:	4.5 kg.	3.6 Kg.
Hen	:	3.4 Kg.	2.7 Kg.
Cockerel	:	3.6 Kg.	3.1 Kg.
Pullet	:	2.7 Kg.	2.2 Kg.

INDIAN BREEDS

India is the ancestral home of the modern breeds of chickens. The common country hen, the desi is the best mother for hatching, a good forager, but a poor layer. They are small in size and they can adopt climatic condition for their rearing. The rate of laying eggs increases during the harvesting period of cereal crops. They produces good quality flesh having resistance to the common diseases of poultry.

ASEEL OR INDIAN GAME

Assel, which is the equivalent of English 'real' or 'true', is perhaps a pure game. The body of this breed is round and short with broad breast, straight back and close set setting tail root. The out standing characteristics of this breed are small and pea shaped comb, thick and long neck, long and slender face and not covered with feathers, short beak, bright red wattles and ear lobes, compact and well set eyes and compact in appearance. Aseel is one of the best table birds having well flavoured and plentiful flesh. They are not good layer, but are superior as sitters and they also possess good parental qualities, pugnacity, high stamina, majestic gait and dogged fighting qualities. The legs are strong, straight and set well apart and the tail is small and drooping. The plumage colour may be black, white, duck wing, black and red and mottled. The general feahtering is close, scanty and almost absent on the breast. The most popular varieties of this breed are peela (Golden red), Yakub (Black and red), Nurie (white), Kajal (black), Chitta (Black and white spotted) Java (Black), Teekar (Brown), Reza (light Red) and Sabja (white and

Table 3.3. Poultry breeds and their characteristics

Breed	Standard Weight		Plumage	Colour of skin	Type of comb	Colour of ear lobe	Colour of shank	Colour of eggs	Shank Feath-ered or not
	Cock	Hen							
1. American									
Plymouth rock	3.5-4.0	2.5-3	White	Yellow	Single	Red	Yellow	Brown	No
Rhode Island Red	3.8	3.0	Red	Yellow	Single & Rose	Red	Yellow	Brown	No
Wyandotte	3.8	3.0	White	Yellow	Rose	Red	Yellos	Brown	No
New-Ham-pshine	3.8	2.9	Red	Yellow	Single	Red	Yellow	Brown	No
2. Asiatic Brahma (Light)	5.4	4.3	Columbian	Yellow	Pea	Red	Yellow	Brown	No
Cochin (Buff)	4.9	3.8	Buff	Yellow	Single	Red	Yellow	Brown	Yes
3. Mediterranean									
White Leghorn	3.5	3.0	White	Yellow	Single & Rose	White	Yellow	White	No
Minorca	3.5	2.9	White	White	Single	White	Dark slate	White	No
4. English									
Australorp	4.0	3.0	Black	White	Single	Red	Dark state	Brown	No
Cornish (White)	1.5	3.4	White	Yellow	Pea	Red	Yellow	Brown	No

golden or black with yellow or silver). The Standard body weight of this breed is as follows :

Cock	:	4.0 kg.	5.0 Kg.
Hen	:	3.0 Kg.	4.0 Kg.
Cockerel	:	3.5 Kg.	4.5 Kg.
Pullet	:	2.5 Kg.	3.5 Kg.

CHITTAGONG OR MALAY

Chittagong or Malay is mostly found in Eastern India. It is a large bird measuring sometimes 75 cm from beak to toe. The adult birds are very strong, hardy and quarrelsome. The outstanding characteristics of this breed are as follows : Small pea comb, head is long, beak is long and yellow, ear lobes are small, usually red and at times admixtured with a little white. Wattles are red and hardly visible in the hen, breast is broad, deep and fleshy, the shoulder is broad with small narrow loins, legs are yellow and featherless, plumage is close to the body, firm, short and glossy. The colour of adult bird is white with splashed of golden colour marking on the wings. The birds of this variety possess excellent fleshing properties and good laying abilities. The standard body weight of this breed is as follows :

Cocks	:	3.5	4.5 Kg.
Hen	:	3.0	4.0 Kg.

4

HATCHING OF EGGS

Chickens are grown from fertile egg. The fertile eggs are called as hatching egg. The hatching is a process by which in the span of 21 days, a microscopic germ is changed into downy chick, capable of walking, eating and expressing its needs by its voice and action. In order to obtain fertile eggs, it is necessary to mating the female with the males. One male is usually run with about ten females and a breeding pen for this number should measure at least 20 sq. yards. The ordinary breeder can get good results with mating two or more males with a flock of females and in flock mating normally one male is used for every 20 females allowing 20 sq. yards run space per bird. The hen can produce egg naturally without the mating with male. This type of egg do not contain embryo and is known as unfertile egg. Chick do not grow from this egg. But this types of egg is equally suitable like fertile egg from the nutritional point of view as a food.

Production of chicken from fertile egg is a special grieft of nature. The development of embryo of poultry bird is also complex process as that of mammals. But the difference is that the embroynic development takes place in mother's worub in mammals and the embroynic development of poultry bird takes place out side the mother's worub i. e. in the fertile egg. The fertile egg provides food to developing embroyo. In order to obtain first class hatching eggs it is necessary to have good, strong and heatlhy fowls. The future of poultry industry depends upon to a large extent on the quality of chicks, Produced by the hatcheries working all over the world.

SELECTION AND CARE OF GOOD HATCHING EGGS

The fertile egg containing embryo produces chicken. The hen lays fertile egg after 24 hours of mating with male. Production of fertile egg depends mainly on the following factors

(i) **Nutrition of breeding flock :** The embryonic development of eggs depend mainly on the food containing in the egg. The hen can produce egg without providing the complete food to them. But this type of egg do not produce good chick. The hen should be provided complete food for 6-8 weeks with a view to get good quality hatching eggs. The cocks also be provided breeder's diet at least three months before mating with female.

Table 4.1. Nutritional requirements of Breeders and Layers

Feed Ingredient	Laying hen	Breeding hen
Crude protein (%)	15	15
Vitamins :		
Vitamin-A (IU/lb)	3300	3300
Vitamin-D (ICU/lb)	340	340
Riboflavin (Mg/bird)	0.9	1.6
Pantothenic acid (Mg/lb)	2.5	5.0
Pyridoxine (Mg/lb)	1.6	1.6
Biotin (Mg/lb)	-	0.07
Minerals :		
Calcium (%)	2.25	2.25
Phosphorus (%)	0.75	0.75
Salt (%)	0.50	0.50
Magnese (Mg/lb)	-	15.0

(ii) **Disease free stock :** Disease spreads from generation to generation through egg. Egg acts as a carrier of disease inoculum. Some poultry diseases such as Fowl typhoid, Fowl Paralysis etc. are spread by eggs of disease affected birds. The hatching eggs should be collected from birds free from attack of those diseases.

(iii) **Age of parents :** The breeding ability of cock having good vigour becomes good. So the age of the cock have no or little effect on the hatchability of egg and vigour of the chicken. The old cock can mate with little number of hen. On the other hand, the hatchbility of eggs depend on the age of the hen. Maximum hatchability has been observed in eggs produced in the first year of laying.

(iv) **Egg Production in Breeding Flock :** It is observed that when the hen produces more eggs, the eggs become fertile and rate of production of chicken from those egg becomes more. This characteristic are retarded as the egg production decreases. Besides this the fertility and hatchability of eggs depend on some factors.

(a) **Seasonal Condition :** The fertility and rate of hatchability of eggs produced in summer and early spring becomes low.

(b) **Number of cocks to hens in the flock :** As stated earlier, one male is usually run with 10-12 females produces fertile egg. But in flock mating one male is used for every 20 females. The male should be good, strong and healthy.

(c) **Physical condition of the breeding stock :** The eggs produced by matting with strong, healthy and vigorous males and females naturally becomes fertile and more chickens are produced from those eggs.

(d) **Storage condition before incubation :** Hatching eggs should be collected several times daily from the nests and stored, untill required, in a cool moist place. The eggs should not be kept for more than three days in hot weather. But they can be kept seven to ten days in cold weather. The best storage temperature for hatching egg is 55°F (10°C)

(v) **External Characteristics of hatching eggs**

(a) **Egg size :** The size of the chicks hatched depends on the size of the eggs used for hatching. So the size of the eggs used for hatching is very important. Too small or too large eggs should not be selected for hatching as they create hindrance in setting in incubation trays and also do not hatch properly. The optimum size of hatching, egg is about 53 gm. But it can vary from 50-55 gm for chicken egg, 65-70 gm for duck egg and 80-85 gm for turkey egg. Eggs in which the proportion of white to yolk is about 2 : 1 usually hatch better than eggs having wider or narrow ratio. The shape of hatching egg should be oval.

(b) **Shell colour :** The white shelled eggs used for incubation should be free from tints. In case of brown coloured egg, medium and dark brown eggs hatch better than light brown eggs.

(c) **Shell texture :** The shell texture becomes thin due to deficiency of calcium or vitamin - D in poultry bird and this type of egg is associated with low hatchability. The eggs having thin shell texture should not be selected for hatching. It is advisable to select eggs having thick shell texture and fully developed.

(d) **Cracked eggs :** The cracked eggs should not be selected for hatching. The cracked eggs are easily detected by tapping two eggs together. If there is a resonant sound, both eggs are sound in shell. But if there is dull sound, one of the eggs is cracked. The cracked eggs are also easily detected at the time of candling. Eggs with sound shell should be selected for hatching.

(e) **Tremulous air cells :** Excessive shaking of selected eggs during transit should be avoided as they sometimes result in a condition known as 'tremulous air cells', It is a condition that tends to lower hatchability.

(f) **Soiled eggs :** Soiled eggs should not be set for htching. It is not advisable to wash the soiled eggs with water. Because the washing with water opens up the pore and this interferes with the hatching. The eggs with small dirt should be cleaned with a knife or rubbing with a cloth.

(g) **Age of egg :** The eggs should not be kept for more than three days in hot weather. But they may be kept for 7 to 10 days in winter. The eggs that are obtained from healthy, strong and vigorous hen of improved varieties, should be selected for hatching. The breeding males should also be healthy, strong and vigorous.

(h) **Turning of eggs :** There is no practical value in turning eggs during storage period when stored for seven days or less.

CARE AND HANDLING OF HATCHING EGGS

It is important to handle hatching eggs properly and carefully before incubation to achieve maximum hatchability of viable and strong chicks.

1. **Collection of eggs :** The eggs should be collected as frequently as possible, particularly in severe weather. Three or four gathering of eggs from poultry shed will be necessary to avoid undue effect of weather on embryo.
2. **Storing of eggs :** The eggs should be stored in a cool moist place. The best storage temperature for hatching eggs is 55°F (10°C). Hatchability starts declining rapidly when eggs are stored at 0°C and the embroys are completely destroyed when eggs are stored at 32°C for seven days. High humidity of storage is preferred as it helps to avoid drying of the eggs. A relative humidity of 80 to 85 percent during storage appears to be the best. Eggs should be properly stored in ventillated room before setting the same in the incubator.
3. **Handling of eggs :** The hatching eggs should be stored in hard, clean filler flats keeping narrow end down. The clean eggs hatch better than the soiled eggs. The disease producing organisms harbour in the dirty eggs. Sufficient space should be provided in the nest box for producing clean eggs. One nest box measuring 14" x 12" x 12" is suitable for every five layers. Dry cleaning of soiled eggs with rough cloth or sand paper may be done before setting of egg in the incubator.
4. **Care of hatching eggs during incubation :** Care should be taken after

setting the eggs for incubation. It is necessary to inspect the eggs every day to see that they are all right. When the weather is very hot and dry, it may be necessary to sprinkle warm water of 102°F over the egg in order to maintain proper moisture of the egg. In West Bengal, it is generally not necessary due to normal humidity. Rats causes damage to the hatching eggs by steeling them from under the hens. The only remedy is to keep the hen with her eggs in a box having strong bottom and surrounded by ½" mesh wire netting. Sprinkling flower of sulphur over the nests and egg just a day or two before the chicken appears seems to be beneficial.

EGG TESTING

It is necessary to know whether the egg is fertile or not before setting them for hatching. Of all the methods of testing egg, candling of eggs is the most common.

The eggs should be tested on the seventh day of incubation in order to remove the infertile egg or any embryos which have dried at an early stage. The fertile egg under the candling lamp at this stage show a small dark spot with radiating blood vessels similar to spider web. The infertile egg, on the other hand, appears quite clear of such spots while the dead embryo has either a conspicuous blood ring or a much reduced embryo spot. The eggs should be again candled on the 18th day in order to remove dead embryo chicks. By this time, the live embryo will have practically filled the egg, excpet for the air space, where as the dead embryo will be less well developed (Iyer, 1962).

The other method of testing fertile good eggs is as follows:

On the 19th or 20th day of hatching, a large bowl is filled with hot water (exactly at 102°F) and the testing eggs are placed in the water. After a minute, the fertile eggs containing live chickens will wriggle in the water. This is caused by the chickens endeavouring to make escape from the shells. The infertile and addled eggs will float about, but will not wriggle. The eggs must be allowed to remain only one minute in the water and then taken out, properly dried and put back under the hen. (Banerjee, 1992).

METHODS OF HATCHING EGGS

There are two methods of incubation usually practiced in our country

(i) **Natural hatching :** In this method eggs are incubated with the help of broody hens. It is a primitive method. But it is most effective method to get a high percentage of success. Natural hatching or hatching of eggs by hen is still popular with small poultry keepers in remote rural areas in many parts of our country.

SELECTION OF HATCHING HEN

The ordinary 'desi' hen is ideal for hatching chicken as she is a close sitter and owing to her light weight, there is a little possibility of eggs being broken.

The hens hould be throughly broody and she may be tested with the help of dummy eggs for her interest to sit on the eggs. The broody hen used for hatching eggs should be healthy, quiet, a good sitter and have a good body size with all feather in her body. The hens in moult should always be rejected. The hen should be treated for internal and external parasites before allowing her to sit on eggs. The hens should be dusted with a good insecticides such as gammaxane or sodium flouride. A further dusting ten days latter will ensure her complete freedom from lice and ticks.

THE NESTS

The nest should be made of fine, soft hay, straw or leaves and placed near the ground so that the hen can enter it without difficulty. An earthen pot, about 15 inches in diameter and eight inches deep is filled three quarters with earth or ashes and latter is pressed to make a hollow. A quantity of flowers of sulphur or an insectides powder is sprinkled over the nest and after the eggs have been placed on the hollow, the hen is gently seated on them and left undisturbed. The nest should be roomy, fairly dark, cool and well ventilated, readily accessible and easy to clean. The nest should be in a place where the hen will be safe from dogs, cats, rats and other vermin. (Iyer, 1962)

BEST TIME TO SET HENS

The best time to set hen is at a night as at this time she is more likely to settle down to her job. Besides, when eggs are put under the hens at night, the chicken are more likely to appear on the night of 21st day and will have the whole night to rest and grain strength.

NUMBER OF EGGS UNDER A HEN

Depending on the size of hen, 10-15 eggs can be placed under one bird. The ordinary desi hen will only cover eight to nine eggs (two ounce eggs).

CARE OF SITTING HENS

The sitting birds should receive clean cold water, twice daily and adequate amounts of whole grains and limestone grits. Sloppy foods of all description should be avoided, as they tend to produce loose droppings and consequently soiling of eggs. The hen should be taken out at least twice a day for about 30 minutes to be feed and watered. The temporary change from the cramped position is good for the hen and the exposure to the fresh air gently benefits the eggs.

ADVANTAGES AND DISDVANTAGES OF NATURAL HATCHING

Advantages

1. Natural hatching is profitable for hatching small number of eggs.
2. There is no need of any implement for hatçhing of egg by this method.
3. The broody hen will take care newly hatched chicks if they are left to them.

DISADVANTAGES

1. The broody hen sometimes leaves the hatching eggs before the eggs are hatched. The total number of eggs are spoiled in this case.
2. The breaking of eggs may occur due to faulty sitting of broody hen.
3. This method is not suitable for hatching large number of eggs at a time.
4. The hen do not lay egg so long they are engaged in hatching of eggs. The total production of eggs may be hampered for this.
5. It is not always possible to get broody hen as and when required.

ARTIFICIAL HATCHING OR INCUBATION

The small Poultry farmers generally use the broody hen for hatching the egg. The desi hens are ideal for the purposes. The broody hen can hatch 10 to 12 eggs. But at present the incubators are used for large scale chick production. Following are two type of incubator generally used for hatching large number of eggs :

1. Hot water tank incubator
2. Hot air incubator

The water or air inside the incubator is heated by kerosene lamp or electric heater and accordingly the incubators are of two types :

(a) Kerosene incubator,

(b) Electric incubator.

Kerosene incubator is generally used in rural area where there is no electric supply. The electric incubator is used in big poultry farm for hatching large number of eggs.

1. HOT WATER TANK INCUBATOR

The cabinet of the incubator is made of wood. The wall of the incubator is made with wood, tin or asbestor sheet in such way that there is some space in between them and this space is filled with glass wood or glass fibre. The insulator preserve the heat inside the incubator. The incubator have the followings compartment.

(i) **Hot water chamber :** Hot water is kept in water chamber made of copper or aluminium which is placed on upper side of the incubator. The heat radiated from water chamber falls on egg and the embryo develops slowly by getting heat.

(ii) **Flue :** Flue remains at the side of the incubator. A oil lamp is attached on the beneath of the flue. The hot air entered into incubator through the flue. This hot air maintains the temperature of water in the water chamber. The upper end of the flue is open and a damper remains on it.

(iii) **Arrangement of automatic heat control :** The incubator have the heat regulating arrangement. When the temperature of the incubator rises above the level to which it is previously adjusted, the capsul expands and forces the pus rod upwards and this in turn lifts the damper off the exhaust flue, but as soon as the inside temperature falls below the required point, the damper closes down and all heat goes into the incubator.

(iv) **Arrangement of maintaining humidity :** The optimum and uniform humidity is very essential for successful incubation. The relative humidity should be around 60 percent during the first 18 days of incubation and 70 percent in the last three days for optimum hatchability. A water tray with sponge or hessian over or in it is kept inside the incubator and is filled with water about hatching time. The air get entered into the incubator through the opening on the bottom and become moist during flowing through the bottom hole of the water tray. This moist air maintains the required humidity of the eggs. Moisture content of the incubator affect the hatchability.

(v) **Thermometer :** A thermometer is fitted in inside the incubator for maintaining proper temperature. The incubator have a glass window fitted infront of the hatching egg tray, through which the temperature reading is taken.

(vi) **Egg Chamber :** A wire bottom tray is fitted at 6-8 inches below the hessian of the heating chamber. This is meant for eggs tray.

(vii) **Nursery tray :** There is also another tray which is known as the nursery tray. The newly hatched chicks may be kept in this tray for about 36 hours.

2. HOT AIR INCUBATOR

Hot air incubator is generally used more than that of hot water incubator. The structure and function of this incubator is similar to that of hot water incubator. The only difference is the presence of heat chamber in place of hot water chamber which is present in hot water incubator. Heat is provided by lamp or electric heater.

3.CABINET TYPE INCUBATOR

Cabinet type incubator is generally used for hatching large number of egg at a time in Government and non-government poultry firm. The demand of this incubator is increasing gradually. The egg trays are fitted in stacks. As a result, the incubator beecomes smaller in size. The incubator have the automatic egg turning device. Electricity is used for providing heat.

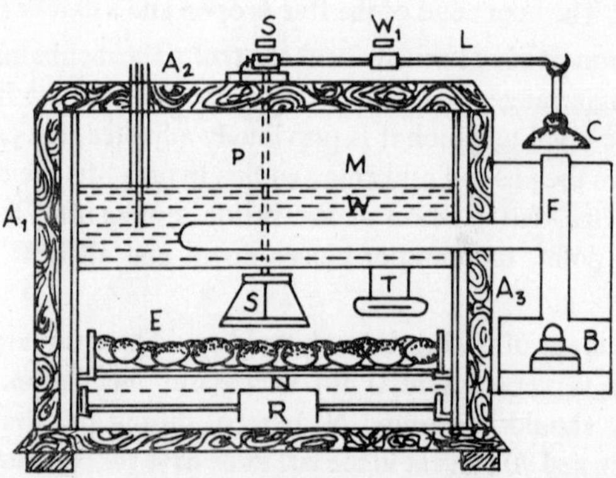

Fig. 4.1. Kerosene incubator

A_1, A_2 and A_3 : Wooden box, W_1 : Weight, L : Liver rod, C: Damper, F : Flue, T : Thermometer, W : Water tank, S : Capsule, M : Chick tray, P : Push rod, E : Egg, R : Water trays, N : Napkin, B : Lamp.

MANAGEMENT OF INCUBATORS DURING INCUBATION

(i) **Fumigation :** The main object of fumigation is to kill disease producing organism to decrease the disease infection of the chicken and to control the speread of organism in the hatching house. Formaldehyde is generally used for this purposes. Fumigant is made by mixing formaldehyde and potassium permanganate. These chemical are required in the following rate for fumigation of incubator meausuring one hundred cubic foot.

Formaldehyde	:	45 gm (Liquid)
Potassium permanganate	:	30 gm.

Fumigate should be used very cautiously.

(ii) **Levelling of the incubator** : Levelling of the inocubator is very essential. The damper rod will not function normally if the level of the incubator is not even. As a result the temperature regulation of incubator is affected. Levelling may be accomplished by the use of a spirit level.

(iii) **Regulating incubator** : A trial run of the incubator at the beggining of each hatching, regardless of the incubator new or old is a must. The thermometer of the incubator should be checked. Comparing with a standard thermometer.

(iv) **Placing eggs** : Fertile eggs are placed in egg tray in rows with broad end up in cabinet incubator. The hatchability decreases if the eggs are placed in the egg tray with narrow end up. The eggs should be placed in the incubator early in the morning. This will faciliate the inspection of the incubator during day time and adjustment may be made accordingly.

(v) **Regulating temperature** : The optimum and uniform temperature is essential for successful incubation. The hatchability is more with a temperature of 101°F during first week followed by 102°F during the second week and 102°F during the third week of incubation. Abnormal temperature conditions over a long period adversely affect the hatchability.

(iv) **Regulating ventilation** : Developing embryos require oxygen for their metabolism. Ventilation ensures oxygen supply in the incubator. Oxygen concentration above or less than 21 percent effects hatchability. The ordinary air contain 21 percent oxygen. Carbon-di-oxide concentration should not exceed more than 0.5 percent inside the incubator. Carbon-di-oxide concentration more than 0.5 percent decreases the hatchibility. The incubator should be placed in a room having adequate ventilation.

(vii) **Regulating moisture** : The optimum and uniform humidity is essential for successful incubation. The incubator should have the moisture regulating arrangement. At low moisture, the developing embryo becomes dry and hatchability decreases.

(viii) **Care of the lamp** : The lamp should have new wick having sufficient length to last during the incubation period. The oil lamp should be provided with oil daily.

(ix) **Turning of eggs** : Turning of eggs in the incubator increases hatchability. Eggs should be turned at least four times daily, starting with third day of incubation. No turning is required after 18 days of incubation. Turning of eggs at regular interval helps to prevent the embryo sticking to the shell membrane.

(x) **Testing of eggs** : The incubated eggs should be tested on 7th and 14th days. Egg testing helps to eliminate the infertile egg.

Fig. 4.2. Egg tester

(xi) **Care during hatching :** A good hatch is that when the chicks are out of their shells before the end of 21st day. The eggs should be sprinkled with flower of sulpher. The nursery tray should be placed in the incubator on 19th day. The door of the incubatorr should be kept close untill hatching is complete. The chicks after hatching access to the nursery tray.

(xii) **Care of new hatch :** The chicks which have hatched should be kept in incubator without providing any food for atleast 18 to 24 hours. The temperature of incubator should be gradually reduced to 93°F to 95°F when the chicks are dried off and fluffed out. The chicks become hardern before transferring them into the brooder. Proper care is required during transferring the chicks from the incubator to the brooder. Culling of weak, disease affected and lamb bird is to be done at this time.

1 2 3

Fig. 4.3. Fertility test of egg

1. Fertile eg (7 days), 2. Fertile egg (14 days). 3. Infertile egg.

ADVANGATES AND DISADVANTAGES OF ARTIFICIAL INCUBATION

Advantages

(i) Large number of eggs are hatched at a time.

(ii) Hatching of eggs may be done as and when required.

(iii) The diseases of broody hen may transmit to chicks in the case of natural hatching. But there is no such possibility of transmission of disease in case of artificial hatching.

(iv) There is no need of broody hen.

(v) The rate of hatchability of incubator is more. The artifical incubation is profitable from economic point of view.

(vi) The artificial incubation is most useful for the hatchery.

DISADVANTAGES

(i) Incubator and brooder are needed for aftificial incubation and thereby it needs extra cost.

(ii) Artificial incubation needs skilful management. Otherwise the whole programme will be upset.

(iii) The machinary defects at any time of incubation period leads to heavy loss.

(iv) Disease may be transmit through the incubator.

(v) The newly hatched chicks need special nourishment. The broody hen performs this function in case of natural hatching.

Table 4.2. Incubation period of different bird

Name of the bird	Incubation period (days)
Fowl	21
Duck	28
Muscovy duck	35-37
Goose	28
Turkey	28
Cotunix quail	17

BROODING AND REARING

The young chicks should be kept warm and comfortable and fed on a well-balanced diet. The care and management of chicks during early part of their life (upto 4-6 weeks of age) constitutes brooding. Successful brooding results in the production of healthy pullets in terms of egg and meat production. The chicks should be brooded as far away as possible from older birds to reduce spreading of infection to young flock. Completely isolated brooding arrangement is a must.

PRINCIPLES OF BROODING

The success of poultry industry mainly depends on the proper management and brooding of young chicks. Brooding is the method of applying heat, specially at night to the chicks during early part of their life. The chicks hatched artificially i.e. in incubator are kept in brooder to provide them requisite temperature.

Successful brooding depends to a considerable extent upon providing the chickens with an adequate and steady source of heat. The heating unit is known as brooder or foster mother. Brooder is the substitute for the mother hen.

The success of brooding depends mainly on the following things :

(i) **Disease free chicks and healthy stock :** To start with healthy high quality chicks is of prime importance. Day old chicks are purchased from hatchery and reared in a poultry farm. It is essential for ascertaining the health status of parent stock. They should be free from pullorum, Typhoid, Mycoplasma gallisepticum (M.G.) and Mycoplasma Synoviae (M.S.) The chicks must be vaccinated with Mereks F1. vaccine.

(ii) **Maintenance of proper temperature :** Desi hens as a class are ideal mother and they reared the chicks by providing with their body heat. But in artificial brooding, the chick comfort is the criterion to determine the proper brooding temperature. It is essential to watch the behaviour of chicks four times during the day and three times during the night for the first one week to determine wheather brooding temperature is correct. The chicken, if huddle, the temperature may be low, if they are away from brooding hover, the temperature may be very high and if they move around evenly, the temperature is just right. The temperature under the brooder is to be reduced at the rate of 5°F (3°C) every week of age after the first week (from 95°F) untill approximately 70°F (21°C) is achieved. Comfortable chicks will be quiet and uncomplaining.

Table 4.3. Brooding temperature necessary for various ages of chicks

Age of the chicks (week)	Brooding temperature
0 - 1	93° - 95° F (33.8° - 35° C)
1 - 2	80° - 90° F (26.6° - 32.2° C)
2 - 3	83° - 85° F (28.3° - 29.2° C)
3 - 4	78° - 80° F (25.5° - 26.6° C)
4 - 5	75° F (23.8° C)
5 - 6	70° F (21° C)

(iii) **Fresh air and ventilation control :** Fresh and pure air is essential for proper growth of young chicks. Ventilation at slow rate is necessary for the chick of 2-3 weeks of age. As chick grow, they need ample supply of fresh air. The chicks feel discomfort in humid, hot house. So they need dry, fresh air and pure water in the brooder.

(iv) **Keeping the chicks busy :** Chick guard of 18" (45 cm) high corrugated cardboard roll or hand board (laminated) all round the brooder about 2 ft away from the edge of brooder must be placed. Feeder and waterer should be placed in between the chick guard and wall of the brooder. Feeder and waterer should be big enough to provide opportunity large number of birds to take food and drinking water at a time. Otherwise, they will overcrowded to take food and drink water, leading to cannibalism.

(v) **Safety from fire :** Electric, gas, kerosine, hot water etc. are used to keep the brooder and brooder house hot. Care should be taken to avoid the fire hazard.

(vi) **Dryness :** The Brooder house should be clean and dry. The chick may be affected in paralysis if they are keept in damp brooder house.

(vii) **Sanitary condition :** The poultry farm and its surroundings must be kept clean. The litter must be clean and free of mould. This helps to prevent aspergillosis (brooder pneumonia) and reduce other disease risks. House where flocks live should be disinfected and should be kept ideal and clean for at least one week of brooding.

A large, deep disinfecting pan and also a bucket filled with fresh disinfectant solution and scrub brush, should be kept just inside all entry doors and used to clean the attendant's boots each time he enters the building. Visitors should not be allowed on the farm. Farm attendants should wear separate boots and coveralls for each flock they care for. If an attendant remains responsible for more than one flock, the younger birds always should be cared for first. The entire building including litter and all equipments should be fumigated, if the previous flock had a serious disease problem.

(viii) **Proper feeding and management :** The growth of young chicks depends mainly on the properly balanced diet. Crushed maize may be feed in the paper or chick boxes lids or plastic filler for first two days. Two inches feeder space in chick size feeder troup type for the chicks up to 6 weeks is ideal. One feeder (four feet long feeder) is sufficient for 100 chicks.

The birrds should be provided with fresh and clean water. Two waterers of one gallon capacity should be sufficient for 100 chicks. Chicks should have at least 2 cm. of linear watering space per bird. The waterer should be washed daily.

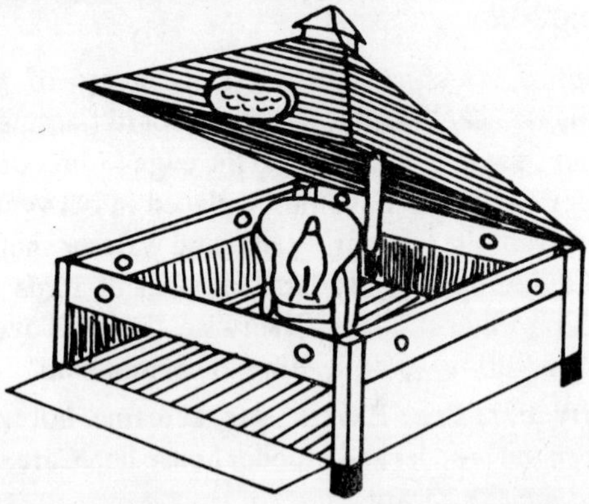

Fig. 4.4. Brooder for newly hatched chicks

(ix) **Proper housing and case of attendant :** The hosue should be prepared in such way that permits easy accession of attendents for cleaning and disinfection. The house should have cement floor and all windows and doors should be screened to prvent the entry of wild birds. The poultry house should be big enough. The house should be such that permits entry of sufficient sunlight. The poultry house should have lighting arrangement @ one 15 watt bulb per 200 sqft. This will provide sufficient heat to the chicks, opportunity of getting more food and they do not huddle.

(x) **Litter :** Litter is spread on the floor to prevent the direct contact with the floor. Straw, wood dust, paddy husk etc are generally used for making the litter. The litter should be dry and free of moulds. The floor of the house is covered with new absorbent type litter to a depth of approximately 5 cm (2 inches). The old litter should be handled well away from the area. Lime is used @ 500 gm per 100 sq. ft. to keep the litter dry. This will also help to keep the litter free from disease organism. The dusty or excessively wet litter should not be used and caked or mouldy materials should be removed. The wet litter harbour the disease producing organisms and act as a agent of spreading various diseases.

(xi) **Protection from enemies :** Some animals such as cat, rat, owls and other predatory animals etc. are the common enemies of the poultry birds. They are harmful to the poultry birds. Flies and rodents are also major sources of infection. They must be controlled.

(xii) **Skilful management :** The success of poultry farming depends on skilful management. The experience of poultry production may be helpful for smooth and profitable running of poultry farm.

(a) **Vaccination :**

(i) At day old stage either F_1 or Mareck's vaccine should be given.

(ii) On 5th day F_1 vaccine should be given if Mereck's vaccine is administrated on first day.

(iii) At the end of 6th week, Fowl pox vaccine is to be given.

(iv) At the end of 9th week, vaccination against Ranikhet (R B strain)

(v) At the end of 17th weeks once again against Ranikhet (same as iv)

(b) **Precision Debeaking :** The most important management function next to vaccination is debeaking. It is done to prevent feed wastage and reduce picking. About one half of both the lower and upper beak is removed keeping the lower beak slightly longer than the upper. Precision debeaking at the 6th to 10th day of age is ideal with less stress on birds and better labour efficiency.

SYSTEM OF BROODING

The system of brooding depends mainly on the method of incubation followed and accordingly there are two method of brooding :

1. Natural brooding or hen rearing
2. Artificial brooding

1. NATURAL BROODING

The natural brooding method is adopted where only few chickens are raised by natural hatching. The brooding of chicken is done under the hen. Desi hens as a class are ideal mothers as they possess a strongly developed maternal instinct and as they are comparatively small they seldom injure the young chicks by trampling on them. So desi hen has no rival in this regard. Desi hen will brood 15 to 20 chickens. The chickens get warm under feathers of the hen. The chickens get infected with various diseases if they are not provided required temperature during their early period of growth. This method is good from the practical standpoint as it needs no extra cost and management.

Brooding Coop

Probably the most desirable system of natural brooding is to kept the hen in a coop. The brooding coop is made of packing box material at a dimension of 2 x 2 x 2 feet, keeping slight slope from front (i.e. 2 feet height) to back (i.e. 1½ feet height), The brooding should have a wire door at one side, which is remain close during night. The hen and chickens are placed in brooding coop after spreading straw on its bottom. The essential requirements of brooding coop are dryness, durability, ventilation, roominess, safety and cheapness. In order to protect the young chickens from wild animals and bird it is best to confine them to a small area of land. The broody hen supplies her young with necessary heat by means of her own body and feathers.

Feeding Chickens and Hen

The chickens should be given small quantities of feed frequently for the first week. The feed should consist of chick mash which is mixed with water or milk to a crumbly consistency.

The hens must get blanced growers mash. Clean water must be available for hen and chicks.

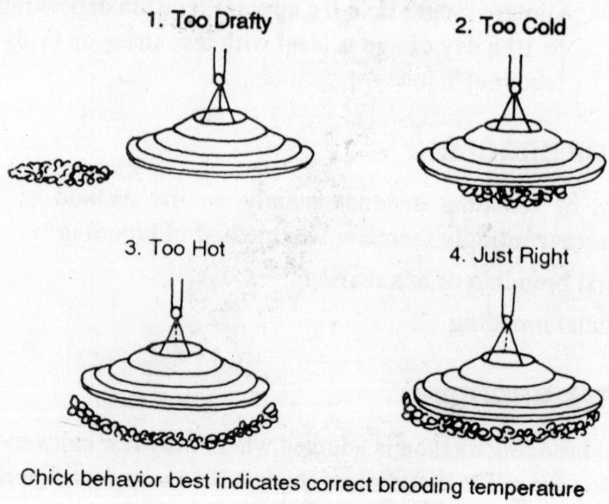

Fig. 4.5. Brooding temperature

2. ARTIFICIAL BROODING

Artificial brooding is followed on a farm where a large number chickens are raised by artificial hatching. Here the rearing of young chickens is done without the aid of a hen. Successful brooding depends to a considerable extent upon providing the chickens with an adequate and steady source of heat. The heating unit is known as a brooder or foster mother. Brooder is a substitute for mother hen. Artificial brooding has the following advantages over the natural methods :

(i) Large number of chicks may be brooded at a time.
(ii) Chicks may be reared at any time of the year.
(iii) No need of broody hen.
(iv) Sanitary condition may be controlled.
(v) Temperature may be regulated as required.
(vi) Feeding may be under-taken according to plan.
(vii) There is no possibility of spreading insects from mother hen to the chickens.

Day old chickens, can be reared very successfully by artificial method without additional heat being supplied to them. The brooder should have the following essentials :

Dependable mechanism for controlling temperature and regular supply of fresh air, economic in construction, durable, adequate light and space, dryness, safety from fire, easy disinfection, and protection against chick enemies.

Brooders may be different kinds in accordance with the nature of source from which the heat is supplied. Such as :

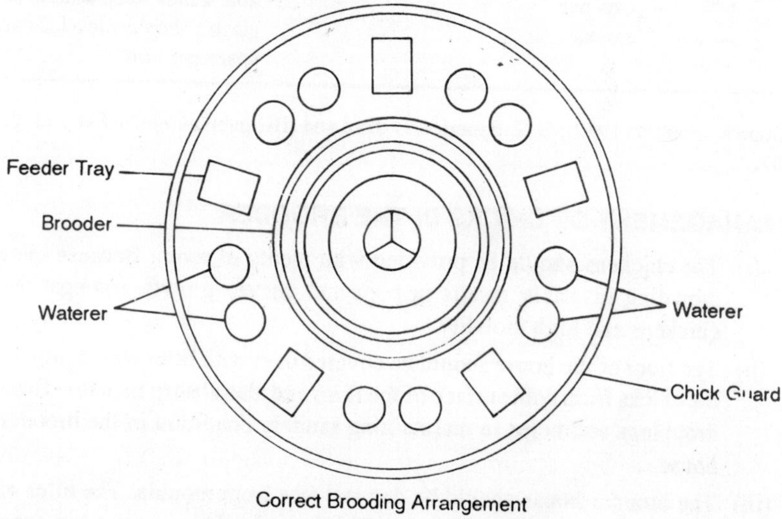

Correct Brooding Arrangement

Fig. 4.6. Brooder Stove Arrangement.

1. Hover brooder, 2. Coal brooder, 3. Oil brooder, 4. Electric brooder, 5. Batery brooder

Out of these, electric brooder are very convenient and can be kept economically where the cost of electricity is low. Continuous and regular supply of electricity is essnetial for this brooder. The main disadvantage of this brooder is that the break down of current for a few hours during night may result in heavy losses by chilling. Kerosene lamp brooders are generally used when chickens are reared artificially on a small scale.

Table 4.4. Floor spare, temperature and water space for chicks in artificial brooding.

Age	Floor space	Brooder temperature	Water space
1st Week	100-120 sq cms per chicks	95° F	Start on shallow pans to avoid crowding, use 4 waterers per brooder.
2-4 weeks	250-300 sq. cms per chick	90° F : 2nd week 85°F : 3rd week 80° F : 4th week	Provide 4-6 waterers of three litre capacity per brooder. Fill waterer at least twice daily.
5-8 weeks	700-800 sq. cms per chicks	80° F	Use water trough with adjust-able stands Keep waterer at chick's shoulder level, 2 cm space per bird.

Source : Poultry (1992), G.C. Banerjee, Oxford and IBH publishing Co. Pvt. Ltd. P. 67.

MANAGEMENT OF CHICKS IN THE BROODER

(i) The chickens should be provided with plenty of room. Because over crowding invaribly results in poor and uneven growth amongst the chickens and high motality.

(ii) The floor of the house should be covered over with litter which protect the chicks from cold surface of the floor and also absorp moisture from droppings and helps in maintaining sanitary condition in the brooder house.

(iii) The brooder house should be dry and free from moulds. The litter of high quality keeps the room dry. The litter should be renewed as soon as it becomes damp or very dirty with droppings.

(iv) The young chicks should be removed from the incubator and transferred as quickly as possible to the brooder which should have been running for at least 24 hours previously.

(v) The temperature should be adjusted as per requirements of the chicks.

(vi) The chicks should be provided plenty of good water in a convenient container which should be placed between the guard and the brooder other wise the chicks may sometimes peck each other and also pick up litter and other materials which may cause digestive troubles in them. After few days the guard should be removed and the chickens are allowed into the entire compartment.

(vii) As the chicks grow, increased space area should be given. They should also be provided sufficient hopper. Lack of hopper space leads to feather pecking and cannibalism.

(viii) The young birds should be given chopped green grass every day from one week onward.

(ix) Some form of calcium such as limestone, grit and Oyster shell, should also be fed *ad libitum* from day old onwards.

(x) The brooder including feed hoppers and waterer should be cleaned daily. The waterer should be filled with clean and fresh water at least twice daily.

(xi) The brooder should be placed in such a place where cold winds and rain water does not get in.

(xii) Chicks may be taught to roost when they are 4 weeks of old. Early roosting will help to reduced over crowdig and prevent litter borne infections.

(xiii) Brooder may be removed after 4 to 5 weeks depending upon the weather.

SEXING OF CHICKS

Sexing of chicks when they are day old is profitable for the hatcheries dealing with egg type chickens. Because of most poultry farmers starts their enterprise with the female birds. There are two method of chick sexing :

(i) Vent or Japanese method and

(ii) Auto sexing

(i) **Vent or japanese method :** Vent method of sexing is very popular method and is commonly used for sexing of chick. This method is originally developed in Japan. Sexing of chicks at day old is possible with very considerable accuracy by means of differences in the cloca. The typical male chicks possess a small rudimentary testes in the cloaca, which is wanting in female chicks. The persons highly skilled and experienced in sexing can do this work accurately.

(ii) **Auto sexing :** Auto sexing is done with the help of any sex linked external character. In this method plumage colour or growth of an organ or any other character such as rapid and slow feathering, barring and non barring etc. linked with sex chromosomes are taken into account to determinet the sex. For example, when a Rhode Island Red is mated with Barred plymouth Rock hens (barring of feather is sex linked), all the female progeny will be black and the males barred. Adults males usually have larger combs and wattles than femates and usually posses spurs which are small or absent in female birds. The male birds is usually considerably longer and more rugged and has a bolder appearance and longer and more pointed feather on lower neck, saddle, sickle and tail.

Table 4.5. Indication of sex in Poultry

	Males	Females
Head	Usually large with large and longer attachments such as combs and wattles, coarser than that of females in appearance.	Smaller, rather fine and delicate in appearance compaiired with hens, Hen turkeys have hair on centere line of head.
Plumage	Feathers usually long and pointed at the ends. Tail feathers in chickens is long and curved. Parti-Coloured varieties have more brilliant colour than females. Most duck have a curl in the tail feathers	Feathers inclined to be shorter and more blunt than those of male. Tail feathers short and straight in compirson with the male. Modestcolours in parti coloured varieties.
Body	Larger and generally more angular than the female. Depth from keel to back greater on same weight birds. Bones including shanks, longer, larger and coarser.	Fine boned, body more rounded.
Skin	Slightly coarser particularly in old birds, Feather follicles larger. Less fat under skin between heavy feather	Smoother, generally a better distribution of fat between feather tracts. Feather tracts narrower but carrying more fat.

Contd.

	Males	Females
Keel	Longer with fleshing leading to tapper at the base.	Shorter with more rounded appearance over the breast.
Legs	Drumstick and thigh relatively long with flesh leading to show less full until mature	Drumstick and thigh relatively shorter with drumstic more inclined to roundness, increasingly so with age.

Source : Poultry grading Manual, Ag. Hdbk No. : 31. USDA, 1971, P4 and 5.

5

HOUSING AND EQUIPMENT OF POULTRY

The chickens were the Wild jungle birds and lived in the forest. The forest provide their protection against the hot sunlight. They lay very few eggs and maintain their race to which they belong on the basis of survival of the fittest. The domestricated birds required proper housing, for their protection as well as the production of more eggs. The poultry house should be designed to protect birds from extreme weathers, parasites, predators and thieves and also to avoid the spread of infections and contagious diseases. It should also provide convenience of poultry man to work efficiently without wasting time in unnecessary movements.

ESSENTIAL OF GOOD HOUSE

The traditional method of poultry rearing was free range in the past. This method have both the merit and demerit. But with the introduction of intensive method of poultry rearing, more birds are kept in a limited space. A suitable house is the prime needs for the rearing of poultry birds in the intensive method. The housing arrangement varies according to the prevailing weather condition of the locality and system of poultry rearing. Followings are the essential of good housing of poultry birds.

(i) **Comfort** : The birds that are comfortable and happy produce more eggs. There should be adequate accomodation in the house to provide them comfort. The house should be reasonably cool in the summer, free from drafts and sufficiently warm during winter. It also provide adequate supply of fresh air and sunshine and must remains dry through out the year. The house should be east or south facing. It protects the birds from scorching sun and western wind. The houses having open in the eastern or southern side permits the sunshine to enter into room. The chickens prefers the morning sunlight.

(ii) **Protection :** Thieves, dog, fox, crow, cat and kite etc. are the natural enemies of poultry bird. The poultry house should have safe guard against them. The birds should also be protected against parasites like lice, ticks and mites.

(iii) **Relation of other building :** The poultry house not be too close to the dwelling houses. Because it creates the unsanitary condition. On the other hand it should not be too far away from the dwelling houses as it requires more time in going to the poultry house for feeding, watering and collection of eggs. The poultry house should be located at convenience distance.

(iv) **Shady and cool environment :** Poultry birds suffer much in hot weather and they require cool condition during the day time. Trees planted in the western and northern side of poultry hosue serve as a wind break in the winter and for shade in the summer. The tree should be tall witu no low limbs. Otherwise, the soil under the tree remain damp which produces suitable condition for disease attack. Generally guava, Custard apple, Lemon, Jaba etc. are planted in the run of the poultry house. The birds take shelter under shade during hot weather.

IMPORTANT PRINCIPLES OF SOUND POULTRY HOUSING

The following principles should be taken into consideration at the time of preparation of poultry houses :

(a) **Selection of site for poultry farm :** The followings should be taken into consideration in selecting the site of pultry farming :

(i) The poultry house should be located at a convenient place where there is good market for eggs and meat and at the same time the common poultry feeds should be readily available at cheaper rates.

(ii) The poultry farm should be well connected with roads and other modes of transportation having no poultry farm nearby.

(iii) The poultry farm should be located at a place where electricity and water should be available at reasonable cost and easy.

(iv) The high land with loamy soil should be selected for poultry farm as they provide good drainage.

(v) The poultry farm should have enough space for future expansion.

(vi) The poultry farm should be located in the open space as it provides good ventilation

(b) **Housing requirements**

(i) **Floor space :** The requirements for floor space may vary according to age, size, breed, type and number of birds to be maintained and method of rearing. The bigger house have more usable space per bird compared to smaller house. It is advisable to allow lesser floor, space in large house and more floor space in smaller house. It is better to keep the laying birds in a small unit of 15 to 25 birds. The number can go up to a maximum of 250 birds. The long poultry house should have a partition at every 20 feet to eliminate draft etc.

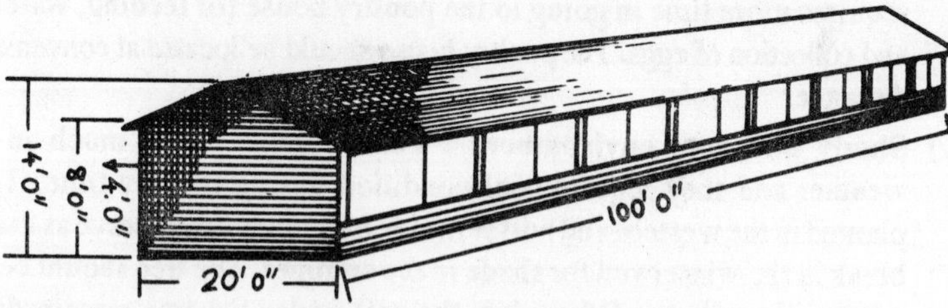

Fig. 5.1. Poultry house

Table 5.1. Floor space requirement for poultry birds

Birds per pen	Area of the house (sq. ft.)		Floor space per bird (sq. ft.)	
	Light Breed	Heavy Breede	Light Breed	Heavy Breed
25	88	100	3 ½	4
100	300	350	3	3 ½
200	500	600	2 ½	3
500	1,000	1,250	2	2 ½

The house should be long in east-west direction. The floor of poultry house should be kept dry at all times. The poultry birds feel discomfort in damp floor and is being attacked with various disease such as cough, Pneumonia etc. Besides, the feeds get mouldy in the damp floor and becomes unfit for poultry. The floor of pultry house should be one foot high from the soil level. Cement concrete floor is the best. The mud floor becomes damp shortly. The dampness in poultry house is caused by

(i) Moisture rising through the floor,
(ii) Rains entering through the window,
(iii) Leaky roofs and walls
(iv) Leaky water container and
(v) Exhalation of birds

Overcrowding creates the following difficulties in poultry farming :

(i) Epidemic may occur due to spread of contagious and infectious diseases.

(ii) The poultry house becomes damp.

(iii) Feather picking and cannibalism may occur

(iv) Malnutrition of poultry birds.

VENTILATION

There should be proper ventilation arrangement in poultry house as it is necessary to provide the birds with fresh air. Proper ventilation require for the movement of fresh air into the building and removal of stale air out of the building in such a way to produce healthy atmosphere in all parts of the house. Proper ventilation during summer months is very much important. Ventilation is reduced during winter to avoid, the loss of heat from the shed. But this type of practice should have limitation. Poultry bird requires more air per unit of body in comparison with that of other animals. A hen weighing 2 kg and on full fed produces about 52 litre carbondioxide in every 24 hours. The expired air contains 3.5 percent carbondioxide, and the total air breathede amounts to 0.5 litre per kilogram live weight per minute. Proper ventilation help to remove this and other undesired gass formed in the poultry house. This also includes the removal of moisture given off by birds in thei dropping, exhaled gases, spilling from water etc. to keep the humidity of the atmosphere down to an acceptable level. Wire mesh is fitted on the upper side on the wall of all sides to provide proper ventilation. Cross ventilation arrangement is the best. Wet litter due to poor ventilation is often predisposing factor for out - break of coccidiosis and other helminth infestation.

Table 5.2. Daily requirement of fresh air per 100 lbs live weight of different animals.

Name of animals	Requirement of fresh air (cubic foot)
Man	2,833
Cow	2,804
Horse	3,401
Fowl	8,278

TEMPERATURE

Poultry birds should be kept at their comfort in the house. For this, it is necessry to protect the birds from extreme heat during summer and extreme cold during winter. Growth and production of poultry birds reduce at extreme heat and cold condition. Hen needs a moderate temperature of 50° - 70° F. (10 - 21° C). The poultry birds need a warmer temperature at night. A temperature of 21° C appears to be the ideal during growing period. The poultry house should be kept cool during summer and hot during winter as far as possible. The use of insulation with straw pack or other materials help to keep the house warmer during the winter months and cooler during the summer months. Cross ventilation also aids in keeping the house comfortable during the hot weather.

LIGHT

Light stimulates the chicken's sexual development and egg production. The birds remain active and consume more feed and produced more egg or meat if proper light is provided. Light stimulates the pituitary gland which release certain hormones necessary forovulation. The poultry house must have proper lighting arrangement. Day light is good for the comfort of chicken. The sunlight kills the organisms and keeps the litter dry and it has an effect on the health of chicken. Day length varies throughout the year and hence the performance of birds is also expected to vary accordingly. The eg production decline during winter season due to short day lenth.

SANITATION

Some external parasites such as lice, ticks, flies and mites are abundant in poultry houses and they are the worst enemies of birds. They live on the body of the poultry birds and retard growth and laying capacity. Besides, they also transmit the poultry diseases and cause damage the poultry birds. The external parasites produce the stress of the pountry birds and they become restless. There should be proper sanitation measure in poultry houses to get ride of their harmful effect. The design of the poultry house should be such which admits easy cleaning and spraying of insecticides.

AVAILABILITY OF LABOUR

Labour is one of the most important input of poultry production. Poultry industry will be profitable if labour is available as and when is needed. Failure of which directly affects the poultry production. The poultry farms should not be constructed in a place where the availability of labour is problem.

SOCIAL CONDITION

Social condition should be taken into consideration before the starting of poultry farm. Thieves and un-social men causes difficulties of smooth running of poultry farm. Poutltry farm should not be constructed near religious areas where there is no demand of egg and meat.

POULTRY HOUSES

DIfferent types of houses are needed to run the poultry farm successfully Although one type of building can be used for several purposes. Following buildings are usually found in poultry farm.

1. Hatchery
2. Brooder house
3. Broiler house
4. Layer house.

1. Hatchery

Hatchery is a place where artificial hatching of eggs is undertaken. The size of hatchery may vary according to the capacity of eggs. The hatchery should preferably be located in a place where there is a demand for chicks. The hatchery may be located at a far distance from actual users provided transportation facilities exist. The hatchery should consists the following rooms.

(i) **Office room** : Office room is meant for keeping records, correspondence and order supply. It must be comfortable for efficient working of staff. A waiting room for the visitors and customers may be provided with a display unit showing the working of hatchery, advertising its products and providing a supply of advertising literature.

(ii) **Working room** : Hatchery includes different activities and accordingly it may have the following rooms or sections. Egg Receival Room, Egg Traying room, Egg cleaning and washing room, Fumigation chamber, Incubator room, sexing room, packing and despatch room and store room etc.

2. Brooder House

Poultry farm should have proper brooder house. Brooding is a process of care and management of chicks during early part of their life (upto 4-6 weeks of age). Layer or broiler house can also be used as brooder house. The brooder house should be well protected. The brooder house should be constructed with such material which can be readily and throughly cleaned. The brooder house should be well ventilated and lighted.

3. Layer House

Pullets should be housed in layer house between 16 to 18 weeks of age. Floor space @ 1.5 sq. feet per bird in litter floor house should be provided. Laying hens are able to adjust to a wide range of envorinmental condition. Optimum house temperature for laying bird is between 55° to 75°F (11.7° - 23.8° C). The layer house should be well ventilated and lighted. Flock health and performance are highly dependent on temperature control and good ventilation.

4. Broiler House

A broiler or fryer is a young chicken of either sex below 6 to 8 weeks of age. Broiler inherit the most desirable and profitable, meat type traits in Poultry industry. They grow and gain weight rapidly, convert feed more efficiently and reach market size at an early stage. The broiler birds spend their entire life in one house. The broiler house should be well ventilated and lighted.

STYLES OF POULTRY HOUSES

Rectangular house is most suitable for rearing of poultry bird. The length of poultry house may vary according to the size of the flocks, but the width of the house should be between 4.5 to 90 metre. The house should be constructed preferably east to west dirction lengthwise. East or South facing house is the best as it permits sunlight to enter into the house. There are several styles of poultry houses according to the types of roofs. Followings are the different styles of poultry houses :

1. Shed tyres

It is one of the most simple type of poultry houses and easy to made. This type of poultry house is by far the most useful and practical type of house that can be used under different climatic condition and for different system of poulltry keeping. The shed types of house may be stationary or portable. Straw, asbestors and corrugate sheets are used for making roof. Cement concrete roof is best.

(i) **Appex hut or portable house :** It is generally a small house, not exceeding 8 feet x 6 feet. This house can be replaced from one place to other place as and when needed. This type of house is most suitable for free range and semi-intensive system of poultry rearing. The poultry birds spent most of their time during daytime outside the house and take shelter in this house during night. Apex hut is made by woods with a roof made by any kind of materials. The wire mesh is fitted on all sides and floor of the house. Apex hut measuring 8' x 6' with 5 ft. high is suitable for rearing 16 poultry birds.

(ii) **Stationary type** : The stationary type house can be made of any dimension. This type of poultry house is suitable for back yard poultry farming, intensive and semintensive system of poultry keeping. This house is permanently fixed in a particularr place. The poultry birds are confined to in the house.

2. Gable type

Gable type may be stationary or portable. More labours and materials are required for construction of this house. Hence it requires more cost. This type is more suitable in rainfall areas. The roof of this house becomes slopy.

3. Combination type

Combination type house has double pitch roofs and requires more material and labour. Hence it requires more cost. Most of the houses have long slope to the rear.

4. Monitor or semi-monitor type

This type of roof is made for the house that have wide width and pen on both sides of the house. This type of house is meant for brooder house and grower's house. Cost is more for construction of this types of house.

CONSTRUCTION OF POULTRY HOUSES

FLOORS

The floor should be strong and durable, free from damness with smooth surface and having no cracks and crevises, easy to clean and disinfect and rat proof. Floor may be of two types : General floor and improved floor.

(a) **General floor** : This type of floor can be made by various' method. such as

(i) **Katcha floor** : The poor village farmers sometimes prefer this type of floor, due to low cost. But the main demerits of this type of floor is that it is difficult to keep clean. The rat may make holes in this type floor. The floor becomes dirty shortly and harbours disease germs and vemins and provides favourable conditions for the onset and spread of disease.

(ii) **Brick or Tali floor :** Bricks or talies are spread on the floor of the house and the gap between the two bricks and talies is sealed with cement-sand mixture.

(iii) **Concrete floor :** Concrete floor is recommended in preference to any other kind of floor. It is a floor of superior type. 8 - 10 centimeters thickness of well mixed concrete (1 parcent, 2.5 part gravel or stone chiff and 5 part sand) laid on well tamed base is usually sufficient for making concrete floor. It is essential to keep six inches slope per 20 ft. for easy drainage. The floor should be 25 cm higher than outside surrounding elevation. Initial cost is higher for preparation of this tpe of floor. But this floor is very strong and durable. This type of floor is easy to disinfect.

(b) **Improved floor :**

(i) **Wire mesh floor :** Wire mesh floor is the best floor for portable house. The wire having 3" x 1" mesh with 10-12 gange is fitted on the bottom of the house to make this type of floor. It makes excellent flooring through which all the excreta drop out and thus ensures best sanitary condition.

(ii) **Slatted floor :** This type of floor is made with wood having thickness of one inch. Floor made with sal wood is durable provided they are not subjected to dampness.

(iii) **Battery cage :** Battery cage is best for keeping small number of Poultry birds. The bird is confined in a cage. Battery cage have the following advantages.

(i) Egg production is more.
(ii) Culling of non layer and disease affected bird is possible.
(iii) Large number of birds can be kept in limited space.
(iv) Less problem due to parasites, predators and other diseases. Because the birds do not come in contact with each other and litter. But it needs more capital. For this reason this system of Poultry keeping is not found in our country.

WALLS

The walls of poultry house may be made with mud, bamboo, wood, darma, brick and wire mesh. Mud or brick wall is good. The lower portion of the house upto 0.6 metre should be made with brick by masonary works. The upper portion of the walls may be made of chicken wire mesh. The interior surface of the wall should be finished in such way that aids easy cleaning and disinfecting. In winter, it is a necessary to cover the upper portion of the wall made with wire mesh with gunny bags etc. The walls should be strong and durable. In plains open type house with necessary adaption is considered best.

DOOR

The door of the house must be on the south. It may be made with wood or an angle iron frame which is covered with half inch mesh wire netting. The size of the door should be always large enough to allow a man to conveniently get through.

WINDOWS

The windows of the house must be on all four wall of the house, made with mud or bricks. The window should be covered with one inch wire neeting. Window of equal size should be placed on opposite side of the closed type house. The open type house needs no window.

POULTRY HOUSE EQUIPMENT

The poultry house should be equipped with necessary equipment which are essential for the satisfactory production of poultry birds. The equipment used in poultry hosue should be simple in construction, easy to use, cheap, movable, durable, easily cleaned and disinfected whenever necessary. Followings are necessary equipments needed for poultry house : Feed hopper, water containers, roosts, nests, Grit and shell container and sand birth.

FEED HOPPER

Feed hopper is meant for providing food to the poultry bird. They should be designed in such a manner that they can control the feed wastage to a consideral extent, provide the proper space for getting food and prevent the birrds for getting their feet into the feed and for roosting on the hopper. Each bird should be provided three inches space in the feed hopper and accordingly one feet long feed hopper is needed for four birds and it should not be more than six feet long for the convenience. The feed hopper should be such that it can provide the opportunity of two or three birds to eat at a time from the bottom of the feed hopper. Pans, pots and troughs are used as feeding utensil. They should be of suitable size depending on the age and size of birds as follows.

Age of the bird	Measurement of feed hopper		
	Length	Breadth	Depth
Chicks of one day to one week old	1'	2"	1"
Chicks of one week to 45 days old	2'	3"	1 ½
Chicks of 45 days to 120 days old	4'	5"	3"
Adult birds	5"	6"	4"

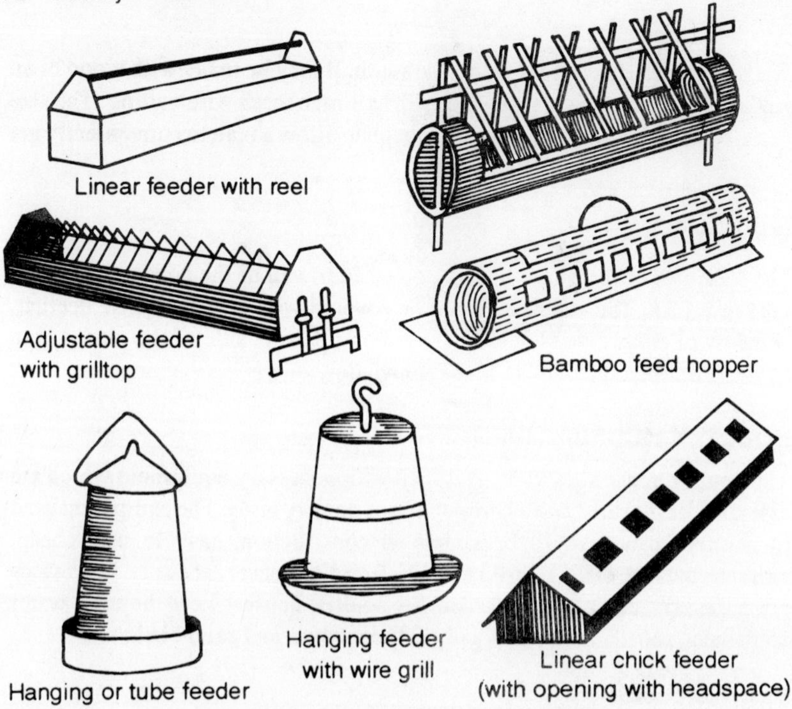

Fig. 5.2. Different types of feeding equipment

Automatic feed hopper is best for avoiding feed wastage. It permits the birds to eat from the bottom of the hopper as and when they need to eat.

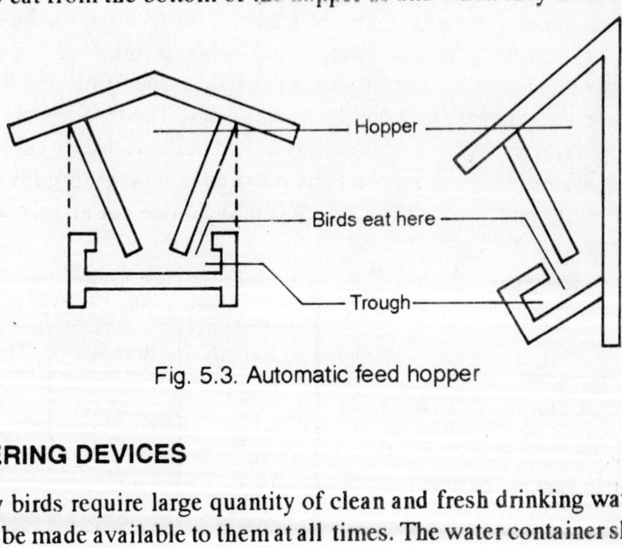

Fig. 5.3. Automatic feed hopper

WATERING DEVICES

Poultry birds require large quantity of clean and fresh drinking water. This should be made available to them at all times. The water container should be large enough for full day supply, kept the water clean and cool in summer, easy to empty, clean and refill. The contaminated water tends to spread certain disease from bird to bird. The warer container does not canode, break or rust and they should be cheap. The water container may be of three types;

(i) Fountain type
(ii) Trough type
(iii) Permanent channel type

Water trougn with wire grill top

Bottle and Bowl waterer

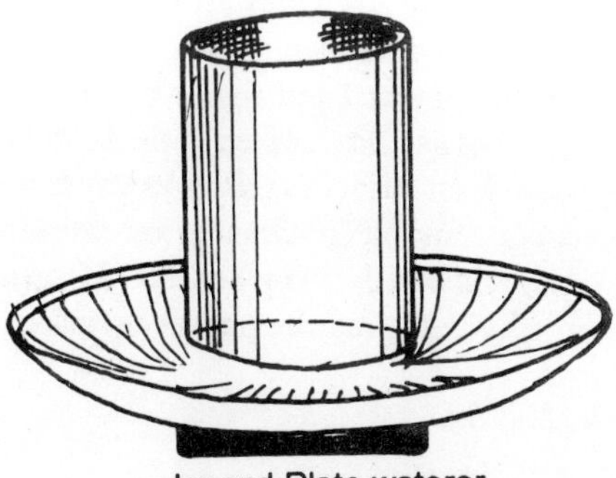

Jar and Plate waterer.

Earthen pot and bowl

Fig. 5.4. Watering devices

Following are the common design of watering devices of poultry birds:

(i) Earthen pot and bowl.
(ii) Jar and plate waterer.
(iii) Bottle and bowl waterer.
(iv) Simple water fountain made of galvenised iron.
(v) Water trough with wire grill top.
(vi) Earthern waterer with hood.
(vii) Automatic linear water trough with float valve assembly.

Waterer made with earthen pot and bowl is very simple and successful waterer as it keeps water cool during hot weather. The demand of water increases with the increase age of poultry birds.

Table 5.3. Water requirement of 100 Poultry birds

Tyep of Poultry bird	Age (week)	Water requirement (litre)
Chicken	0 - 5 5 - 9 9 - 24	1.5 - 8.0 3.0 - 12.0 12.0 - 30.0
Layer	After 24 weeks.	30.0

PERCHES OR ROOSTS

The chicken as a wild jungle fowl, sought safety and rest on the high limbs of a tree or in the thick under bush. The poultry birds prefer roosting as they are habitual to do so. The chickens start roosting when they are eight weeks old. The perches may be made from long wooden bars of two square inches rounded at the top and flat at the bottom or from round baboos having diameter two inches (5 cm). The perches should be fixed at the height of 16 inches (40 cm) above the ground and at least 10 inches (25 cm) away from rear walls in such a way that they are easily removable for cleaning and disinfection. The distance between two perches should be 12 - 14 inches (30 - 35 cm). The perches should be painted occasionally with creosote to prevent insect.

NEST BOXES

The laying birds of almost all breeds prefer dark and separate place for laying eggs. The hen lays egg every day at a place where she starts laying egg at first. The laying birds should be provided with nest boxes for laying eggs in the ration of 1 : 5 i.e. one nest is sufficient for five laying hens of commercial flocks. The nest boxes should be roomy, cool, well ventilated, dark and movable. They should be conveniently located for easy accessible for laying birds. The nest boxes can be made with wooden box, earthen pot or kerosene tin. Out of these, empty kerosene tins makes excellent nest boxes. It is essential to place sand, soft hay or straw inside the boxes which provides comfort to the laying bird and less egg breakage. The nest should be 30 cm square, 15 cm deep and with 37.5 cm head room.

Trap nest box is used in commercial poultry farm in the ratio of 1 : 3 or

4 i.e. one nest is sufficient for 3 or 4 laying birds. The trap nest having trap door is very useful to identify the laying bird in commercial laying farms as the laying bird shot herselves in when she enter in the box. The poultry man can identify the hen and mark her leg band number on the egg when he releases the hen from the trap nest box.

GRIT AND SHELL CONTAINER

The grit is provided to supply additional surface area of the feed by grinding those inside the gizzard. Most grinding takes place in the thick muscled gizzard as the poultry birds do not have teeth for grinding of feed. Lime stone, oester shell etc. are common grits that are provided to the poultry birds. Calcium is required for formation of egg sheel and that can be provided through lime stone, oester shell etc. These should be provided in a ordinary hopper made either of wood or metal as *adlibitum* feeding.

DUST BIRTH

Dust birth resembles the water birth of other animals. Poultry birds prefers dust birth and this do the function of water birth. The poultry birds of free range system makes their place and materials for dust birth. But the poultry birds of intensive system do not get this opportunity. So it is essential to provide the arrangement of dust birth. An earthen pot or a hole in the ground, 2 feet in diameter, filled with dry, clean sand or ashes makes the excellent dust birth which should be placed on east side of the shed. Flower of sulphur and coarse dry tobacco leaves should be added to the sand or ashes. It is useful for destruction of some harmful insects.

OTHER EQUIPMENTS

(i) Weighing balance
(ii) Egg tray and busket
(iii) Egg grader and egg tester
(iv) Rake
(v) De-beaker
(viii) Fleat sprayer
(viii) Brash
(ix) Lamp
(x) Water cane

SYSTEM OF POULTRY FARMING

There are four system of poultry farming generally found to follow among the poultry keepers :

1. Free range system
2. Semintensive system
3. Folding unit system
4. Intensive system
   (a) Cage system
   (b) Deep litter system

1. FREE RANGE SYSTEM

The poor farmers keep small number of poultry birds in this system. It is one of the oldest method. This method generally adopted where there is no shortage of land. Rearing of desi fowls in this systems is profitable enterprises. The poultry birds find appreciable amount of feeds in the surroundings during day time and take shelter in a house during night. This method is not suitable for commercial poultry farming.

Advantages

(i) The poultry birds meet their food requirement from the surroundings. So feed cost is minimum.
(ii) Elaborate housing is not required.
(iii) Rearing cost is minimum.

Disadvantages

(i) The hen lays egg here and there. So losses of egg may be a problem.
(ii) Predatory animals causes loss of poultry birds.
(iii) Infectious diseases including parasitic infestation may occured.

2. SEMI-INTENSIVE SYSTEM

This system is adopted where the amount of free space availability is limited. The poultry house and run is situated in small land surrounded by wire mesh. The poultry birds spend the day time in the run and take shelter in apexhut during night. The birds should be provided 3-4 sq. ft. per birds in the house and 150-200 sqft in the run. The space may be divided giving a run on either side of the house.

Advantages

(i) Protection against predatory animals is possible.
(ii) The birds gets the opportunity to move in the fresh ground.

Disadvantages

(i) The run may get infested with the droppings.

(ii) The poultry birds may be infected with infectious and cotagious disease.

3. FOLDING UNIT SYSTEM

This system of poultry farming is an innovation of recent years. The birds should be provided one sqft. space in the house and 3 sq. ft. in the run. The folding house measuring 5 ft. wide and 20 feet long is suitable for 25 birds. The whole area. (Side and top) is surrounded with wire neeting.

Advantages

(i) Spreading of disease is minimum as the birds being confined to one small run.

(ii) No fear of predatory animals.

Disadvantages

(i) Labour cost is high

(ii) Feeding, watering and collection of eggs needs more time

4. INTENSIVE SYSTEM

This system is usually adopted where land is limited and expensive. The birds are entirely confined to the house.

(a) **Cage or battery system :** The cage system is the latest contribution of the inventor for the poultry lover of the town. The cage system is gradually graining popularity and is useful for those having small quantity of floor space at their disposal. In this system, the birds is confined in a cage just large enough to permit very limited movement and allow the bird to stand and sit comfortably. The usual floor space of cage is 14 x 16 inches and the height is 17 inches. The floor is made with strong galvanised wire and a tray is fixed underneath of the floor for collection of dropping. The feeder and waterer remains outside of the cage. California type of cages are better than the three or four-tier cages as it saves labour. But the later is most commonly used for commercial egg production. Cage system can be used for birds of all age groups and in all climate conditions.

Advantages

(i) Cage system of rearing allows better flock supervision.

(ii) The performance of each bird can be noted and culling is easily carried out as and when required.

(iii) Vegetative egg (i.e. unfertilised egg) may be produced as there is only one pullet in each cage. This egg can be preserved for a longer time than fertilised egg at ordinary room temperature.

(iv) Cage system of rearing offers economy in space, reduce feed consumption and labour, helps in prevention and control of certain diseases like coccidiosis and increase the efficiency of production.

(v) Clean and uniform egg production throughout the year is possible.

Disadvantages

(i) Cage fatigue is one of the problem.

(ii) Malnutrition may be the problem, if the feeding of birds in cages is not carefully performed.

(iii) The eggs produced by the hen keep in the cage can never be used for hatching purposes.

(iv) Feeding and watering requires more labour.

(v) Housing and equipment cost per bird is high.

(b) **Deep litter system :** Deep litter system is widely used for scientific and successful poultry farming in all over the world. In this system, Poultry birds are kept in large pen upto 250- birds each in a house, whose floor is covered with dry litter. Up to a depth of 20 - 30 cms. Rice husk, saw dust, dried leaf, chopped straw and ground nut shells depending upon their availability, can be used as litter materials. Deep litter resembles to dry compost. Followings precautions should be taken into consideration for getting success of this system :

(i) The floor of the house should be 45 - 60 cm high from the ground level. Concrete floor is preferable.

(ii) The birds should be provided floor space @ 3-4 square feet per bird. A house measuring 15 feet long and 10 ft. broad can accommodate 150 birds.

(iii) The floor should not be damped. Precaution should be taken to keep it dry.

(iv) The house should be well ventilated. The house should be south facing as it aids well ventilation.

(v) The litter materials should be used in sufficient quantity to give a depth of 6 - 8 inches (15 - 20 cms). This is reduced to 5 - 6 inches

(12.5 - 15 cm) during summer. The deep litter should always be kept dry.

(vi) The poultry house equipment such as feeder, waterer, roost, nest box, shell and grit container, sand birth etc. Should be arranged in specific place of the house. The waterer must be placed near the drainage channel.

(vii) The poultry house should have door of 6' x 3' size for easy accessible.

(viii) The poultry birds should be provided food having vitamin A and D as they do not synthesize vit. D for want of sunlight due to their confinement in the house.

MANAGEMENT OF DEEP LITTER

(i) The floor of the house should be disinfected by Phenyl, lysol, bleeching powder or lime water before placing litter materials.

(ii) The depth of litter should be 6 inch (15 cm) in summer and 8 inch (20 cm) in winter.

(iii) The deep litter should be kept dry. Wet litter in early stages of growth leads to the sporulation of coccidia. Lime or super phosphate @ 500 gm lime or 1 kg. superphosphate per square feet is applied to make the litter dry.

(iv) Cacking of litter should be avoided as far as possible by keeping the humidity low and strirriing of litter at least once in a week.

(v) Fresh litter should be used for rearing pullets and new batches of birds should be placed in clean litter. The time of starting deep litter should be in the dry period of the year.

(vi) The old, built up litter should be replaced after the rainy season and beginning of winter season. The litter may be kept for one year only.

(vii) The waterer should be placed in such a way to keep the litter dry. Leaking of water from waterer or roof, upsets the whole process and it would have to start over again.

ADVANTAGE OF DEEP LITTER SYSTEM

(i) Deep litter system of poultry rearing aids safety of bird as the birds remain in enclosed and protected house.

(ii) Litter itself act as a source of food supply. The built up litter provides animal protein, vitamin and hormone to the birds.

(iii) The level of coccidiosis and worm infestation is much lower in deep litter system. The disease producing organism can not grow in deep litter if they remain dry. The poultry birds remain engaged for scratching of litter. This is good for their health and cannibalism may not developed due to their engagement in this work.

(iv) Deep litter system needs no cleaning out of poultry pen daily. So it is a labour saving system.

(v) Deep litter is a valuable fertilizer. The built up litter contain about 3 percent nitrogen (nearly 20 percent protein), 2 percent phosphorus and 2 percent potash. Its value is about three times than that of cattle manure. A poultry bird can produce 25 - 30 kg of deep litter manures in one year.

(vi) The deep litters maintain its constant temperature. The birds burrow into the litter when the air temperature is high and thereby cool themselves. Conversely, they can warm themselves in the same way when the weather is very cool.

6

MANAGEMENT OF POULTRY FARMS

Poultry farming has becoming very encouraging enterprise in modern India for small Farmers, Landless labourers and educated unemployed as well as for big enterpenures keeping birds on industrial pattern. It is no more a taboo as used to be in earlier days. As a matter of fact poultry is an old associate of Indian farmers, especially for the poor people and they were kept in small flocks of few on range since long without any particular attention of breeds, feeds and management resulting in poor production (50 to 60 eggs per year) out of indigenous birds.

At present, it has become imperative to know the technique of scientific poultry keeping as modern poultry keeping has become as much science as an art. It is essnetial to combine scientific principles with art of poultry keeping to reap the best harvest.

CHICKS MANAGEMENT

1. Purchase of chicken

The improved and high yielding chicken should be purchased from a reputed farm or farm maintaining high yielding birds superivised by expert genetist who are producing these hybrid high yielders through proper breeding. The farmers may purchase such chicks only from such farms who can supply duly vaccinated chicks against 'Marek's disease and other viral diseases.

2. Brooding (0 to 6 weeks)

After receipt of the chicks, they should be put in well heated brooder which should be run 24 hours before the arrival of chicks with proper temperature of 90° to 95°F with adequate dry litter on the floor duly covered with thick papers to avoid litter eating by these young chicks during first three or four days of their lives. The brooder should be provided with chicks guard to avoid straying of chicks for off places away from heat zones, during these earlier stage. During the first 6 weeks of chicks life the temperature of the booder is to be reduced by 5° F every week starting from 90°F from the first day as per season.

CAUTIONS

(i) Chicks should be brooded as far away as far possible from older birds to reduce spreading of infection to young flock. Completely isolated brooding arrangement is a must.

(ii) It is essential to cheek all equipment carefully that they are clean, and washed with deisinfectant and dried.

(iii) The house of poultry bird should be clean and the house should be white washed and sprayed with malathion before the arrival of chicken.

(iv) No visitors should be allowed in the brooding house.

(v) A separate attendant, only meant for the rearing of baby chicks, should be entrusted with brooding management.

(vi) It is essential to observe the condition of the chicks four times daily during day and three times during night for the first one week. If they huddle, the temperatuure may be low, if they are far away from brooding hover, the temperature may be high and if they move around evenly, the temperature is just right.

(vi) Good movement of air should be ensured in the brooder house for adequate ventilation.

(vii) Temperature under the brooder is to be reduced at the rate of 5° F every week of age after the first week (from 95° F).

(viii) It is essential to maintain an even room temperature by fixing room heaters.

(ix) As the chicken grows, increased space area should be given.

(x) Clean fresh water should be provided to the chicks.

(xii) The guard area should be expanded gradually after three days as the chicks grow and the waterers and feeders should be moved out away from the hover. After 7 to 10 days, the use of brooder guards may be discontinued.

HOUSING

The chicken should be kept in a clean, dry and well ventilated room. Poultry house should have proper ventilation as this provide the birds with fresh air and to carry off moisture. Fresh air is needed without drafts. The poultry house should have wire screening.

Overcrowding is often a problem in growers. The floor space requirement for chicken of various ages is given below :

Table 6.1. Floor space requirement for growing chicken on deep litter.

Type of birds	Floor space/Bird (sq. m.)
(i) Egg type pullets (small strain) :	
0 to 18 weeks	0.13
18 to 21 weeks	0.18
(ii) Egg type pullets (Medium and large strains) :	
0 to 18 weeks	0.18
18 to 22 weeks	0.20
(iii) Egg type breeder pullets	0.22
(iv) Egg type breeder cockerels	0.25
(v) Meat type pullets	0.30
(vi) Meat type cockerels	0.40

The litter should be dry and free of moulds. The caked or mouldy material should be removed and refilled with fresh materials. Excessively wet or dusty litter should not be used.

3. Feeds and Feeders

The growing birds should be provided balanced ration. Crushed maize may be fed in paper or chick boxes lids or on plastic filler flats for two days. chick-size feeders-trough type is ideal. Small quantities of feed should be feed at a time but often, during first 2 to 3 days. The chicks should be feed starter mash containing 20 - 22 percent protein and 2400 to 2500 calories/kg metabolished energy for the first 6 weeks of age.

Table 6.2. Composition of starter mash

(i) Carbohydrate	:	Maize (crushed)	:	30 part
		Wheat (crushed)	:	20 part
		Wheat bran	:	10 part
		Molasses	:	5 part
(ii) Protein	:	Groundnut cake	:	30 part
		Fish meal	:	2 part
(iii) Minerals	:	Oyster shell	:	1 part
		Steamed Bone meal	:	1 part
		Common salt	:	1 part
		Total	:	100 Parts.

Rovisol is to be feed to the chicks two days in a week. 5 ml. Rovisol mixed with 5 litre of water will suffice for 100 birds.

Just before arrival of chicks, waterers filled with lukewarm water with glucose or sugar should be placed in brooder area. With the arival of chicks, they are to be release under the brooder maintained at 95°F after dipping their beaks in water in the water fountain containing Vitamin (Rovisol : 5 ml.) antibiotics (Terramycin or Auromycin 2 A at 100 to 125 gms) and Glucose D (Two teaspoonful per 100 chicks) along with feed spread on the paper and low trays under the brooder. Water and feed are to be provided simultaneously along with adequate heat in well ventilated, clean, dry room on dry litter protected from draft. Feeds, water and light should be provided at proper time. Sudden break of this operation practice will affect production as birds are very sensitive and nervous during the laying period which common people do not observe strictly resulting poor production affecting the very economy of the farmer (Mukerji, 1980).

VACCINATION PROGRAMME

(i) At day old stage either, F_1 or Mareck's vaccine is administrated.

(ii) On 4th day, the chicks are required to be given F_1 strains vaccine through nasal drop to protect them against disease if Mareck's vaccine is administered on first day. This vaccination is done at farmers end on the 4th day when the maternal antibody against Ranikhet is in declining phase and best result of F_1 strains vaccination is obtained by this type of vaccine.

(iii) At six weeks these chicks are again given a short of R 2 B vaccine to protect them for life against Ranikhet disease.

(iv) At eight weeks they are to be protected against fowl pox.

(v) At the end of 17th weeks, when the final selection is made for putting them in laying house, these are to be given a booster dose of R 2 B vaccine again to protect them against any break down in immunity.

DEBEAKING

The most importantmanagement function of poultry bird next to vaccination is debeaking. Chicken should be debeake at the hatchery to prevent feed wastage, feather picking and cannibalism. 6th to 10th day of old is ideal age for debeaking. A combined hot blade debeaker or electrical debeaker should be used to perform this job. About one half of both the upper and lower beak is removed, keeping the lower beak slighty longer than the upper.

GROWER MANAGEMENT

1. Housing

The pullets are transferred in grower house. The house should be clean and well protected. The requirement of chicken is giiven in the following table.

Table 6.3. Floor space, feeder space, waterer space, perch space and nest space per bird.

Age	Floor space	Feeder space	Waterer space	Perch space	Nest space
0 - 4 weeks	½sq. ft.	1"	¼"	x	x
4 - 8	1sq. ft.	2"	½"	x	x
8 - 12	1½sq. ft.	2 ½"	$^3/_4$"	x	x
12 - 16	2 sq. ft.	3"	1"	x	x
16 weeks and above	3 sq. ft.	4"	1"	6" for adult	2' x 2' x 6' for every 50 birds (Layers)

2. Feeds and Feeders

The grower should be feed a good quality well balanced growing ration containing 15 per cent protein, 2600 calories of metabolizable energy per kg. and 5 to 10 percent fibre with proper vitamins and minerals in convenient feeder. 2.6 inches feeder space per bird or one tubular feeder for 25 birds should be provided. The feeder height should be kept adjusted as birds grow to avoid feed wastage. The feeder and waterer should be placed in such a way so that birds need not move more than 10 feet for either feed or waterer. One inch of waterer space for drinking water should be provided and waterers should be cleaned every day.

Table 6.4. Particulars of feed and water requirement (Mukherjee 1980)

Age	Amount of feed per bird	Waterer capacity	No. of of waterers required/ 100 birds	Remarks
0 - 4	30 gms (1 Oz)	1 Quart	8	These feed and water requirements on average basis depend on good quality of feed and fresh,
4 - 8	60 gms (2 Oz)	2 gallons	2	
8 - 12	90 gms (3 Oz)	5 gallons	2	

Contd.

Age	Amount of feed per bird	Waterer capacity	No. of waterers required/ 100 birds	Remarks
12 - 16	100 gms (3½ Oz)	5 gallons	2	Clean and sweet water which too varies as per season and rate of growth and production when these are to be adjusted accordingly.
16 week & above	120 gms (4 Oz)	5 gallons	2	

Table 6.5. Suggested feed analysis

Item	Starter Ration	Growing Ration	Leghorn Layer Ration Controlled Feed	
			Summer	Winter
Protein (Percent)	20 - 21	13 - 15	16 - 18	15 - 17
Calories Me per lb	1280 - 1330	1250 - 1330	1280 - 1330	1300 - 1400
Fat (Percent)	4 - 5	3 - 4	4 - 5	4 - 7
Fibre (Percent)	3.5 - 4.5	5 - 10	3 - 5	3.0
Calcium (Percent)	1.20	1.00	3.00	2.75

The feed should be provided in a convenient feeder so that all birds get their equal share and flock grows uniformly. Adequate feeder space is required to enable all birds to eat at one time. A minimum of 2.6 inches space per birds should be provided. Birds may be feed twice daily at fixed hours without any change or break.

The starter and growing rations feed for the first 14 weeks (98 days) should contain coccidiostat level that allows the flock to develop an immunity against coccidiosis. During the periods of stress, disease and medication, place the birds on full feed. Return to controlled feeding as soon as the flock has recovered.

TIME OF CHANGING RATION

Changing from chick mash to growing mash any time between the beginning of 6th week to the beginning of 8th weeks (36 to 50 days of age) should be done. Continuation of growing ration through 21 week (147 days) using controlled feed programme is to be done.

CONTROLLED FEED PROGRAMMES

The controlled feeding could be done by two methods :

(i) Skip every other day and

(ii) Limited every day

When properly and carefully managed each programme gives excellent result. Careful attention should be given to condiitions of birds, weather and equpiments available. Change from starter to growing mash at 36 to 50 days of age is to be done.

FEEDING HARD GRAIN

Birds grown on 'Skip day' programme may be given small whole or particle size grains to keep them active and it help to maintain good litter condition. Feed it in the litter, one pound per 100 birds, on no feed days only (deduct this from total feed amount the flock is allowed). Do not feed hard grains on excessively hot days.

FEEDING OF GRITT

Grit feeding should be practised for both birds reared in cage as well as on floor. Feed one pound of hen size grit per 100 birds per week, beginning from the 7th week (43 days). Feed the grit on a feed day in hanging tube feeders. Allow one feeder per 250 birds.

FEED AMOUNTS

Approximate feed intake levels are furnished for each week of age during growing period. This will vary according to feed formulation, weather conditions and stress factors. Weekly average body weight of the growers should be thumb-rule guide to determine feed intake. Feed to maintain the recommended body weight for that age level.

DETERMINING CORRECT BODY WEIGHT

Arbor Acres' suggested weight standard are furnished in Table : 6.6 as average flock body weight by weeks of age.

Sample weight of 50 to 100 birds in each pen; find out average feed to maintain flock body weight. Collect birds from different areas of pen. Take individual bird sample weight in a similar manner, each week throughout the growing period. Birds should be weighed on the same day of each week at approxdimately the same time of day, preferably in the afternoon.

Table 6.6. Arbor Acress suggested Leghorn Pullet body weights and feed allowance guide during growing period.

Age of Flock Week	Days	Average Flock body Weight Kg..	Approximate Feed Amounts per 100 bird. * Skip every other day or Limited other day. Kgs.	CUM Kgs.
1st	1 - 7		0.58	4.12
2nd	8 - 14		1.18	10.80
3rd	15 - 21		1.36	20.33
4th	22 - 28		2.71	41.00
5th	29 - 35		3.4	64.92
6th	36 - 42	0.453	3.85	91.71
7th	43 - 44	0.481	4.50	123.48
8th	50 - 56	0.58	4.50	153.26
9th	57 - 63	0.64	4.6	188.86
10th	64 - 70	0.72	4.6	222.06
11th	71 - 77	0.82	4.6	255.60
12th	78 - 84	0.86	4.9	290.50
13th	85 - 91	0.90	5.0	326.88
14th	92 - 98	1.0	5.4	365.00
15th	99 - 105	1.04	5.7	405.00
16th	106 - 112	1.09	5.7	444.47
17th	113 - 119	1.13	5.9	485.78
18th	120 - 126	1.18	5.9	527.94
19th	127 - 133	1.22	6.1	570.22
20th	134 - 140	1.27	6.1	612.90
21th	141 - 147	1.32	6.3	657.39
22nd	148 - 154	1.36	6.5	703.70

Skip feeding programmes should not begin before the birds are six weeks of age. * When using the skip every other day programme double the feed amounts shown the Limited every day.

LAYER MANAGEMENT

Pultets should be housed in layer house between 16 to 18 weeks of age. The pullets should be housed in different pens according to their size and growth. The poutltry house should be well ventilated, resonable worm in winter, cool in summer and free from drafts. South or south-east facing house is good as it get maximum sunlight. The poultry house should be cheap, durable, comfortable and safe. In layer house, two third of the area of the side walls are kept open and fitted with wire mesh for proper ventilation. The height of the house is ordinarily 2.6 to 3.3 m from the foundation to the roof line. Optimum house temperature for laying bird is 55° F to 75°F (12.7° C to 23.8° C).

FLOOR SPACE

Floor space @ 1.75 sq. ft. per bird in the deep litter floor house is to be provided.

FEEDERS

Feeders space @ 2.6 inches per bird or 4 large tube feeders per 100 birds should be provided. It is important that distribution of feed is done uniformly throughout the area as quickly as possible, so that all birds get their equal share. One tube feeder for shell grit/oyster shell should be provided for every 250 pullets. This should be provided @ 1.5 kg per 100 birds per week beginning 22nd week (148 days) The requirements of feed during lay depends on the rate of egg production and the body weight of layer birds. The birds may need more feed in winter and less feed in summer. During summer months when it will be extensively hot or if the flock is under severe stress it will be necessary to stimulate feed intake and even temporarily change to ration containing higher level of protein and other nutrients. The actual feed consumption may be influenced by several factors as follows :

(i) Body weight of the hen.
(ii) Rate of egg production.
(iii) Season and weather condition.
(iv) Health and physical condition of the hen.
(v) Feed quality such as protein content, caloric value of feed etc.

The feed intake increase as the pullets flocks increases their egg production.

LIGHTING

Light affects growth and reproduction of poultry birds by different physiological actions. Correct lighting boosts up egg production by 5 to 10 percent. The duration of the light period should not be decreased during laying period. Lighting encourages the chicks to feed more which will lead to better growth. Even distribution of poultry house is important for proper utilization of all space available in the shed. Irregular lighting results in drop in egg production. One foot candle should be provided at birds eye level. This is equivalent to one watt for each four square feet of the floor space with lamps well distributed. Lighting should be increased gradually from 21 weeks till it reaches 16 - 17 hours per day and maintained at that level thereafter. Light should be 8 feet above the floor and good reflectors should be used to direct all light to the bird areas. The light bulbs should be cleaned and checked regularly. The defective bulbs should be replaced immediately.

WATERER

Minimum of one inch of drinking space with through type of waterer should be provided per bird. The waterer should contain fresh, clean and cold water. It is necessary to provide extra water during summer and extremely hot weather. The top edge of the waterer should be about level with the backs of the birds. This will help to keep water spoilage to a minimum and keep the water clean.

LITTER

The litter should be dry and free of moulds. The extensively wet and dusty litter should not be used for laying birds. The new litter for the layer flock should be provided unless the birds have been grown in the same house.

SANITATION

Sanitation is the maintenance of surroundings conductive to good health. The poultry house and its equipment should be cleaned and disinfected with disinfectant solution before placing the pullets. Poultry disease are highly contagious. So the cleanliness and precautions aginst disease hazard inside and outside of laying hourses are essential.

CULLING

Culling is the procedure of selection and rejection of unproductive and poor producers. Culling is very important job for running poultry farm profitably. Poor layer should be culled to minimize the cost of production. The birds that have laid well for short period but have stopped laying for one reason or other should also be culled out. The characters that should be taken into consideration for distinguishing good and poor layers are as follows :

(i) **Appearance :** We can get an idea about the health and vigour of the birds by its appearance. The healthy bird is more active, more alert, virgours, well fleshed but not fatty, tight feathering with tail and wings carried up. Deviation of any of this characteristics is the indication of poor layers. The main chatacteristics for distinguishing a layer and poor layer is given in Table : 6.7.

(ii) **Moulting :** Moulting provides an indication about the laying capacity of a bird. It is natural and physiological process to renew old feathers at the end of first year of laying. Early moulters are usually poor layer, whereas late moulters are usually good layers.

(iii) **Pigmentation :** Yellow pigmentation of the skin surface especially vent, eye ring and ear lobes, breaks, shanks etc is due to carotenoid pigment known as Xanthopyll coming from the ration of poultry bird containing yellow maize. It provides an indication about the laying ability of poultry birds. The pigment tends to disappear during egg production in the yellow skinned breeds such as white leghorn and Rhode Island Red. Birds come in egg production, lose their pigment and the body parts starts bleaching in the following order :

(i) Vent

(ii) Eye-lids,

(ii) Ear-lobes,

(iv) Beak - starting at the base and gradually extending to the tip,

(v) Shanks - first at the front and then at the rear.

Table 6.7. Relationship between depigmentation of body parts and number of eggs laid.

Order of depigmentation	No. of egg laid to bleach the body part	Time to bleach (after first egg is laid)
1. Vent	0 to 10 eggs	0 to 2 weeks
2. Eye ring and ear-lobe	10 to 15 eggs	2 to 3 weeks.
3. Beak	about 35 eggs	6 to 8 weeks
4. Shanks		
Bottom of feet	about 68 eggs	12 to 16 weeks
From of shanks	about 98 eggs	16 to 24 weeks
Entire shank	about 175 eggs	24 to 32 weeks.

Source : Poultry Production (1985), R.A. Singh, Kalayani Publishers P.P. 90.

(iv) **Sexual maturity :** Sexual maturity is meant the duration between the date a pullet is hatched and the date she lays her first egg. The birds that mature early make good layers. Early sexual maturity is determined by at least two dominant genes, one is autosomal and other is sexlinked (Hays 1924)

MANAGEMENT OF BROILER

A broiler or fryer is a young chick of either sex between 8 to 10 weeks of age weighing 1.5 to 2.0 kg body weight, with tender meated soft, pliable smooth textured and flexible breast (Banerjee, 1991). They grow and gain weight rapidly, convert feed more effeciently and reach market size at an early age, having excellent feather coverage, Now a days, the broiler production is progressing at much faster pace than layer.

BROILER CHICKS

The chicks should be of uniform size, active, alert and bright eyed. The shank or leg covering (skin) of healthy chicks appears bright and shinny. Whenever possible broiler chicks should be hatched from eggs that weight 52 grams each or larger, since there is a direct correlation between egg size and broiler chick weight.

According to the Random Sample Tests of U.S. department of agriculture, performance of some of the leading broiler stocks are as under :

Average body weight at eight weeks : 1.8 to 1.9 kg. (Both sexes combined)

Feed require to produce one kg.

live weight : about 2.0 kg.
Mortality : about 2.0 %

BROILER HOUSING

The broiler house should be prepared for the next group of chicks as soon as possible. The entire building including litter and all equipment should be fumigated, if the previous flock had a serious disease problem. Proper cleaning and sanitizing and then allowing the house to lie vacant for one or two weeks, will break the cycle of most disease producing organisms. Using of new litter for each flock is good for raising disease free broiler. The litter only from previous flock that was in good health may be reused. Chicks should never be brooded on old litter if the previous flock was infected with a contagious diseases that adversely affected its performance. The litter must be clean and free of mould, as they helps prevent aspergillosis (booder pneumonia) and reduces other disease risks. The litter must be raked occasionally to remove caked and crusted area as well as feathers and other debris. Raking also loosens and improves the litter texture. If the depth of old litter is insufficient for brooding, new clean litter should be added.

The broiler house should be sweept down to remove all cobwebs and dust from celling, side walls, curtains and windows.

The males grow faster than females and become ready for market a week earlier than females. So the males and females should be reared in a separate house.

MANAGEMENT PRACTICES FOR BROILERS

(i) **Broiler house temperature :** Chick comfort is the criterion to determine the proper brooding temperature. On the first weeks 95°C is quite comfortable. As chicks grow, the temperature may be reduced at the rate of 5° F (3°C) untill approximately 70° F (21°C) is reached on the sixth week. Comfortable chicks will be quite and uncomplaining.

(ii) **Ventilation of Broiler house :** Proper ventilation aids in removal of dust or moisture or ammonia from the house and maintains required temperature and oxygen. Unless these management factors are carefully controlled, significant damage to the flock is possibleand performance may be greatly impaired.

(iii) **Lighting for Broilers :** Most broiler growers provide 24 hours light during brooding and early growing period. Recent research contducted in windowless buildings, using intermittent lighting of 1 - 2 hours period, has indicated significantly improved feed efficiency. The initial period light intensity (1 - 15 days) should be 40 - 60 watts per 20 squaremeters (200 square feet) of space and this can be replaced by 15 watts bulb in beginning of third week.

(iv) **Floor space requirement :** Floor space requirement depends on the size of the birds to be grown. The approximate bird placement rates is given below :

Anticipated body weight (Kg.)	Birds per square metre	Square feet per bird.
1.4	18	0.6
1.8	14	0.8
2.3	11	1.0

Table 6.8. Floor space conversion

Square feet per bird	Number of birds per Square metre
0.5	22
0.75	14.4
1.00	10.8
1.25	8.6

* 1. Square meter = 10.76 square feet.

(v) **Broiler feeding :** Feed represents 60 - 70 percent of total live production. Broiler are usually feed with the following two types of ration :

(a) **Broiler starter :** It is feed to the broiler up to five weeks of age.

(b) **Broiler finisher :** It is feed to the broiler of more than five weeks of age and continued till the age of marketing.

Feeding three or four times each day will stimulate feed intake and prevent waste. It is essential to provide adequate feeder space (5 cm per bird in case of trough feeder and one pan per 50 birds in case of pan type feeders).

Table 6.9. Broiler starter diet

Ingredients (Kg/100 kg.)	1	2	3	4	5	6
Maise	44.25	43.75	45.47	44.42	50.88	57.10
Rice Polis	10.00	10.00	10.00	15.00	10.00	-
Groundnut cake	15.00	14.00	30.00	26.00	14.00	-
Sunflower cake	15.00	14.00	-	-	8.00	15.00
Mustart cake	-	-	-	-	-	10.00
(Solvent extracted) Fish meal (40% pro)[1]	6.00	10.00	10.30	7.00	8.00	6.00
Meat meal (50% pro)	6.00	-	-	-	-	7.00
Meat-cum-bone meal (54% pro)	-	-	-	-	3.00	-
Silkworm pupaemeal deoiled (70% pro)	-	-	-	5.00	5.00	3.00
Blood meal (73% pro)	-	3.50	-	-	-	-

(Contd.)

Ingredients (Kg/100 kg.)	1	2	3	4	5	6
Lysine HCl·D.L. Melhionine	-	-	0.10	0.10	-	-
Animal fat	2.00	3.00	-	-	-	1.00
Bone meal	0.75	1.15	0.75	1.00	-	-
Lime stone	0.50	-	-	0.30	0.40	0.50
Salt	0.25	0.50	0.40	0.40	0.40	0.30
Choline chloride	-	-	-	0.03	-	-
Mineral[2] and Vitamin mixture[3]	0.10	0.10	10.10	0.10	0.10	0.10
Total :	100.00	100.00	100.00	100.00	100.00	100.00

1. The quality of fish meal can be reduced if good quantity of fish meal is available.
2. Mineral Mixture contains : Ferrous sulphate : 20 gm, Manganese sulphate : 25 gm. Zinc sulphate : 25 gm Copper sulphate : 15 gm, and potassium iodate : 100 mg.
3. Vitamin mixture provides : Vitamin - A : 800, 000 I.U., Vitamin - D_3 100,000 ICU, Riboflavin : 400 mg, and Folic acid : 100 mg.

Table 6.10. Broiler Finisher diet.

Ingredients (Kg./100kg.)	1	2	3	4	5	6
Maize	44.10	45.30	46.80	50.38	49.90	65.10
Rice Polish	20.00	20.00	20.00	20.00	20.00	-
Groundnut Cake	11.00	9.50	19.00	13.00	8.00	-
Maize gluten meal	-	-	-	-	8.00	-
Sunflower Cake	11.00	9.50	-	-	-	12.00
Mustard cake (Solvent extracted)	-	-	-	-	-	10.00
Fish meal[1] (43% pro)	5.30	9.00	13.00	10.00	10.00	5.00

(Contd.)

Ingredients (Kg./100kg.)	1	2	3	4	5	6
Meat meal (56% pro)	5.50	-	-	-	3.00	5.00
Meat-cum-bone meal (54% pro)	-	-	-	-	-	-
Blood meal (73% pro)	-	3.00	-	-	-	-
Silk worm pupae meal deoiled-70% pro)	-	-	-	5.00	-	1.20
Fat	1.25	2.00	-	-	-	-
Bone meal	0.60	1.10	0.70	1.00	0.70	0.60
Lime stone	0.70	-	-	-	-	0.60
Salt	0.25	0.50	0.40	0.50	0.30	0.40
Choline chloride	-	-	-	0.02	-	-
Minerals[2] and Vitamin mixture[3]	0.10	0.10	0.10	0.10	0.10	10.10
Total :	**100.00**	**100.00**	**100.00**	**100.00**	**100.00**	**100.00**

*** 1, 2, 3 same as Table : 21**

Source : Panda, B; Mahapatra, S.C. Poultry Production (1985)

Table 6.11. Estimated growth and feed consumption rates of broilers.

Age (Weak)	Feed consumption per (Week)	Camula tive	Average Grain in body weight (kg)	Average weight per bird (kg)	Kg. Meat per 100 (kg) feed	Kg. Feed per kg. Meat.
1.	0.11	0.11	0.09	0.13		
2.	0.18	0.30	0.10	0.24		
3.	0.32	0.61	0.17	0.17	0.41	
4.	0.43	1.04	0.20	0.61		
5.	0.50	1.54	0.25	0.86		
6.	0.60	2.25	0.27	1.14	53.0	1.89
7.	0.70	2.85	0.27	1.41	49.5	2.02
8.	0.78	3.63	0.30	1.70	47.5	2.13
9.	0.92	4.55	0.30	2.00	44.0	2.27

Source : Lankford L.T. and T.L. Barton; Guide to Broiler production, leaflet No. 180, University of Arkanass, April 1974.

Table 6.12. Feed and water consumption

BROILERS : PER 1000 GBIRDS

Age (Week)	Water Litres	Water Gallons	Daily Intake Feed (Kg.)
0 - 2	50	11	38
2 - 3	62	14	64
3 - 4	114	25	85
4 - 5	133	30	108
5 - 6	176	39	126
6 - 7	212	47	141
7 - 8	227	50	161

REARING BIRDS : PER 1000 BIRDES

Age (Week)	Water Litres	Water Gallons	Daily Intake Feed (Kg.)
0 - 2			14
2 - 4	44	10	24
5			33
6	66	15	39
7			49
8			57
9			61
10			61
11			66
12	112	25	66
13			67
14	120	27	67

Laying Hens :

Daily water intake per 1000 birds : 125 to 235 litres per day (18 to 52 gallons per day)
Daily feed intake per 100 birds : 100 to 125 kg. per day.

7

POULTRY NUTRITION

Poultry birds require food for their growth and development. The fowl is a very efficient converter of vegetable food stuffs into eggs and flesh. The poor rate of growth of fowls, high mortaility and low egg production, reported throughout the whole of the country, can be largely attributed to malnutrition. Nutrition is the process of furnishing the cells inside the animal with that portion of the external chemical environment needed for optimum functioning of the many metabolic chemical reactions involved in growth, maintenance work, production and reproduction. Nutrition encompasses the procurement, ingestion, digestion and aborption of chemical elements which serve as food. Feed cost alone constitute about 60 to 70 percent of total cost of production of poultry meat and eggs., The living organisms have to consume food for maintenance of their life. Foods are of two types according to their function in the living body :

(i) **Proximate principle of food :** The foods that are needed for the formation of living body, growth and energy formation are called proximate principle of food. Carbohydrates, protein, fats etc. are of such type of food.

(ii) **Protective principle of food :** The foods that protect the living beings from the attack of disease are called protective principle of food. Vitamins, mineral etc. are of such type of food.

PRICIPES OF POULTRY FEEDING

The first and foremost function of food is to save the life of living beings. Food performs the most important function in living beings such as :

(i) Food enhances growth and protect the body

(ii) Food maintains the productive capacity of the living beings (Meat and eggs production in case of poultry)

(iii) Food replenished the losses of living beings

(iv) Food maintains the normal body temperature

(v) Food makes it possible to excrete the poisonous substances from the body.

The variation of energy contents of foods depends mainly on the following conditions :

(a) **Body weight of the birds :** Food requires for the body maintenance. It is observed that 60 k Cal/kg metabolizable energy is needed for the maintenance of normal life. So the required energy may vary according to the body weight.

(b) **Activity :** The energy releases from foods controls the function of the involuntary muscles (i.e. Heart, gizzard etc.) and voluntary muscles (i.e. Feather, leg, neck etc.). The energy requirement increases as the activity is increased. The activity of deep litter bird is more than that of cage bird. For this reason, the deep litter bird requires more energy.

(c) **Environmental temperature :** The body temperature of poultry birds is normally 105°F. The required temperature is produced due to digestion of food and helps to maintain the normal body temperature. The requirement of heat evaluation will be less under high environmental temperature.

(d) **Rate of growth :** The surplus energy beyond meeting the body maintenance uses for the body growth. The energy requirement depends on the rate of body growth. As for example it is said that chicks of light breed requires less energy than that of broiler chicks. Because the rate of growth of chicks of light breed is less than that of broiler chicks.

(e) **Rate of lay :** The laying birds require more energy for production of egg in addition to their body maintenance. The energy requirement varies on the rate of laying eggs. The hens that lays more eggs requires more energy in comparison to the hen that lays less eggs. So the hens should be provided foods to keep the egg production at a normal in addition to maintaining body growth.

Poultry birds have many precularities, both anatomical and physiological, which governs their feeding habits and feed utilization. The following facts should be considered while computating ration for poultry birds :

(i) The poultry birds are omnivorous. They are habituated of eating both of vegetables and animal products.

(ii) Poultry birds have simple stomach unlike ruminants which is comparatively short. The digestion is quite rapid in poultry bird.

(iii) Poultry birds have no lips or teeth and they can not chew their feed.

Hence they require a more concentrated ration.

(iv) Poultry birds are small in size. Hence they feed collectively rather than individually.

(v) Due to higher rate of metabolism, poultry requires a more exact ration as compared to other farm animals in order to avoid any nutritional problem.

(vi) The poultry birds have crop for storage of foods and gizzard for grinding of food. No other animals than that of poultry bird possess such alimentary organs.

(vii) The hen lays egg. Calcium, protein, vitamins and minerals are required for formation of egg shell and yolk and albumin of egg. So the poultry birds should be provided such elements sufficiently.

(viii) The growth rate of chicken and egg laying rate of laying birds depend on the quality and amount of foods provided. The poultry birds should be provided food as per their daily requirement.

NUTRITIONS - THEIR NATURE AND FUNCTION

The term nutrient means any single class of food or groups of like feeds, that aids in the support of life and makes it possible for birds to produce meat and eggs. Foods are generally composed with the following six nutrients :

1. Carbohydrates
2. Proteins
3. Fats
4. Vitamins
5. Minerals
6. Water

1. CARBOHYDRATES

Carbohydrates are a group of organic compounds containing the elements carbon, hydrogen and oxygen generally in the ratio of 1 : 2 :1. However the above criteria for this group has been widened to include compounds containing nitrogen and sulphur and the compounds that do not conform to a strict 1 : 2 :1 ratio of carbon, hydrogen and Oxygen. Because of this, carbohydrates are no longer exclusively thought as "hydrates of Carbon", but are grouped in a more general category as polyhydroxyaldehydes or Ployhydroxyketones and their dervatives.

Classification of Carbohydrates

The carbohydrates may be divided into three following large groups :

(i) **Monosaccharides :** Monosaccharides are the least complex of the carbohydres and do not yield simpler carbohydrates on hydrolysis. They are the building units for the more complex oligosaccharides and polysaccharides. Monosaccharides are simple sugar, The important members of this carbohydrates are Glucose, fructose and glactose.

(ii) **Saccharides or oligosaccharides :** The disaccharides are also relatively simple, being made up to two or more monosaccharides held together by glycocide linkage. They yield two monosaccharide molecules upon hydrolysis. Disaccharides are compouund sugars composed of two monosaccharides. The important members of this carbohydrates are Lactose, Sucrose and maltose.

(iii) **Polisaccharides :** The polisaccharides are complex molecules of high molecular weight composed of a large number of monosaccharides joined through glycosidic linkage. They yield many monosaccharide molecules upon hydrolysis. These are the most abundant carbohydrates found in nature and they serve as reserve food substances and as structural components of plants. The most important members of this carbohydrates are starch, glycogen, cellulose, dextrin and insulin.

Sources of Carbohydrates

Carbohydrates are available from cereals and by-product of cereal crops. The abundance of carbohydrates in nature is relatively more. The sources of different types of carbohydres are as follows :

Starch : Rice, wheat, Maize, Bajra, Potato, Edible arum, Beet, Carrot etc.

Glucose : Apple, grape, sugarcane juice, date palm juice etc.

Sucrose : Sugar, Sugar beet etc.

Cellulose : Vegetables, water melon, custard apple etc.

Lactose : Milk etc.

Glycogen : Liver of bucks, muscles of animal etc.

Importance in Nutrition or Function

(i) The primary function of carbohydrates is structural support of living plants.

(ii) Carbohydrates acts as a fuel of living body i.e. heat and energy is produced on its combustion.

(iii) When the intake of carbohydrates is morre than what is required by the body, the excess is utilised for the transformation of fats or even for the carbon skeleton of proteins.

(iv) Carbohydrattes provide the energy of the body.

(v) The carbohydrates having cellulose removes the constiption.

One gram carbohydrate produces 4.2 K Cal heat energy.

2. PROTEIN

The term protein is taken from Greek word proteus whose meaning is first. The terminology was suggested in 1840 by Mulder, who clearly recognised that protein was necessary for life in a more fundamental way than could be attributed to either carbohydrates or lipid : "Without it no life is possible". Protein are high-molecuular weight substances made up of carbon, hydrogen, Oygen, nitrogen and sulphure. Proteins are made of the combinations of 20 naturally occuring amino acids in unique manner. The common amino acid has a general structure as follows :

$$\begin{array}{c} \mathrm{H} \\ | \\ \mathrm{R} - \mathrm{C} - \mathrm{COOH} \\ | \\ \mathrm{NH_2} \end{array}$$

Proteins are classified into three groups according to their chemical composition :

(i) **Simple protein :** The proteins which yield only amino acids on hydrolysis are called simple proteins. Albumin, Globulin, Prolamine, Glutelin, Protamine, Histone, scleroprotein etc. are the important siimple protein.

(ii) **Conjugated Protein :** The proteins which yield amino acids and other chemical substances on hydrolysis are called conjugated protein. Nucleoprotein, Lipoprotein, Mucoprotein, Cromoprotein, Phospho protein, Glycoprotein Metalloprotein etc. are the important conjugated protein.

(iii) **Derived Protein :** The intermediate proteins that are developed by the partial analysis of simple or conjugated proteins are called derived proteins. Peptone, polypeptides, Proteose, Metaprotein, Coagulated protein etc. are the important derived protein.

Amino Acid

The amino-acid constitutes the protein. Unlike plants, animals cannot synthesize all 20 amino acids. Accordingly amino acids are of two types :

(i) **Essential or indispensible amino acids :** The amino acids which are not shythesized in animal body are called "essential or indispensable amino acids" and they are needed to be supplied through feed for optimum growth and well being of animals.

(b) **Non-essential or dispensible amino acid :** The amino acids which are synthesized in animal body are called non-essential or dispensible amino acid.

The complex protein is converted to simple and liquid amino acid.

The complex protein is converted to simple and liquid amino acid by the action of enzymes.

The proteins that contains the essential amino acid are termed "First class protein". Such as fish, Meat, Milk, Egg and other animal protein. The proteins in which one or more essential amino acid remains absent are temred second class protein or incomplete protein. Such as plant protein. Generally lysine and methionine is absent in cereals and pulse crops respectively.

Sources

(a) **Plants source :** Rice, Pulses, wheat, soyabean etc.

(b) **Animal source :** Fish, Meat, Egg, Milk etc.

The carcass of poultry bird contain about 21 percent protein and egg contain about 13 percent protein. The poultry ration should contain 15-20 percent protein. Animal protein should be included in poultry ration. It is essential to include 5 percent fish meal in poultry ration. In fact, the amino acid requirement of growing chickens and of laying hens, are meet by proteins from plant and animal sources.

Importance In Nutrition or Function

(i) Proteins are essential for both structure and function of every living cells.

(ii) Protein replenished the losses of the body and enhances growth of living beings. Protein is essential for formation of muscles and albumin of eggs of poultry birds.

(iii) Protein acts as a partial fuel in respiration as a result heat energy is produced.

(iv) Protein meets the amino acid requirement of the body.

(vi) Any excess protein consumed by the bird can be burned in the body to yield energy in some what the same manner as carbohydrates and fats.

One gram protein produces 4.2 K Cal. heat energy.

Table 7.1. Essential and non-essential Amino-acids for chicken.

Not synthesized (Essential)	Synthesized from limited Substrate	Synthesized from simple substrate (Non-essential)
Arginine	Tyrosine [1]	Alaxine
Lysine	cystine	Aspartic acid
Histidine	Hydroxylysine	
		Asparagine
Leucine		Glutamic acid
Isolenine		Glutamine
Valine		Hydroxyproline
Methionine		
Theonine		Glycine[2]
Tryptophane		Scrine[2]
Phenyla lanine		Protein[3]

1. Tyrosine is synthesized from phenylalanine, cystine from methionine, hydroxylysine from lysine.
2. Under certain conditions glycine and serine synthesis may not be sufficient for most rapid growth.
3. When diet is composed of carystalline amino acids, proline may be necessary to achieve maximum growth.

Source : Poultry producion by R.A. Sing, Kalayani Publishers, 1/1 Rajinder Nagar Ludhina - 141 008. 1985

3. FATS OR LIPIDS

Fats are really the easter of fatty acids and glycerol. Fats are rich in energy and gross energy value of pure fat or oil is about 9.4 K Cal per gram, approximately 2.25 times that of starch. The fat contain the elements carbon, hydrogen and Oxygen. Fats produce much more heat than carbohydrates or proteine. Fat is solid and oil is liquid at room temperature. Fats and oils are generally of animal and plant origin respectively. The term lipids is used for all other soluble materials. Excess of both carbohydrates and proteins are also converted to fat in the body. Generally the inclusion of fat as true fats or oils in the ration is seldom practised. It is due to its high cost and risk of rancidity which develop on prolong exposure to air, heat and sunlight etc. The fat requirement of poultry birds can be meet up by the inclusion of other feed ingredients (e.g. Rice bran, wheat, barley (maize etc.) as they contain 2 - 5 percent fat. The carcas of poultry bird contain 9 percent fat and egg contain 10 percent fat.

Source

Plant source : Mustard, Seasame, Linseed, Ground nut, coconut oil. Corn oil and other vegetables oil.

Animal source : Animal tallow (Beef), Butter, Ghee, etc.

Importance in Nutrition or Function

(i) Fats are the concentrated forms of stored energy in animal kingdom. Energy in the body can be stored mainly in the form of fat.

(ii) Fat supply concentrated form of energy. It supply 2.25 times more energy than that of carbohydrate and protein.

(iii) Fats provide insulation for the vital organs, Protecting them from mechanical shock and maintaining optimum body temperature.

(iv) Fats that are stored in the body, can be utilised in future.

(v) Fats improves the palatability of feeds for all classes of animals.

(vi) Fat acts as dissolvent of some vitamin (i.e. vitamin - A, D, E, K etc.) and help their absorption.

One gram fat produces 9.3 K Cal heat energy.

4. VITAMINS

Vitamins are organic compound which are essential for development of normal tissue and for normal health, growth and maintenance. "No animal can live upon a mixture of pure protein, fat and carbohydrate, and even when the necessary inorganic material is carefully supplied, the animal still can not flourish" (Hopkins, 1906). Frank established the term 'Vitamin' in 1911 According to Rosenberg's definition, Vitamins can be defined as organic compounds required in very minute amounts for normal growth and maintanance of animal life. Some vitamins are essential for transformation of energy but do not themselves supply energy to the body. The vitamins are generally divided into two major groups as follows :

(a) **Fat soluble vitamins :** The fat soluble Vitamins which are usually found asosociated with the lipids of natural foods. Vitamin A, D, E and K are the fat soluble vitamin.

(b) **Water soluble Vitamins :** Vitamin C and Vitamin B Complex comprise the water soluble group. The members of Vitamin B Complex are B_1 (Thiamine), B_2 (Riboflavin), B_6 (Pyridoxine), Nicotinic acid, Pantothenic acid, Biotin, Folic acid, Choline and B_{12} (Cyanocobalamine).

Table 7.2. Vitamin deficiency symptoms in Poultry and the principal natural source of these vitamins.

Vitamin	Deficiency symptoms	Principal natural Source.
Vitamin - A (Retinol)	Retarded growth, general Weakness, emaciation, staggering gait, ruffled feather, mortality, Watery or sticky eyelids, Xerophathalmia, Creamy white pustules on roof of the mounth and along esophagus, Ureates in Kidney tubules and ureters. In young and adult birds, a cheesy exudate from eye and sticky discharge from nostrils is often observed. Egg production and hatchability are markedly reduced.	Cod-lver and other fish oils, animal liver meals, green grasses, yellow corn leucern green or dried maize gluten meal, leaf meal, leaf meals from tropical legumes.
Vitamin-D (Calciferol)	Rickets-leg Weakness, stiff le-gged gait, crooked keels, beaded ribs, swollen hocks, soft bones, Ungainly manner of balancing body, appear unthrifty, depligmentation of feathers and mortality; in adults fragile bones, thin shelled eggs, reduced egg production and hatchability.	Cod-liver oils and certain other fish oils or concentrates. Deactivated animal sterol. Sun shine by irradiation of sterols under the skin. Ultraviolet ray lights by similar irradation.
Vitamin-E	Encephalomacia (" Crazy Chick" disease), incordination of movement, frequently unable to stand, turns in circles, edema beneath skin and hae-morrhage in cerebellum, In turkeys, enlarged hock disorder and dystrophy of smooth muscles of gizzard lining reported. In ducks, dystrophy of skeletal muscle. In adults, reduced hatchability in chickens & turkeys.	Green forage Vegetable oils whole and sprouted grains, lucern meal.
Vitamin-K	Prolonged blood clotting time. Haemorrhages develop internally and subcutaneously on the legs, breast, abdomen, neck, under the wings and in intestinal tract.	Lucern, Kale, green leafy Vegetables, meat scraps, fish meat.
Vitamin-B	Polyneurities - retracted head,	Whole grain, wheat by-

Contd.

Vitamin	Deficiency symptoms	Principal natural Source.
(Thiamine)	retarded growth, reduced appeptite, extreme weakness, alaxia emaciation, impairement of digestion, convulsion and death.	products, yeast, liver meal groundnut meal, molasses, grasses, lucern, rice by products.
Vitamin-B_2 (Riboflavin)	"Curled toe" paralysis (Toe curl inward) and paralysis of legs, retarded growth, diarhoea, tendency to walk on hock, hypertrophy and softening of brachial and scitic nerves and dry scale skin, severe dermatitis, in poults at corner of the mouth, vent, eyelids and footpads. In audlts, reduction in egg production and hatchability, dwarfed embryos, showing edema, degenration of wolfian bodies and 'clubbed down' condition. Embryo motality peak at about the eleventh day of incubation.	Liver meal, yeast, milk by products, concentrates made from fermentation residues, lucern leaf meal, young grasses, kidney, some fishmeals, distillers' solubles.
Vitamin-B_6 (Pyridoxine)	Retarded growth, hyper-excitability, tend to run aimlesely, flapping their wings with head down, repeated convulasions with distended or twisted neck, complete ex-haustion and death. In adults loss of appetite reduced egg production and hatchability, loss of weight and death.	Liver meal, yeast, rice bran, meat (muscle tissue and glands), cane molasses, fish, whey and rice by products, lucern.
Vitamin B_{12} (Cyanocobalamine)	Reduced growth, poor feathering and mortality in young chicks. In adult hens poor hatchability of fertile eggs, chicks that do hatch have low carryover and show high early mortality unless injected with or fed with levels of Vitamin B_{12}.	Fish meal, liver, whey, soyabean oil meal, cow manure, egg yolk egg white various fermentation products.
Pantotheric acid	Retarded growth, ragged feather development, dermatitis, lesions on eyelids, at corner of mouth, around Vent and sometimes on top of the feet, liver damage and changes in	Liver meal, yeast, cancemolasses, ground nut meal milk by-products wheat bran, rice bran, soyabean meal, lucern leaf meal, kale, cabbage,

Contd.

Vitamin	Deficiency symptoms	Principal natural Source.
	spinal cord may develop. In adult fowls, lowered hatchability and impaired egg production result.	broccoli, cauliflower, cucumbers, fermentation residues, maize, distillers solubles grasses
Nicotinic acid (Niacine)	Poor growth, poor feathering, inflammation of the mouth and tongue (Black tongue"), perosis, reduced feed consumption and occassionally dermatitis on skin, and feet of young chicks and poults. In poults, enlarged hock disorder; In ducks and goslings, bowed legs occur. In adults poor egg production and reduced hatchability.	Yeast, liver meal, rice bran wheat feeds, groundnuts, greens, meat (Muscle tissue), maize distillers' solubles.
Folic acid (Folacin)	Retarded growth, poor feathering depigmentation of feathers in coloured chicks and poults, reduction in red blood cell numbers and hemoglobin (anemia), reduction in white blood cells, occasionlly perosis and high mortality. In poults, cervical paralysis (Paralysis of neck) also observed. In adults, anemia, weight loss, reducd egg production and lowered hatchability.	Green leafy plants, grass, spinach, lueern etc. Yeast, liver, kidneys, whole grain supplies enough in poultry rations.
Biotin	Poor growth, perosis and severe dermatosis. Bottoms of feet become roughened and crack open, then dermatitic lesions also appear, at corners of mouth and on eyelids as described for pantothenic acid deficiency. In adults, impaired hatchability with embryos showing skeletal deformities including parrot beak and short legs.	Liver, yeast, potatoes, kidneys and other glands, milk, cane molasses, lucernleaf meal, grasses, whole grain supplies enough in the poultry ration.
Choline	Poor growth, perosis (slipped tendon), poor feed utilisation, unthrifty appearance and slight increase in liver fat. Practical rations for adult fowl appear to contain adequate levels of choline.	Liver, meal, meat, fish, whole grain, wheat by products, milk by products, ground nut meal, soyabean oil meal.

Source : Poultry Feeding in Tropical and subtropical countries, F.A.O. Rome, 1964.

5. MINERALS

There are about 40 inorganic clements found to exist in various parts of the animal. Out of these, 14 elements have been observed to have specific function in animal body and the metabolic roles of the rest is not fully established.

(a) Macro or major minerals

(1) **Calcium (Ca^{++}, at wt. 40) :** Calcium is present in body especially in skeleton and teeth in large amounts than any other cations. Skeleton contain 99 percent of calcium.

Source : Wheat, cereals, vegetables, Milk, Channa, Fishmeal, Oyster shell, Limestone, Dicalcium phosphate, Hard water, Bone meal.

Function and importance

(i) Calcium is required for growth, bone formation, blood clotting, and egg shell formation.

(ii) Calcium regulates the heart beat and working of muscles.

(iii) Calcium maintains acid-base balance.

(iv) Calcium controls the irritability of neuromuscular system.

Symptoms of calcium deficiency

(i) Calcium deficiency will result in rickets in young and obsteomalacia in adults.

(ii) Normal function and growth of the body is retarded.

(iii) In laying hens eggs are laid with thin shell followed by drop in egg production and low hatchability.

2. **Phosphorus (P^{+++}, at wt. 31) :** Phosphorus is found in every cell of the body but most of it (about 80 percent of the total) is combined with calcium in bones and teeth.

Source : Wheat, soyabean, fishmeal, meat meal, dicalcium phosphate, steamed bone meal, phosphoric acid, monosodium phosphate, defluorinate phosphate.

Functions or importance

(i) Phosphorus have a role of bone and teeth formation.

(ii) Phosphorus is a component of all living cells.

(iii) Phosphours regulates the metabolism of carbohydrates and fats.

(iv) Phosphorus maintains the acid-base balance of the body and calcium transport in egg formation.

Symptoms of phosphorus dificiency

(i) Phosphorus deficiency causes rickets, anorexia, weakness, cage-layer fatigue and osteomalacia.
(ii) Normal growth is retarted.
(iii) In chronic phosphorus deficiency birds may have stiff joints and muscular weakness.
(iv) Phosphorus deficiency is also responsible for pica in animals.

3. **Sodium : (Na^+, at wt. 23)** : Sodium is present in the extracellular fluid.

Source : Vegetables, water, fishmeal, common salt (Nacl) etc.

Functions and Importance

(i) Sodium is involved in the functioning of muscles.
(ii) Sodium is essential for the hydrochloric acid formation in the stomach.
(iii) Sodium promotes growth and improves appetite.
(iv) Sodium helps to regulate the body fluid pH.

Symptoms of sodium deficiency

(i) Sodium deficiency in layers results in decreased egg production, Poor growth and cannibalism.
(ii) The severely low sodium diet results in eye lesions, reproductive disturbances and finally death.

4. **Potassium (K^+, at wt. 39) :** Potassium occurs in blood cells in higher concentraion than in plasma. Nerve and muscle cells are specially rich in potassium.

Source : Cereals, Corn, Vegetables, meat meal etc.

Function and Improtance

(i) Potassium is involved in maintenance of osmotic pressure and acid-base equillibrium.
(ii) Potassium ion is necessary for carbohydrate and protein metabolism.
(iii) Potassium activates certain enzyme.
(iv) Potassium regulats the muscle activity.

Symptoms of potassium deficiency

(i) Retarded growth and high mortality.
(ii) Weakness and tetany followed by death.

5. **Magnesium (Mg^{++}, at wt. 24) :** About 70 percent of the total magnesium is present in skeleton and the remainder being distributed in soft tissues and fluids.

Source : Wheat bran, dried yeast, cotton seed cake, Linseed cake, Magnesium Oxide or Magnesium sulphate etc. Limestone is a principal source of magnesium for laying hens.

Functions and Improtance

(i) Magnesium is closely associated with sodium and potassium metabolism.

(ii) Magnesium is an essential component of bones.

(iii) Magnesium is involved in the activation of several enzymes, usually in the form of metal enzyme complex.

(iv) Magnesium controlls the irritability of neuromuscular system.

(v) Magnesium is neeeded for normal growth

Symptoms of magnesium deficiency

(i) Depressed growth

(ii) Chicks grow slowly for about a week, then ceases to grow and become lethergic.

(iii) Decreased egg production..

(iv) Chicks show a brief convulsion and later coma that end up with death but usually ceases in few minutes.

6. **Chlorine (Cl^-, at. wt. 35.46) :** Chloride is evenly distributed in all cells and extracellular fluids.

Source : Vegetables, common salt.

Functions and Importance

(i) Chloride is essential for hydrochloric acid formation in the stomach.

(ii) Chloride promotes normal growth.

Symptoms of chlorine deficiency

(i) Chloride deficient chicks show extremely poor growth rate, high mortality, dehydration and reduced blood chloride level.

(ii) Chloride is involved in nervous symptoms.

7. **Sulphur (S^{++}, at. wt. 32) :** Sulphur is present in all cells of the body. The hormone insulin and the two vitamins biotin and thiamine contain sulphur. The intake of sulphur is mainly done in the form of protein

sulphur is a constituent of enzyme and some vitamins.

Source : Vegetables, fish meal, meat meal, egg etc.

Functions and importance

(i) Sulphur makes the cartilage, feather and nail hard.

(ii) Sulphur eliminates the Poisonous effect of the body and takes part in various organic oxidation process.

(iii) Sulphur resists athe blood clotting.

Symptoms of Sulphur deficiency

(i) The deficiency of sulphur would indicate a protein deficiency.

(ii) The normal growth of cartilage, feather and nail is retarded.

(b) Micro minerals or trace minerals

1. **Manganese (Mn^{++} at wt. 55) :** Kemmerer, Elvehjem and Hart (1931) Were probably the first to demonstrate that manganese to be an essential element in nutrition.

   Source : Rice, Wheat bran, alfalfa meal, Grain by-Product, distillers' solubles. In practice Poultry feed is always supplemented through inorganic sources like manganese sulphate, manganese chloride, manganese carbonate.

   Functions and Importance

   (i) Manganese is necessary for growth, bone formation and reproduction.

   (ii) Manganese is involved with several enzyme like orginase, eysteine, desulphydrase etc.

   (iii) Manganese is related with amino acids transport accross the gut.

   Symptoms of manganese deficiency

   (i) Manganese deficiency is responsible for perosis or slipped tendon, skull deformation and Parrot beak.

   (ii) Shortening and thickening of the longbones of the wings and legs are also observed.

   (iii) In laying and breeding hens, manganese deficiency results in lowered egg production, egg shell strength and hatchability (Singh, 1985).

2. **Iron (Fe^{++} at wt. 56) :** Major portion of body iron is present in the form of haemoglobin in blood.

   Source : Meat meal, liver meal, fish meal, Green fooders, Pericarp of cereals grains, Rice bran, wheat bran, cotton seed cake, linseed cake, alfalfa meal etc.

Functions and Importance

(i) Iron is necessary for formation of haemoglobin, an iron containing compound which enables the blood to carry oxygen.

(ii) Iron is also important for maintenance of oxidative enzyme system within the tissue cells.

Symptoms of Iron deficiency

(i) Iron deficiency is responsible for microcytic, hypochromic anemia in chicks and poults.

(ii) Due to iron deficiency, complete depigmentation of feather in red feathered chickens occurs.

3. **Copper (Cu^{++}, at wt. 64) :** Copper is necessary for haemoglobin formation (Hart et. al, 1982).

Source : Liver and glandular meal, dried whey, peanut meal, fish meal, cotton seed meal, etc. In poultry feed copper sulphate, copper carbonate, and copper oxide are about equally effective.

Functions and Importance

(i) Copper is necessary for synthesizing haemoglobin and preventing nutritional anemia.

(ii) Copper is an essential elements in a number of enzyme system.

(iii) The relation of copper with the growth of born is noteworthy.

Symptoms of copper deficiency

(i) Anemia is the result of copper deficiency in the chick ration as that of Iron.

(ii) Due to copper deficiency depigmentation of feathers and digestive disorders and marked cardiac hypertrophy occurs.

4. **Iodine (I^-, at. wt. 127) :** Iodine is recommended as a remedy for goiter, a disease result in a swelling of the thyroid gland (J. Francois, Coinder, 1920)

Source : Fishmeal, meat and bone meal, molasses, Stabilized iodized salt etc.

Function and Importance

(i) Most of the iodine is concentrated in the thyroid gland as a component of thyroxine. Thyroxine is an Iodine containing hormone which controls the rate of body metabolism or heat production.

(ii) Iodine influences physical and mental growth and metabolism of food nutrients, including various minerals and water.

(iii) Thyroxin has an effect on integument and its outgrowth, hair, fur and feathers.

Symptoms of Iodine deficiency

(i) Iodine deficiency is responsible for enlarged thyroid gland.

(ii) Lack of thyroid activity cause hens to cease laying and to become very fatty.

(iii) Eggs produced from Iodine deficiency breeders hens have a lowered hatchability, prolonged hatching time and subsequent retardation of yolk sac absorption.

(iv) Iodine deficiency causes the growth of abnormally long and lacy feathers.

5. **Zinc (Zn^{++}, at wt. 65) :** Zinc has been found in every tissue, specially in bones in animal body. Most of the zine in the blood is present in erythrocytes.

Source : Safflower seed oil meal, fish meal, wheat standard middlings, etc. Poultry feed is supplemented through Zinc Carbonate or Zinc sulphate.

Functions and Improtance

(i) Zinc is a component of several enzyme system, including peptidases and carbonic anhydrase.

(ii) Zinc is required for normal protein synthesis and metabolism.

(iii) Zinc is a component of insulin

Symptoms of Zinc Deficiency

(i) Zinc deficiency causes retardation of growth, shortening and thickening of bones and poor feathering (feather fraying occurs near the end of feathers) and latter, on Keratosis.

(ii) Zinc deficiency results in loss of appetite, delayed sexual maturity, sterility and loss of fertility and also disorder of feathers.

(iii) Leg abnormality in Poultry is a common features of Zinc deficiency.

(iv) Eggs from deficient hens have a low hatchability and abnormal embryos. Egg production is also reduces.

6. **Cobalt (Co^{++}, at wt. 59) :** Cobalt is also an essential mineral nutrient.

Sources : Vegetables, legnumenous fodder, liver meal etc.

Functions and Importance

(i) Cobalt acts as anti-pernicious anemia factor in liver.

(ii) Cabalt acts as the activating ion in certain enzyme reaction.

Symptoms of Cobalt deficiency

(i) Starvation and gradual wasting of animals.

(ii) Cobalt deficiency causes severe anemia with almost complete appetite failure.

7. **Selenium (Se^{++++}, at. wt. 79) :** Selenium was reported in 1957 as an essential eliments at low levels, despite its toxicity in large intake.

Source : Fish meal, brewers' dried yeast etc. Poultry feed is supplemented through sodium selenite or sodium selenate.

Functions and importance

(i) Selenium is involved in Vitamin-E absorption and/or retention.

(ii) Selenium plays primary role in the prevention of exudative diathesis in chicks.

(iii) Selenium is also involved in the destriction of peroxides within the cell as a constituent of glutathione peroxidase.

(iv) Selenium has also been reported to reduce the incidence of encephalomalacia in chicks. (Singh, 1985)

Symptoms of selenium deficiency

(i) Selenium deficiency causes pancreatic fibrosis, exudative diathesis, steatitis and muscular dystrophy.

(ii) Growth rate is reduced and mortality is increased due to severe selenium deficiency.

(iii) Myopathies of the gizzard and heat of trukeys occurs.

6. WATER

Water is a life of living beings. No animal can survive without water. It is not possible to think of life without water. Water aids in performing all physiological function of life. Water is a compound which contain hydrogen and oxygen in the ratio of 2 : 1. Living things are comprised mostly of water. Water is an universal solvents. Water aids in intake of food materials, absorption of food materials from intesttine and reaborption from kidney tubules, transport of various food stuffs, from place to place in the living system, manufacture of various secretions such as digestive juices etc, carrying the water soluble hormone to their place of activity, excretion of the end products of metabolism, hydrolysis process involved in digestion and other metabolism, regulation of body heat etc. Defficiency of water delays digestion, assimilation and excection of wasteproducts through urine. Prolonged water deficiency causes the normal life abnormal and finally death.

Water is provided to the poultry birds *adlibitum.*

FEEDSTUFFS OF POULTRY

The feeds given to poultry consist chiefly of cereals, cereals by products, proteins of plant and animal origin, minerals and green food. Under Village conditions, birds pick up by themselves considerable amounts of supplementary foods but in commercial farms, it is necessary to feed all the essential elements for proper production.

A. Carbohydrates

(i) **Wheat :** Wheat is rich in carbohydrate and it is easily digested. Wheat meal and wheat bran is generally used in poultry ration. Wheat bran is a superior food of Poultry birds, as it provides certain minerals and vitamins.

(ii) **Maize :** Maize is a valuable grain for poultry feeding. It is palatable and highly digestible. Due to this property, poultry birds prefer it very much. Maize must be fed to the poultry bird in conjuction with a protein supplement. Maize contain less protein and minerals. Maize is easily digested due to its little fibre content. The yellow maize containing carotene (Vitamin-A precursor) is best for egg Production. Carotene has a influence on the colour of egg yolk. The white variety of maize may be used for fattening of table chickens. Prolonged use of maize in larger quantities will result in cannibalism and feather picking in young chicken.

(iii) **Oats :** Oats is an useful cereal owing to its oil and mineral contents. It is also rich in carbohydrate. But it is not so palatable as that of maize and wheat. It is less valuable due to its high fibre content. Poultry ration should not contain more than 30 percent of oats.

(iv) **Bajra :** Bajra is a very small millet akin to wheat in food value and composition. It may be used, either as grain or meal, in rations for chick and adult stock.

(v) **Jowar :** Jowar is suitable poultry food on the point of its food value. It contain more protein than maize. It is used as meal. Jower is not very good cereals owing to the presence of some toxic elements in it. But it may used in the ration of older birds along with other cereals such as maize, paddy, barley and oats.

(iv) **Rice :** Rice and its by-products are rich in carbohydrate. It contain less protein. It is highly digestible food materials. Broken rice or rice bran may be used in ration for chicken and laying bird. Rice bran contain about 13 percent fibre. So it is not advisible to use more than 10 percent rice bran in poultry ration.

Rice polish is also a good poultry feed. It is an excellent substitute for maize and can easily substitute maize upto 40 - 50 percent in chick starter or layer ration.

(vii) **Vegetables :** Green vegetables contain carotin, Vitamin and minerals. The peelings of different fruit vegetable can savely be used in Poultry ration. It should be cooked and mashed before use. Feeding of these enables the poultry birds to get large quantity of vitamin at a free of cost. The poultry birds should be provided 25 - 30 gm green vegetables daily. Leaves of spinach, amaranthus sp. radish, cabbage, cauliflower, beet and carrot and grasses may be fed to the poultry birds. 4 kg. green vegetable is equivalent to one kg. mash on food value. Poultry ration containing no greens may cause the eggs to be inferior in Vitamin-A potency.

(viiii) **Molasses :** Molasses is rich in sucrose. It can be used upto 10 percent in poultry ration. It makes the ration sweet and palatable. Molasses contain large amount of potassium and less amount of Calcium and some Vitamin (i.e. Pantothenic acid, riboflavin, niacine, choline etc.). Over feeding of molasses causes the diahorrea of poultry bird. So it should be used in limited amount.

B. Proteins

Proteins are nitrogenous products. Proteins are of two types according to the source of protein :

(a) Animal proteins and

(b) Plants proteins.

Animal protein is superior to plant protein in Poultry feed.

(a) Plant proteins

(i) **Mustard oil cake :** It is a by-product of mustard seeds. Lysine is absent in the protein of this cake. The taste of this cake is good and it has its special flavour. It is widely used as cattle feed. The poultry feed should not contained more than 5 - 10 percent mustard cake.

(ii) **Sesame (Til) Cake :** Sesame cake is also a good poultry food. This cake contain methionine and tryptophane in large quantity. But lysine is absent in this cake.

(iii) **Groundnut cake :** Groundnut cake contains more protein (about 47 percent). It is one of the most palatable food. Besides protein, this cake also contains 24 percent carbohydrate. This cake may be used in Poultery ration upto 40 percent. This cake contains 46.5 percent digestable crude protein, 8 percent fat, 0.28 percent calcium and 1.28 percent phosphorus.

(iv) **Linseed Oil Cake :** It is a valuable plant protein. It contains 27 percent protein. This cake may be included @ 10 percent in layer and breeder ration and @ 5 percent in chicken ration. This cake contains toxic factor which inhibit growth and develops disease. So it should not be used in Poultry ration in a large quantity.

(v) **Coconut meal :** Coconut meal may be used in poultry ration. But the main disadvantages of this cake is the risk of rancidity which develops under prolonged storage condition. The rancid cake should not be used in Poultry ration.

(vi) **Soya bean meal :** Extracted soyabean meal is a valuable protein food and nearly as good as milk. It is one of the most valuable ingredient of layer mash.

(vii) **Pulse chuni :** Pulse chuni is obtained as by-product of pulse crop. Five percent pulse chuni may be included in poultry ration.

(viii) **Yeast :** Yeast is obtained as a by-product of disteller industry. Yeast is a good source of animal protein. It contains Vitamin B.2 (28 mg/kg) and 4 percent protein. Inclusion of yeast @ 5 percent Poultry ration improves growth and egg production capacity.

(ix) **Penicillin mycellium :** It is the waste product of penicillin industry. It contains penicillin in large quantity and 37 percent protein. It is a good plant protein. It has good germicidal property. It can be used in poultry ration at the rate of 5 percent.

(b) **Animal Proteins :**

(i) **Blood meal :** Blood meal is very rich protein food, which can be obtained from slaughter house. It contains 75 percent protein in which Lysin present in abundance. But methionine and isoleucin are absent in blood meal. It is an excellent substitute for plant Protein, deficient in lysine. Blood meal upto 3 to 5 percent can be satisfactorily used in chicken ration.

(ii) **Fish Meal :** Fish meal is a protein rich food suitable for chickens upto six weeks of age. It contains 50-55 percent protein and abundant amount of minerals which render it a satisfactory supplementary food to cereal grains. It should be used upto 3 percent in Poultry ration.

(iii) **Termites :** Termites is cheapest source of animal protein for poultry bird. It is a good food fro growing birds. Poultry birds under free range system can meet their protein requirement by eating the termites.

(iv) **Bone meal and meat meal :** Bone meal and meat meal contain 7 percent and 55 percent protein respectively. They are protein rich good food for poultry birds. They are desirable supplement for laying stock.

(v) **Milk :** Milk is a good source of animal proteins and do good for growing birds upto 5 - 6 days. Milk also contains some growth promoting substances. Milk may be used in different form : such as whole milk, skimmed milk, whey, stone milk etc. It may substitute meat to a great extent.

(vi) **Silk worm pupae meal :** It is also used as animal protein for poultry bird. Satisfactory growth and egg production have been obtained with silk worm pupae meal.

C. MINERALS

(i) **Oyster shell :** Oyster shell is a good source of calcium. Ground oyster shell is provided to the poultry and they feed it *ad libitum.*

(ii) **Bone meal :** Bone meal is a good source of calcium and phosphorus. It contains 32 percent calcium and 15 percent phosphorus. Sterilised bone meal should be used in poultry ration. It is fed to the poultry bird alone and mixed with other food.

(iii) **Common salt :** Common salt makes the food palatable and takes part in digestion. Besides, it increases the water intake capacity. It should be used with food at the rate of one percent. There is no need of using common salt separately if fish meal and bone meal is mixed with food.

(iv) **Grit :** Grit aids in grinding of food. It does not work as food. Under free ranged condition, fowls consume considerable amount of grit. But under intensive system of poultry rearing, grit should be provided to the poultry bird. A poultry bird consumes one kilogram of grit anually.

(v) **Manganese salt :** Of this salt, manganese sulphate and manganese chloride is generally used with poultry food. Manganese sulphate mixed (i.e. 100 gm manganese sulphate per ton of food) food meet the manganese requirement of growing chicks.

D. VITAMIN

Vitamin has also an important role in poultry bird. The vitamin is available from fresh vegetable grass, yeast etc.

Under free range system, poultry birds meet up their vitamin requirement by eating green vegetables and grasses. But under intensive system of poultry rearing, vegetables and grasses should be provided to the poultry birds.

The vitamin requirement of poultry bird may also be meet by the following feed supplements :

1. Avivita : (Feed supplement containing Vitamin A, B_2, D_3, E and K)

Composition

Each gram contain

Vitamin A	:	80,000 I.U.
Vitamin B_2	:	50 mg.
Vitamin D_3	:	1,200 I.U.
Vitamin E	:	10 mg.
Vitamin K	:	10 mg.

Indication

(i) For good and increased egg production.

(ii) To prevent curled toe paralysis, nutritional rough.

(iii) To prevent crazy chick disease.

(iv) To prevent ricket, thin shelled eggs.

(v) To prevent pataechial haemorrage in G.I. tract due to coccidial and helminthic infestation.

Instruction for use : 100 gm per ton of feed.

2. **Cadiplex-C :** (Liquid feed supplement containing Vitamin B Complex and Vitamin-C)

Composition

Each 5 ml contains

Vitamin B_1	:	3.75 mg.
Vitamin B_6	:	0.62 kg.
Vitamin B_{12}	:	6.26 mg.
Riboflaviin	:	1.25 mg.
Nicotinamide	:	37.5 mg.
Vitamin-C	:	5.0 mg.

Indications : Poultry commonly suffer from Vitamin-B difficiency.

Vitamin B can not be stored in the body. Therefore it is necessary to supplement Vitamin-B every day.

(i) Regular supplementation of Vitamin-B results in proper digestion and metabolism.
(ii) Effective feed utilisation.
(iii) Better growth
(iv) Increased production of egg and meat.

Administration : To be given daily through drinking water or wet meal @ 10 to 20 ml. per 100 birds.

3. **Cadisol :** (Liquid feed supplement containing Vitamin-A)

Composition

Each ml. contains :

Vitamin-A : 1,00,000 in a special water miscible base. This special base helps in rapid absoprtion of Vitamin-A from G.I. Tract and promptly raises Vitamin-A level in the blood.

Indication : Vitamin-A should be supplemented daily for the following:
(i) Increased egg production and stimulate growth
(ii) To prevent blood spot in the eggs.
(iii) To prevent nutritional roupe in chicks
(iv) To reduce the helminthic and coccidial infestation.

Mode of administration : To be given daily through drinking water or as wetmeal @ 1 to 5 ml. per 100 birds.

4. **Vitatone :** (Liquid feed supplement containing Vitamin-A D_3, E, C and B_{12})

Composition

Each ml. contains

Vitamin A	:	50,000 I.U.
Vitamin D_3	:	5,000 I.U.
Vitamin C	:	100 mg.
Vitamin E	:	50 mg.
Vitamin B_{12}	:	20 mcg.

Indication : It contains antistress Vitamin in Synergatic combination. Thus regular supplement of it.
(i) Prevents stress.
(ii) Removes weakness and debility.
(iii) Stimulate production.
(iv) Prevents Crazy chick disease.
(v) Improves reproductive efficiency.

Administration : To be given daiily through drinking water or as wet meal @ 2 to 5 ml per 100 birds.

(*Source :* Veterinary Reference Book, Cadila veterinary, Ahmedabad - 380008. India)

Table 7.3. Nutritive requirement of chickens

Nutrients	Grower	Layer	Breeder
(i) Protein : (%)			
1-6 weeks	18-20	14-16	14-16
6-12 weeks	16-20	-	-
12 weeks onward	14-16	-	-
(ii) Minerals : (%)			
Calcium	1.5	2	2
Phosphorus	0.8	1	1
Sodium chloride	0.5	0.5	0.5
Manganese (PPM)	50	50	50
(iii) Vitamins :			
Vitamin-A (I.U./Kg.)	750	1500	2250
Vitamin-D (I.U./Kg.)	90	360	270
Riboflavin (mg/kg)	600	337.5	-

(Other vitamins are available from cereal and cereal by product food.)

(iv) Fat : Poultry birds gets the fat from the ingreadients mixed in the ration. Poultry bird can not utilise the fat if the feed ingredient contains 5-7 percent fat.

(v) Water : Sufficient fresh and clean water should be provided for all the times.

(vi) Fibre : Poultry can not digest fiber, cellulose or bulky foods and roughages more than 6-7 percent. For this poultry ration should contain starch.

5. **T.M. - 10, T.M. - 50 (Pfizer Ltd.) :** Terramycin Feed supplement.

Terramycin feed supplement are scientifically blended feed supplements containing a guaranteed oxytetracycline activity as detailed below :

T.M. -10 : Contains 10 grams of oxytetracycline activity per 500 grams.

T.M. - 50 : Contains 50 grams of oxytetracycline activity per 500 grams.

Indication : Teramycin feed supplements, added to the rations of poultry provides :

(i) Increased growth rate.
(ii) Improved feed efficiency.
(iii) Earlier marketing and reduced risks.
(iv) Increased production

Mode of administration : To get the best results T.M. - 10 and T.M. - 50 should be added in poultry feed at the following levels

Age Groups	For	Level per ton of feed T.M. 10	T.M. 50
Starting chicks	Improved feed efficiency, faster growth rate and minimum mortality	5 kg.	1 kg.
Broilers and Pullets From 3 weeks to stage of marketing of broilers or till the onset of egg production of pullet.	Faster growth, better conversion of feed into flesh and better overall health.	500 gms. to 2.5 kg	100 gms. to 500 gms.
Pullet at onset of Lay From the day of onset for one month and during laying slumps	Ensuring early peak production and controlling egg production slumps	2.5 kg.	500 gms.
Rest of laying cycle.	Maintaining optimum egg production and better overall health.	500 gms to 2.5 kg.	100 tms. to 500 gms.

* Trade Mark of Pfizer Inc. U.S.A.

6. **Supplevite - M (Sarabhai Chemicals) :** Supplevite-M is mineral feed concentrate for poultry which provides all essential Vitamins and Minerals to ensure balanced nutrition.

Composition

Each 250 gm of supplevite-M provides :

Vitamins :	
Vitamin-A	: 5,00,000 I.U.
Vitamin-D_3	: 1,00,000 I.U.
Vitamin-B_2	: 0.2 gm.
Vitamin-E	: 75 units
Vitamin-K	: 0.1 gm
Cal. Pantothenate	: 0.25 gm
Nicotinamide	: 1 gm.
Vitamin B_{12}	: 0.6 mg.
Choline chloride	: 15 gm.
Minerals :	
Calcium	: 75 gm.
Manganese	: 2.75 gm
Iodine	: 0.1 gm.
Iron	: 0.75 gm.
Zinc	: 1.5 gm.
Copper	: 0.2 gm.
Cobalt	: 0.045 gm.

Antioxidation added to prevent Oxidation in the feed mixtures.

Mode of administration

(a) **For layers :** 1 kg supplevite-I is added to 400 kg feed or 2.5 kg per ton of feed.

(b) **For starters, Finishers and Breeders :** 1 kg supplevite - M is added to 200 kg feed or 5 kg per ton of feed.

7. **T.M. - Forte (Pfizer Liimited) :** Terramycin feed supplement.

TM - Forte is a specially formulated complete feed supplement for poultry to ensure balanced nutrittion by providing the growth promoter. Terramycin plus essential Vitamins and major minerals like calcium and phosphorus and trace mineral, normally not adequately available in Poultry feed.

Composition

Each 5.5 kg of T.M. - Forte contains

Oxytetracycline activity	:	2 gm.
Vitamin-A	:	1,600,00 I.U.
Vitamin-B_2	:	1.0 gm.
Vitamin-D_3	:	240,000 I.U.
Calcium	:	2.0 kg.
Phosphorus	:	0.4 kg.
Manganese	:	11.0 kg.
Iron	:	4.0 kg.
Iodine	:	0.2 kg.
Iodine	:	0.2 gm.
Zinc	:	10.0 gm.
Cobalt	:	0.02 gm.
Copper	:	0.4 gm.

Mode of administration : To get best result 5.5 kg of T.M. Forte is mixed throughly with 200 kg of feed or 55 kg TM Forte with 2 tons of feed.

8. **Vitamin-M (Pfizer Limited) :** This formulation is exclusively designed to meet the requirements of vitamins and trace minerals when added to poultry rations.

Composition

Every 5 kg of vitamin - M contains

Vitamin A	:	10,000,000 I.U.
Vitamin D_3	:	1,500,000 I.U.
Vitamin B_2	:	8.0 gm.
Manganese	:	110 gm.
Iodine	:	2.0 gm.
Iron	:	40.0 gm.
Zinc	:	100.00 gm.
Copper	:	4.00 gm.
Cobalt	:	200 mg.

Mode of administration : To get best result, 5 kg of Vitamin-M is mixed throughly with 2 tons of feed.

9. **Replamin (Merind Limited) : Chelated Minerals**

Nutritional Liquid Poultry feed supplement

Replamin helps to grow birds better and faster and result in increased productivity.

Composition

Each 100 mg contains :

Magnesium	:	**479.14 mg.**
Zinc	:	**149.75 mg.**
Calcium	:	**84.40 mg.**
Manganese	:	**44.17 mg.**
Iron	:	**25.88 mg.**
Copper	:	**10.69 mg.**
Cobalt	:	**1.41 mg.**

All minerals added as Amino acid chelates.

Sodium Chloride : 100 mg.

Mode of administration : 25 ml of Replamin liquid is added to 5 litres of water. The nutritional water is made available to the chicks for the first 10 days after hatching and subsequently it is provided as follows :

Broilers	:	**21st day until disposal**
Layers	:	**18 weeks to 21 weeks**
		30 weeks to 33 weeks
		42 weeks to 45 weeks
		54 weeks to 57 weeks

10. **Roxarsone (Merind Limited) :** This poultry feed supplement stimulates growth and feed efficiency in poultry and potentiates the action of coccidiostat when used in combination.

Composition : Each kg. contains 3- nitro - 4 - hydroxyphenyl arsonic acid; 50 gm.

Mode of administration : 1 kg. of Roxarsone is mixed with one ton of feed.

11. **Furalin (Merind Limited) :** Poultry feed supplement.

Composition

Each kg. contains :

Furazolidon : 200 gms.

Indications : Furalin is effective against the salmonella sp and other infections of gastrointestinal tract. Furalin is active against coccidiosis. Furalin in broiler increases growth rate and improves weight gain by increasing feed conversion. Furalin in layers improves egg production. Furalin also reduces chick mortality and combats stress.

Mode of administration : 250 - 500 gms per ton of feed.

12. **Mericlop (Meriland Limited)**

    Clopidol

    Coccidiostat

    Poultry feed supplement.

Composition : Each kg. contains

Clopidol : 250 gmgs.

Indications : As an aid in the prevention of coccidiosis in chickens by administration in the feed. It should not be used in Poultry from laying age onwards.

Mode of administration :

Chickens : For administration continuously in the feed at a level of 500 gms per ton of complete feed.

13. **Meridot (Meriland Limited) :**

    Dinitrotoluamide

    Coccidiostat

    Poultry feed supplement

Composition : Each kg. contains

Dinitrotoluamide : 250 gms.

Indications : For prevention of coccidiosis in poultry. Continuous administration to broiler and replacement chickens up to 16 weeks of age.

Mode of administration : 500 gm Meridot is added per ton of complete feed to give a rate of 125 mg per kg. Dinitrotoluamide in complete feed.

14. **Merimix (Meriland Limited) :**
Vitamin and Mineral concentration
Poultry Feed supplement.

Composition : Each 2.5 kg contains

Vitamin-A	:	50,00,000 I.U.
Vitamin-D_3	:	10,00,000 I.U.
Vitamin-B_2	:	2,000 mg
Vitamin-E	:	750 mg.
Vitamin-K	:	1000 mg.
Calcium pantothenate	:	2,500 mg.
Niacinamide	:	10 mg.
Vitamin B_{12}	:	6 mg.
Choline chloride	:	150 mg.
Manganese	:	27,000 mg.
Iodine	:	1,000 mg.
Zinc	:	15,000 mg.
Copper	:	2,000 mg.
Cobalt	:	450 mg
Calcium	:	500 mg.
Phosphorus	:	300 mg.

Indications : Merimix ensures rapid growth and heavier, more healthy birds.

Merimix increases feed intake efficiency, egg production and weight gain in poultry.

Merimix helps in prevention deficiency syndromes, deformity of bones, fatigue and lameness.

Mode of administration : 2.5 kg per ton of feed.

15. **Meriplex (Meriland Ltd.)**
Multivitamin Mixture
Poultry feed supplement.

Composition : Each gram contains

Vitamin B_1	:	4 mg
Vitamin B_6	:	8 mg

Vitamin B_{12}	:	40 meg
Vitamin E	:	40 mg. (40 I.U.)
Niacin	:	60 mg.
Calcium pantothenate	:	40 mg.

Indication : To provide Vitamins required by Poultry for growth and production.

To build resistance to fight against disease.

Mode of administration : 200 grams of Meriplex is throughly mixed with one ton of feed.

16. **Merivite-100 (Meriland Ltd.) :**

Vitamin B_{12} concentrate

Poultry feed supplement

Composition : Each kg. contains

VItamin B_{12}	:	100 mg.

Indications : To improve growth and productivity in Poultry.

To improve weight gain and feed conversion in broilers.

To improve egg production and hatchability in hens.

Vitamin B_{12} has a sparing effect on protein quality when adequate levels are added to poultry feeds, fish meal levels can be reduced and partially replaced with less expensive vegetables, proteins and minerals.

Mode of administration : Per 100 kg. geed.

Broiler and Replacement	:	220 g merivite - 100
Layers	:	100 g Merivite - 100
Breeders	:	150 g Merivite - 100

17. **Merivite A D_3 (Meriland Ltd.) :**

Vitamin A and D_3

Poultry Feed Supplement

Composition

Vitamin-A	:	50,000 I.U.
Vitamin-D_3	:	5,000 I.U.

Indications : To provide the vitamins to poultry required for growth and production.

To help maintain growth and production when feed consumption is subnormal.

To build resistance to fight against infection

Mode of administration : 200 gms of Merivite A D_3 is throughly mixed with one ton feed.

18. Merivite A B_2 D_3 (Meriland Ltd.) :

Vitamin A, B_2 and D_3

Poultry feed supplement

Composition

VItamin-A	: 40,000 I.U.
Vitamin-B_2	: 25 mg.
Vitamin-D_3	: 5,000

Indications : To help maintain growth and production when fed consumption is subnormal.

To build resistance to fight against infection. To prevent curled toe Paralysis and to prevent Rickets.

Mode of administration : 200 grams of Merivite A B_2 D_3 is mixed throughly with one ton of feed.

19. Merivite A B_2 D_3 K (Merind Ltd.) :

Vitamin A, B_2, D_3 and K.

Poultry feed supplement.

Composition : Each gram contains

Vitamin-A	: 82,500 I.U.
Vitamin-B_2	: 52 mg.
Vitamin-D_3	: 12,000 I.U.
Vitamin-K	: 10 mg.

Indications : To help maintain growth and production when consumption is subnormal.

To build resistance to fight against infection.

To protect curled toe Paralysis and to prevent rickets.

To ensure proper coagulation of blood.

Mode of administration : 100 grams of Merivite A B_2 D_3 K is throughly mixed with one ton of feed.

20. **Nutrimin (Sun pharmaceutical)**

Composition (per kilogram)

VItamin A	:	50,000 I.U.
Vitamin D_3	:	600 I.U.
Vitamin E	:	15 mg.
Vitamin B_{12}	:	10 mcg.
Vitamin K	:	10 mcg.
Choline Chloride	:	1,000 mg.
Calcium Pantothenate	:	8 mg.
Papin	:	1,000 mg.
Diastase (1 : 250)	:	25 mg.
Pancreatin	:	4 mg.
Niacinamide	:	20 mg.
Galactogogue	:	Q.S.
Lysin mono HCL	:	3,000 mg.
D.L. Methonine	:	2,500 mg.
Vitamin B_1	:	2 mg.
Vitamin B_2	:	2 mg.
Vitamin B_6	:	0.5 mg.
Calcium	:	250 mg.
Magnesium	:	15 mg.
Iodine	:	15 mg.
Iron	:	60 mg.
Zinc	:	90 gms.
Copper	:	50 mg.
Cobalt	:	1 mg.

Indication : To improve resistance to disease, growth and health.

To improve feed efficiency, egg production and weight. Resist mortality in poultry.

Mode of administration : 3 gms per kg. of feed daily

21. **Calcicare (Brihans Laboratories)** : Liquid feed supplement of calcium, Vitamin D_3 and B_{12}

Composition : Each 5 ml contains :

Calcium Gluconate	:	500 mg.
Calcium Lactobionate	:	5 mg.
Vitamin-D_3	:	600 I.U.
Vitamin-B_{12}	:	10 mcg.

Indication : Stimulates skeletal and muscular growth. Helps calcification of bones and eggs. Strengthens muscles and bones. Builds up calcium reserve in the body. Maintains high egg production.

Mode of administration : Daily through drinking water for 100 birds as stated below :

Chicks	: 5-10 ml.
Growers/Broilers	: 15-20 ml.
Layers	: 30-50 ml.

22. **Recovit (Brihans Laboratories) :** Liquid feed supplement containing Vitamins-A, D_3, E, C and B_{12}

Composition : Each ml. contains

Vitamin A	: 50,000. I.U.
Vitamin D_3	: 5000 I.U.
Vitamin E	: 50 mg.
Vitamin C	: 100 mg.
Vitamin B_{12}	: 25 mg.

Indication : Builds up body resistance to infections. Keeps bird healthy. Stimulates growth and production. Provides strength and stamina during vaccination, debeaking, deworming, climatic changes, prolapse, dystocia and cage fatigue, maintains normal fertility in male and female.

Mode of administration : Daily through drinking water for 100 birds as given below :

Chicks	: 0.5 - 1.0 ml.
Growers/Broilers	: 1.0 - 2.0 ml.
Layers	: 2.0 - 5.0 ml.

23. **Minamil (Brihans Laboratories) : Vitamin mineral feed supplement.**

Composition : Each 250 gm contains

Vitamin A	: 5,00,000 I.U.
Vitamin D_3	: 1,00,000 I.U.
Vitamin E	: 80 Units.
Vitamin K	: 0.10 gm.
Vitamin B_2	: 0.03 gm.
Vitamin B_6	: 0.10 gm.
Vitamin B_{12}	: 1 mg.
Cal. Panthothenate	: 0.30 gm.

Nicotinamide	:	2.00 gm.
Choline Chloride	:	15.00 gm.
Calcium	:	80.0 gm
Phosphorus	:	5.0 gm.
Manganese	:	3.0 gm.
Iodine	:	0.10 gm.
Iron	:	0.80 gm.
Zinc	:	2.0 gm.
Copper	:	0.25 gm.
Cobalt	:	0.05 gm.

Indication : Provides all essential vitamins and Minerals. Improves feed conversion. Stimulate growth and production. Maintains normal health and reproduction.

Mode of administration : Daily through feed or with treacle as stated below :

25-30 gms for 100 birds or 2-5 kgs per ton of feed.

24. **Dailymix (Brihans Laboratories) :** Mineral stable vitamin supplement

Composition : Each gram contains

Vitamin-A	:	82,500 I.U.
Vitamin-B_2	:	50 mg.
Vitamin-D_3	:	12,000 I.U.
Vitamin-K	:	10 mg.
Vitamin-B_{12}	:	15 meg.

Indications : Provides all essential vitamins as recommended by NRC. Special process ensures stability of vitamins in the presence of minerals and other organic matter. Builds resistance to infections and parasites. Stimulate growth and reproduction. Improves hatchabiltity. Incorporation of special antioxidants ensures full protency of vitamins.

Mode of administration : 100 gms per ton of feed.

25. **Vetkal + B_{12} (Sarabhai Chemicals) :** Liquid feed soupplement of calcium and phosphorus and vitamin D_3 and B_{12}

Composition : Each 5 ml. contains

Calcium Phosphate	:	0.24 g

[Equivalent to 0.21 gm of $Ca_3\ (Po_4)_2$]

Vitamin - D_3, Cholecalfciferol 400 I.U.
Vitamin B_{12} : 5 ucg.

Mode of administration

Chicks : 200 ml per 100 birds.
Grower : 50 ml per 100 birds
Layer : 100 ml per 100 birds

26. **Concitone (Concept Pharmaceuticals Ltd.) :** Multivitamin and mineral Liquid feed supplement.

Composition : Each 5 ml. contains

Vitamin-A : 60,000 I.U.
Vitamin-B_2 : 5 mg.
Vitamin-B_{12} : 125 mg.
Vitamin-D_3 : 30,000 I.U.
Vitamin-B_6 : 5 mg.
Vitamin-C : 50 mg.
Nicotinamide : 30. mg.
Vitamin-E : 275 mg.
Panthenol : 10 mg.
Elemental sodium : 1.48 mg.
Elemental Phosphorus : 1.00 mg.
Elemental Potassium : 1.10 mg.
Elemental chloride : 1.00 mg.

Mode of administration

Chicks : 5 ml for 100 birds.
Grower/Broiler : 7 ml for 100 birds.
Layer : 10 ml for 100 birds.

To be given daily for seven days in drinking water.

METHOD OF FEEDING POULTRY

A well balanced ration improperly fed will not give the most satisfactory result unless a proper method of feeding is followed. Some of the popular methods of feeding are given below :

1. Whote grain feeding system (Cafetaria or free choice system of Poultry feeding)

This method involves supplying all the ingredients of poultry ration in separate hopper to enable the birds to eat as it wishes. This system permits the birds to voluntarily balance its ration by selectively eating different ingredients according to individual needs. But it appears doubtful as the birds can not be totally relied upon to balance their nutrient intake themselves. This method entails the use of too many hoppers and a considerable amount of time to keep them individually filled. This is a old and abandoned method of feeding poultry birds.

2. Gain and Mash Method

This is a common method of feeding grower and layers birds and slightly better method than the whole grain feeding system. This method involves feeding of grain or grain mixture along with balanced mash. By this one can increase or decrease the protein level as disired. Unless the poultryman is exceptionally skilled, this method will lead to bad performance. The layers should be provided feed having equal quality of grain and mash. The growing birds are usually fed only mash during the first few week of their life, after whcih mixed grains should be provided in sufficient quantity as growth advances.

Table 7.4. Amount of grain and mash to be fed to the poultry birds according to their egg.

Age of the chicks in week	6	8	10	12	14	16	18	20
Percent of mash	95	90	80	70	60	50	40	30
Percent of grain	5	10	20	30	40	50	60	70

3. All mash method or mash feeding

Now-a-days, mash feedingg is the choiest method of feeding poultry. The chicken and growing birds, fed by this method, performs well. The mash is feed in the following two system :

(i) **Dry mash system :** The feed ingredients are ground to appropriate size, mixed in required proportion and fed the poultry bird as a single balanced mixture. The method is desirable for all types of Poultry grown under deep litter and cage system as the birds can not have the opportunity to have selective eating.

(ii) **Wet mash system :** The wet mash system, as the name implies, is the dry mash wetted with water. This system improve the feed consumption during the hotter months of the year and reduced the feed wastage. But it involves extra labour and the return may not generally justify such additional expendature. However, this system is not feasible for very large flocks to be fed.

4. Pellet method

Pellet feeding involves pelleting the dry mash under high pressure. Pellet making involves considerable technology and elaborated equipment. For this, the common farmers can not prepare pellet on the farm. Pelleting has the following advantages

(i) It improves feed consumption due to lack of dustiness.
(ii) It reduces labour and handling cost of feed.
(iii) It reduces labour and handling cost of feed.
(iii) It reduces the feed waste and eliminates selective eating by birds.
(iv) It enhances the availability of energy and increases the acceptability of comparatively unpalatable ingredients of mash. The main disadvantage of pelleting is that pellets are expensive and it is about 10 percent more expensive than that of feed not pellet.

This method is extensively used in wastern countries.

5. Restricted or controlled feeding

This method involves restriction of feeding pullets during 6-20 weeks of age instead of *adlibitum* feeding. This method have the following advantages :

(i) Reduction of feed cost.
(ii) Delay of sexual maturity
(iii) Increases the egg production after the delay in sexual maturity has been overcome.
(iv) Reduction in the number of small eggs laid.
(v) Lower layer house mortality.

Feed restriction should never be practiced during brooding time. The pullets under restricted feeding need enough feeder space. So that all birds can eat at the same tiime, as they are very hungry, ready and anxious for feed.

Table 7.5. Maximum levels of different feed ingredients that can be used in poultry rations (Percent)

	Ingredient	Chicks	Grower/layer
A.	Energy Sources :		
	Maize	60	60
	Wheat	50	50
	Barley	20	40
	Pearl Millet	50	50

(Contd.)

Ingredient	Chicks	Grower/layer
Oats	10	20
Finger millet	10	20
Sorghum (White)	25	40
Molasses	5	10
Rice Polish	40	40
Rice Polish (Deoiled)	20	20
Salseedmeal (Deoiled)	5	10
Tapioca meal	25	25
Wheat Bran	10	15
Poultry manure meal	10	10
B. Vegetable Protein Sources :		
Ground nut Cake	40	40
Groundnut cake (Deoiled)	20	20
Soyabean meal	40	40
Sesame (Til) Cake	20	20
Safflower cake	20	20
Linseed meal	20	30
Cottonseed meal	5	5
Mustard Cake	10	10
Maize gluten meal	20	20
Maize gluten meal	20	20
C. Animal Protein Sources :		
Fish meal	15	10
Meat meal	5	10
Blood meal	5	5
Liver Residue meal	10	10
Silkworm pupae meal	6	6
Feather meal	5	5
Penicillin mycelium waste	5	5
Poultry by-products meal	5	5
Hatchery by-products meal	5	5
Meat cum bone meal	6	6

Source : Poultry production (1989) by B. Panda and S.C. Mohapatra, Indian council of Agricultural Research New-Delhi-110012. PP 63.

Table 7.6. Ingredients for preparing balanced ration for poultry (in percentage)

Ingredients	Chick mash	Grower mash	Layer mash
Wheat	20	20	30
Maize	30	20	20
Groundnut Cake	23	30	18
Wheat bran	8	10	10
Rice Polish	10	10	10
Fish meal	7	6	6
Oyster meal	-	2	4
Mineral salt	1.5	1	1
Dust milk	0.5	-	-
Common salt	-	1	1
Total	100	100	100
Vitamin ($A+B_2+D_3$)	25 gm	25 gm	25 gm

Table 7.7. Formula of ration for different stocks.

A. Chick starter ration and its nutritive composition

Ingredients	Amount (lbs)	Protein (lbs)	Calcium (lbs)	Phosphorus (lbs)	Lysine (lbs)	Methionine (lbs)	M.E. (Kcal/lb)
Ground nut cake	15	6.45	0.03	0.03	0.21	0.18	110
Sesame Cake	15	6.76	0.03	0.08	0.20	0.30	104
Wheat (crushed)	10	1.10	0.01	0.01	0.03	0.03	102
Fish meal	5	2.50	0.25	0.16	0.18	0.11	45
Rice Polish	42	5.30	0.02	0.15	0.27	0.14	431
Maize glutenmeal	5	2.10	-	-	-	0.08	42
Mollasses	5	0.15	0.04	0.01	-	-	35
Lime stone	2	-	0.76	-	-	-	-
Bone meal	1	-	0.26	0.13	-	-	-
Total	100	24.36	1.67	0.57	0.91	0.84	869
Recommended level		20	1.4	0.45	0.90	0.80	880

B. Grower ration and its nutritive composition

Ingredients	Amo-unt (lbs)	Pro-tein (lbs)	Cal-cium (lbs)	Phosph-orus (lbs)	Lys-ine (lbs)	Methi-onine (lbs)	M.E. (Kcal/lb)
Sesame Cake	10	4.5	0.2	0.05	0.13	0.20	70
Maize glutenmeal	4	1.6	-	-	0.10	1.04	33
Fish meal	3	1.5	0.15	0.01	0.10	0.06	27
Maize meal	20	1.8	-	-	0.06	0.06	220
Wheat bran	10	1.5	0.01	0.04	0.06	0.04	49
Mollasses	10	0.4	0.08	0.02	-	-	70
Rice Polish	40	5.2	0.02	0.15	0.27	0.14	420
Lime stone	2	-	0.76	-	-	-	-
Bone meal	1	-	0.26	0.13	-	-	-
Total	**100**	**16.5**	**1.48**	**0.49**	**0.63**	**0.56**	**889**
Recommended level		**16.0**	**1.4**	**0.45**	**?**	**?**	

C. Layer and breeder ration and its nutritive composition

Ingredients	Amo unt (lbs)	Pro tein (lbs)	Cal cium (lbs)	Phosph orus (lbs)	Lys ine (lbs)	Methi onine (lbs)	M.E. (Kcal/lb)
Sesame Cake	7.5	3.37	0.15	0.04	0.10	0.15	72
Groundnut cake	7.5	3.23	0.01	0.01	0.10	0.09	55
Meat meal	3.0	1.44	0.24	0.12	0.08	0.04	22
Maize	35.0	2.25	0.01	-	0.10	0.12	385
Rice Polish	20.0	2.60	0.01	0.07	0.13	0.06	210
Wheat Bran	17.0	2.55	-	0.07	0.10	0.08	83
Mollasses	5.0	0.15	0.04	0.01	-	-	35
Lime stone	4.0	-	-	1.52	-	-	-
Bone meal	1.0	-	-	0.26	0.13	-	-
Total	**100**	**15.59**	**2.24**	**0.45**	**0.61**	**0.54**	**862**
Recommended Level		**15.00**	**2.50**	**0.45**	**0.50**	**0.53**	**840**

D. Broiler starter ration and its nutritive composition (In pounds)

Ingredients	Amo-unt (lbs)	Pro-tein (lbs)	Cal-cium (lbs)	Phosph-orus (lbs)	Lys-ine (lbs)	Methi-onine (lbs)	M.E. (Kcal/lb)
Sesame Cake	15	6.75	0.3	0.08	0.2	0.3	105
Maizegluten meal	7	2.87	-	-	0.02	0.1	37
Fish meal	10	5.0	0.5	0.32	0.35	0.21	90
Rice Polish	42	5.3	0.02	0.15	0.27	0.14	431
Maize	16	1.4	-	-	0.04	0.05	176
Molasses	5	0.2	0.04	0.01	-	-	35
Penicillin mycellium	2	0.5	0.06	-	0.06	-	-
Lime stone	1	-	0.76	-	-	-	-
Bone meal	1	-	0.26	0.13	-	-	-
Total	**100**	**22.0**	**1.94**	**0.69**	**0.83**	**0.8**	**894**
Recommended level	**100**	**23.0**	**1.40**	**0.45**	**0.90**	**0.80**	**950**

E. Broiler finisher ration and its nutritive composition (In Pounds)

Ingredients	Amo-unt (lbs)	Pro-tein (lbs)	Cal-cium (lbs)	Phosph-orus (lbs)	Lys-ine (lbs)	Methi-onine (lbs)	M.E. (Kcal/lb)
Fish meal	25	12.50	1.25	0.80	0.96	0.50	225
Seasame Cake	2	0.90	0.04	0.01	0.03	0.04	14
Maize	50	4.50	0.01	0.03	0.14	0.17	350
Rice Polish	15	1.95	-	0.05	0.10	0.05	153
Molasses	5	0.15	0.04	0.01	-	-	35
Bone meal	1	-	0.26	0.13	-	-	-
Lime stone	2	-	0.76	-	-	-	-
Total	**100**	**20.0**	**2.36**	**1.03**	**1.17**	**0.76**	**982**
Recommended level	**100**	**20.0**	**1.40**	**0.45**	**0.90**	**0.80**	**980**

Source : Hans-Murgi palan O Chikitsa (1989) by P.C. Das. West Bengal State Book Board Calcutta - 700 013.

Table 7.8. Classification and Composition table for Poultry feed.

Feed ingredients	M.E. KCal Kg.	D.M.	C.P.	C.F.	E.E.	N.F.E.	Total ash	Acid insolu-ble ash	Ca	P	Lys	Met	Tryp
	1.	2	3	4	5	6	7	8	9	10	11	12	13
Engry feed :													
Bajra grain	2642	89.6	12.7	2.2	4.9	78.2	2.0	1.50	0.13	0.72	0.42	0.24	0.18
Cashew bran	-	94.4	16.9	6.9	27.1	45.4	3.7	0.10	0.45	0.40	-	-	-
Cashew Kuran	-	95.7	18.4	9.5	52.9	15.6	3.6	0.40	0.50	0.60	-	-	-
Jowar	2645	87.3	10.3	3.6	4.6	78.1	3.4	-	0.18	0.32	0.32	0.28	0.08
Lintil dehusked	-	94.2	24.6	0.7	1.0	71.1	2.6	0.36	0.20	0.83	0.97	0.32	0.26
Maize bran	-	93.7	8.5	14.9	1.4	73.8	1.4	-	0.07	0.13	-	0.03	0.06
Maize damage	-	89.7	10.1	2.8	3.9	80.1	1.7	0.39	0.25	0.40	0.21	0.18	0.16
Maize grit	2742	90.8	13.6	5.3	2.1	76.1	2.9	1.23	0.22	0.35	1.01	1.20	1.35
Maize Opague-2	-	-	9.9	-	-	-	-	-	-	-	0.34	-	-
Metha	-	92.1	20.6	8.6	6.1	60.9	3.8	0.45	0.35	0.80	-	-	-
Molasses	2400	73.6	2.8	-	-	86.3	10.9	0.44	1.51	0.66	-	-	-
Mowha flour	-	80.0	6.0	8.7	0.3	78.7	6.3	-	-	-	-	-	-

(Contd.)

Feed ingredients	M.E. KCal Kg.	D.M.	C.P.	C.F.	E.E.	N.F.E.	Total ash	Acid insolu-ble ash	Ca	P	Lys	Met	Tryp
	1.	2	3	4	5	6	7	8	9	10	11	12	13
Oak kernels	-	-	5.4	2.1	10.2	79.2	2.9	-	0.13	0.15	-	-	-
Oats	-	91.7	14.7	13.5	4.6	60.8	6.4	-	0.11	0.41	0.38	0.23	0.10
Rice deoiled	2235	92.3	14.1	13.8	1.7	53.4	17.0	8.37	0.37	1.80	0.45	0.44	0.15
Rice Kani	2345	90.7	7.9	1.4	1.7	87.1	1.9	0.66	0.11	0.48	0.06	-	-
Rice Polis	2937	91.8	12.7	11.2	13.9	48.6	13.6	6.77	0.27	1.37	0.40	0.38	0.25
Salseed Cake	3096	90.4	10.4	3.4	2.9	79.6	3.7	2.16	0.24	0.16	0.60	0.38	0.41
Starch	3938	89.4	10.6	0.03	0.09	99.4	0.28	0.04	-	-	-	-	-
Tapioca flour	3000	-	2.9	10.9	0.7	77.0	8.5	-	0.58	0.12	0.06	0.006	0.005
Tapioca waste	-	90.4	4.1	15.9	1.5	72.5	6.0	-	0.58	0.19	-	-	-
Wheat bran	1069	88.9	14.7	11.3	3.8	62.3	7.9	-	0.19	1.12	0.50	0.16	0.18
Wheat damaged	-	89.9	9.5	2.3	2.3	81.9	4.0	1.66	0.08	0.41	-	-	-
Wheat dust	-	92.1	12.3	18.3	2.3	57.3	9.6	-	0.52	0.33	0.37	-	-
Protein supplement :													
Blood meal	1420	88.8	73.4	0.7	-	-	6.0	3.0	0.32	0.31	4.79	0.66	0.88
Liver residue meal	-	90.9	65.4	1.3	15.8	11.9	5.6	-	-	-	3.85	0.89	0.50

(Contd.)

Feed ingredients	M.E. KCal Kg.	D.M.	C.P.	C.F.	E.E.	N.F.E.	Total ash	Acid insoluble ash	Ca	P	Lys	Met	Tryp
	1.	2	3	4	5	6	7	8	9	10	11	12	13
Meat Meal	2319	92.5	56.2	2.2	11.9	8.7	21.0	9.17	2.68	2.06	3.73	0.80	0.60
Poultry by-product meal	-	93.0	56.4	0.9	17.8	7.6	17.3	2.20	3.95	1.73	-	-	-
Casein	-	95.6	80.2	-	-	-	-	-	-	-	-	-	-
Coconut cake	1190	91.0	22.6	12.5	8.7	19.4	6.8	-	-	-	0.70	0.32	0.32
Cotton seed cake	1556	92.3	25.9	25.4	8.6	33.7	6.4	0.79	0.52	0.86	0.76	0.45	0.35
Dhaincha	-	91.2	28.3	11.0	5.8	50.7	4.2	0.10	0.30	0.55	2.30	0.60	0.67
Fish meal	1834	93.8	43.1	3.6	4.3	11.5	37.5	22.85	7.16	1.67	3.01	1.19	0.80
Frog meal	-	97.4	68.2	0.4	4.9	2.4	24.1	-	11.75	5.38	-	-	-
Grambaked dry	-	94.5	38.8	10.7	6.6	38.1	5.8	-	-	-	-	-	-
Bengal gram	2496	65.1	14.0	6.5	5.7	68.2	5.6	-	0.20	0.28	0.31	0.29	0.20
Black gram	2614	92.4	20.8	6.1	6.4	60.8	5.9	0.19	0.34	0.51	0.29	-	-
Gram chuni	2320	87.6	29.2	12.1	7.0	45.7	6.0	-	1.30	1.30	0.94	0.23	0.18
Redgram (Arhar)dehusked.	-	93.1	21.7	0.9	1.9	71.0	4.5	0.08	0.19	0.92	0.69	0.74	0.14
Green gram (Mung)	-	93.5	19.7	5.2	1.3	70.1	3.7	0.32	0.25	0.84	-	0.41	0.13

(Contd.)

Feed ingredients	M.E. KCal Kg.	D.M.	C.P.	C.F.	E.E.	N.F.E.	Total ash	Acid insoluble ash	Ca	P	Lys	Met	Tryp
	1.	2	3	4	5	6	7	8	9	10	11	12	13
House grem (Kulthi)	2614	93.6	20.1	8.3	5.7	63.1	2.8	0.12	0.35	0.53	-	-	-
Groundnut cake (expeller)	2569	91.5	40.9	8.9	7.9	36.4	5.9	0.86	0.23	0.59	1.50	0.42	0.53
G.N. Cake (deoiled)	2328	93.3	57.9	11.2	2.2	27.2	10.8	2.24	0.31	0.67	1.51	0.43	0.71
Guardak	-	89.7	48.0	5.3	7.4	23.7	5.7	-	0.26	0.70	-	-	-
Guar meal	-	91.0	42.6	10.9	6.2	35.1	5.8	0.59	0.54	0.70	0.29	-	0.59
Meat scrapwithshell	-	89.7	35.5	1.0	14.5	11.9	17.4	-	-	-	-	-	-
Linseed Oil cake	-	94.0	29.6	11.1	10.4	42.6	6.3	-	-	-	0.94	0.51	0.44
Maize gluten feed	2315	92.3	26.9	5.1	4.8	59.6	2.3	-	-	-	-	-	-
Maize grit	2742	90.8	13.6	5.3	2.1	76.1	2.9	0.21	0.31	0.15	0.33	0.26	0.07
Mustard oil cake	2373	91.3	35.1	8.2	14.1	33.4	9.2	1.20	0.89	1.78	0.99	0.72	0.68
Mustard cake (deoiled)	-	-	41.96	11.68	1.43	35.91	9.02	-	1.01	1.11	2.25	0.79	0.18
Neem seed cake	-	-	34.0	27.4	2.8	29.2	6.6	5.60	0.74	0.57	-	-	-
Ramtil cake	2817	96.6	36.0	18.6	8.9	28.3	8.2	1.85	0.62	0.96	1.37	-	-
Rape seed cake	-	87.6	36.0	10.4	12.8	31.4	9.4		1.12	1.05	-	-	-
Rubber seed cake	-	85.9	25.4	25.0	9.7	50.3	9.6	-	0.37	0.33	-	-	-

(Contd.)

Feed ingredients	M.E. KCal Kg.	D.M.	C.P.	C.F.	E.E.	N.F.E.	Total ash	Acid insoluble ash	Ca	P	Lys	Met	Tryp
	1.	2	3	4	5	6	7	8	9	10	11	12	13
Safflower oil cake (decorated)	-	92.8	42.2	8.5	8.2	32.2	8.9	-	0.40	0.51	-	-	-
Safflower oil cake (Undecorticated)	-	95.0	23.1	29.9	5.5	36.9	4.6	-	-	-	-	-	-
Sesame cake	1882	90.7	39.1	4.7	9.3	34.3	12.6	1.50	2.46	1.42	1.04	0.08	0.72
Spent Coffee cake powder	-	90.8	19.4	17.7	1.2	56.2	5.5	-	-	-	-	-	-
Sunflower cake	2230	89.1	37.2	11.6	10.9	32.6	7.7	0.62	0.43	1.14	-	-	-
Sunhemp meal	-	91.1	40.0	9.3	5.4	40.3	5.0	0.36	0.47	0.68	2.1	0.52	0.57
Taramira cake	-	96.9	40.5	8.0	9.5	35.9	6.1	1.04	0.57	0.71	0.97	-	0.55
Yeast sludge	-	94.8	32.1	1.8	1.3	46.3	18.3	-	6.05	0.41	-	-	-
Minerals supplement :													
Egg shell meal	-	98.2	5.8	-	0.3	1.4	92.5	-	33.63	-	-	-	-
Lime Stone	-	99.9	-	-	-	-	99.6	-	34.42	0.02	-	-	-
Feed additives :													
Penicillin mycellium													

(Contd.)

Feed ingredients	M.E. KCal Kg.	D.M.	C.P.	C.F.	E.E.	N.F.E.	Total ash	Acid insolu-ble ash	Ca	P	Lys	Met	Tryp
	1.	2	3	4	5	6	7	8	9	10	11	12	13
residue	-	-	17.9	5.6	5.5	35.8	35.2	-	3.80	0.17	-	-	-
Penicillin mycellium													
waste	-	91.8	31.9	8.4	6.7	34.5	18.5	-	3.97	1.12	1.24	0.46	0.37
Terrymycin waste	-	96.6	31.7	7.2	4.1	15.4	41.6	-	-	-	0.73	0.84	1.05
Dry Roughages :													
Agathi leal meal	-	-	32.3	6.7	6.1	45.1	9.5	-	3.26	0.22	-	-	-
Berseem leaf meal (Dehydrated)	-	89.7	15.3	23.5	3.7	42.8	14.7	-	-	-	0.66	0.30	0.29
Cowpea leaf meal	-	21.2	.21.1	17.7	9.4	36.1	15.7	3.53	4.45	0.46	-	-	-
Guar leaf meal	-	14.2	22.5	9.7	3.5	49.9	14.4	2.26	3.98	0.33	0.52	-	-
Ground nut plant meal	1812	92.1	14.4	32.5	3.1	37.4	12.6	-	1.69	0.34	-	-	-
Lucern leaf meal	-	95.6	20.3	16.0	4.0	51.1	9.6	0.23	2.25	0.35	-	-	-
Lucern dehydrated	-	91.0	19.1	21.6	2.8	42.1	14.4	-	1.83	0.45	-	-	-
Maize husk	1512	92.3	9.7	13.7	2.0	70.5	4.1	3.17	0.63	0.12	0.43	0.26	0.13

(Contd.)

Feed ingredients	M.E. KCal Kg.	D.M.	C.P.	C.F.	E.E.	N.F.E.	Total ash	Acid insoluble ash	Ca	P	Lys	Met	Tryp
	1.	2	3	4	5	6	7	8	9	10	11	12	13
Mohwa residue	-	-	14.5	30.9	5.4	31.0	1.3	-	-	-	0.76	-	0.55
Sugarcane begasses	-	-	2.5	33.1	3.7	46.4	14.3	-	-	0.74	0.07	-	-
Sunhemp leaves	-	-	34.7	13.6	10.2	30.4	11.1	-	2.17	0.36	-	-	-
Tapioca leaf meal	-	90.0	15.4	22.8	12.2	41.1	8.5	-	1.43	0.25	-	-	-
Miscellaneous :													
Linseed	-	97.9	28.9	6.3	40.5	21.4	2.9	0.03	0.44	0.53	-	-	-
Potato pellings	-	16.9	10.0	2.4	2.1	81.5	4.0	-	0.21	0.32	-	-	-
Salseed	2827	92.0	8.1	3.2	16.4	69.0	3.3	0.96	0.19	0.17	9.48	0.33	0.36
Soyabean meal	-	89.9	41.7	6.3	21.2	26.2	4.8	-	0.36	0.90	2.31	0.51	0.72

Abbreviations :

M.E. = Metabolisable energy,
D.M. = Dry matter,
C.P. = Crude Protein,
C.F. = Crude fibre,
E.E. = Ether extract,
N.F.E. = Nitrogen free extract
Ca = Calcium
P = Phosphorus
Lys = Lysine
Met = Methionin
Tryp = Tryptophan

* Compiled by the Division of Poultry Research, Indian Veterinary Research Institute, Izatnager, Bareilly, U.P.

Table 7.9. Amino acid composition of some Poultry feeds.

Feed ingredients	Lysine	Methionine	Tryptophan	Histidine	Arginine
Blood meal	4.79	0.66	0.88	3.06	2.49
Bone Meal	0.17	0.27	0.45	-	-
Liver residue meal	3.85	0.98	0.50	1.15	2.52
Meat meal	3.17	0.80	0.60	1.86	3.74
Pearmillet grain	0.42	0.24	0.18	0.20	0.62
Berseem leaf meal Early stage	0.48	-	-	0.46	0.76
Dehydrated	0.66	0.30	0.29	-	-
Coconut cake	0.70	0.32	0.32	0.42	0.91
Cotton seed cake	0.76	0.45	0.35	0.68	2.33
Dhaincha	2.30	0.60	0.67	1.80	2.60
Fish meal	3.01	1.19	0.80	0.95	2.83
Bengal gram	0.31	0.29	0.20	0.25	0.69
Black gram	0.29	-	-	0.24	0.58
Green mung	-	0.41	0.13	-	-
Ground nut cake	1.50	0.42	0.53	1.08	3.31
Groundnut cake (deoiled)	1.51	0.43	0.71	8.84	3.36
Cluster bean	1.9	-	0.25	1.6	4.0
Leaf meal	0.52	-	-	0.56	0.65
Meal	2.94	-	0.59	2.11	6.35
Sorghum	0.32	0.28	0.08	0.25	0.62
Lentils dchusked	0.97	0.32	0.26	0.53	1.17
Linseed oil cake	0.94	0.51	0.44	0.47	1.41
Maize opaque-2	0.34	-	-	-	-
Maize bran	-	0.03	0.06	-	-
Maize-gluten feed	5.59	0.45	0.20	0.57	0.69

(Contd.)

Feed ingredients	Lysine	Methionine	Tryptophan	Histidine	Arginine
Meal	1.10	1.20	0.35	0.97	1.48
Grit	0.35	0.26	0.07	2.29	0.56
With steep liquid	0.36	0.56	0.18	0.21	1.21
Husk	0.43	0.26	0.13	0.53	0.34
Oil cake	0.65	0.37	0.27	0.50	0.81
Residue	0.76	-	0.55	1.12	1.40
Mustard oil cake	0.99	0.72	0.68	0.78	1.61
Oats	0.38	0.23	0.10	0.24	0.72
Penicillin mycellium waste	1.24	0.46	0.37	1.67	1.38
Ramtil Cake (niger cake)	1.37	-	-	-	-
Rice Kani	0.06	-	-	0.58	0.58
Rice Polish	0.40	0.8	0.25	0.26	0.64
Rice Polish deoiled	0.45	0.44	0.15	0.23	0.62
Salseed	0.48	0.33	0.36	0.41	0.56
Salseed cake	0.60	0.38	0.41	0.51	0.72
Sesame cake	1.04	0.84	0.72	0.76	3.65
Silkworm pupae meal deoiled	5.36	2.39	0.75	1.94	4.13
Silkwork pupae meal undeoiled	5.7	4.4	-	-	-
Soyabean meal	2.31	0.51	0.72	0.12	3.02
Sunhemp meal	2.1	0.52	0.57	2.12	1.62
Tapioca flour	0.60	0.006	0.005	-	0.07
Terramycin waste	0.73	0.84	1.05	0.91	0.95
Triticale		0.31	-	-	-
Wheat bran	0.50	0.16	0.18	0.25	0.71
Wheat dust	0.37	-	-	0.17	0.24

Source : Poultry production (1989), by S. panda and S.C. Mohapatra I.C.A.R. New-Delhi-110012, P-68

Table 7.10. Mineral contents of foods

Feed Ingredients	Major minerals (g/kg.)					Minor minersla (mg/kg.)			
	Ca	Total P	Available P	Chloride	Na	Mn	Zn	K	Se
Barley	0.4	4	2	1.2	0.05	12	38	3.6	0.4
Naked barely	0.3	2	-	-	0.05	10	28	3.7	-
Malt clums	2.2	7	-	-	-	49	99	15.0	0.6
Brewer's dried grains	3.0	7	2	1.5	0.4	25	64	1.3	0.6
Malt distillers dried solubles	46.0	-	-	-	-	21	26	-	-
Dried distillery concentrate (malt)	1.0	-	-	-	0.6	8	28	0.6	-
Dried distillery concentrate (grain)	0.3	14	12	2.6	3.0	16	64	18.0	-
Dried dreg	0.3	-	-	-	4.0	5	26	10.0	-
Maize	0.1	3	1	0.7	0.1	3	20	3.4	1.3
Maize germ meal	0.7	4	1	0.5	9.0	6	43	1.3	0.1
Maize germmeal (oerim process)	3.0	5	1.5	0.5	0.01	28	128	13.2	0.3
Maize gluten feed	0.7	3	1	0.4	1.0	17	72	6.7	1.0
Maize gluten meal	0.4	4	2	0.7	0.1	8	34	1.5	0.1
Millet	1.4	3	-	0.2	-	35	20	4.5	0.1

(Contd.)

Feed Ingredients	Major minerals (g/kg.)					Minor minersla (mg/kg.)			
	Ca	Total P	Availa ble P	Chloride	Na	Mn	Zn	K	Se
Oats	1.0	3		0.7	0.6	44	32	4.5	0.1
Naked oats	0.8	4	1	-	-	32	35	3.9	-
Rice Rough	0.7	2	-	0.3	-	40	12	3.4	-
Rice bran	1.0	18	2	0.7	0.7	124	57	17.4	-
Rice Polishings	0.4	11	1	0.7	0.7	-	-	11.7	-
Rye	0.5	4	-	0.2	0.2	17	21	5.0	-
Sorhum (Milo)	0.3	3	1	0.8	0.1	13	48	3.4	-
Triticale	0.3	3	-	-	0.03	41	31	3.6	-
Wheat	0.4	4	1	0.8	0.6	21	20	5.0	0.2
Wheat germ meal	0.7	10	3	0.7	0.5	151	146	3.0	0.8
Wheat middlings	0.7	9	4	0.3	0.2	84	106	11.0	0.8
Wheat fine middlings	0.5	7	2	0.6	0.5	95	68	0.6	0.8
Wheat bran	1.4	13	3	0.9	0.6	122	162	12.5	0.6
Beanmeal, *vicia fabe* (spring)	0.9	4	1	0.3	0.4	16	45	10.0	-
Beanmeal, *Vicia fabe* (Autumn)	1.3	6	2	0.3	0.4	16	40	10.0	-
Coconut meal, dec. exp.	3.0	11	4	0.4	0.6	24	55	15.6	1.0

(Contd.)

Feed Ingredients	Major minerals (g/kg.)					Minor minersla (mg/kg.)			
	Ca	Total P	Availa ble P	Chloride	Na	Mn	Zn	K	Se
Ground nut meal, dec. exp.	1.4	13	5	0.3	0.8	52	75	12.0	1.0
Linseed meal, exp.	4.0	7	-	0.9	1.0	37	70	12.5	1.1
Palm kernel meal, ext.	2.1	5	-	1.6	0.2	205	60	6.7	-
Pea meal	0.7	9	4	0.4	0.4	14	40	14.0	-
Rapeseed meal	6.0	9	3	-	0.7	73	70	10.4	1.0
Safflower meal dec. exp.	2.6	18	5	-	0.5	40	42	7.0	-
Sesame meal	20.0	16	3	0.3	0.4	31	70	12.0	-
Soyabean meal, 50 percent	2.0	6	-	-	3.4	22	67	20.0	0.6
Soyabean meal, 44 percent	2.2	6	3	0.3	2.9	31	61	20.0	0.6
Sunflower meal, dec.	2.0	10	2	1.9	0.2	23	98	12.3	-
Blood meal	0.4	3	3	8.5	3.2	1	19	2.3	-
Feather meal	2.0	8	6	-	-	5	89	-	-
Fish meal (white)	66.0	35	35	-	5.0	7	92	5.9	1.8
Fish meal (anchovy)	45.0	25	25	3.0	8.0	22	110	5.0	-
Fish meal (Pilchard)	43.0	25	25	8.0	2.0	9	-	3.0	-
Meat meal	3.0	44	44	2.7	7.0	32	104	5.5	0.4

(Contd.)

Feed Ingredients	Major minerals (g/kg.)					Minor minersla (mg/kg.)			
	Ca	Total P	Availa ble P	Chloride	Na	Mn	Zn	K	Se
Fish solubles	2.0	9	8	-	-	-	-	19.0	2.0
Herring meal	20.0	15	15	10.0	5.0	8	94	4.5	3.6
Liver meal and lung meal	4.0	9	9	-	1.1	8	50	4.0	-
Meat and bone meal	75.0	42	42	14.0	7.0	21	95	5.5	0.6
Milk, dried, skim	13.0	11	11	12.0	5.0	-	45	15.0	0.1
Poultry dressing plant by-product meal	29.0	5	5	4.0	4.0	5	76	6.0	1.5
Whey dried	9.0	8	8	17.1	4.8	1	9	25.0	0.1
Buller milk dried	14.0	8	8	19.7	4.8	3	23	17.0	-
Grass, dried	12.0	8	8	8.0	0.8	53	19	1.0	-
Lucerne, dried	19.0	3	6	3.5	1.8	46	28	20.0	0.2
Molasses	9.0	1	1	20.6	1.2	50	15	41.3	-
Potato meal	10.0	2	1	1.2	0.1	6	9	20.0	-
Tapiocaroot flour (casava)	2.0	1	1	0.2	-	16	-	-	-
Yeast brewers dried	3.0	16	15	0.3	0.7	5	96	15.0	1.7
Yeast, paraffin grown	0.1	8	-	-	0.2	250	1300	12.8	-

Source : Poultry nutrition by W. Bolton and R. Blair, Published by Ministry of Agriculture, Fisheries and Food Bulletion No. 174, Her majesty's stationery office, London 1974.

Table 7.11. Vitamins contents of foods

Feed ingredients	Vita-min-A IU/g	Vita-min-E IU/kg	Chol-ine mg/kg	Nicoti-nic acid mg/kg	Ribof-lavin mg/kg	Vita min-B_{12} ug/kg	Biotin mg/kg	Folic acid mg/kg
Barley	0.7	5	1110	52	1.3	3.3	0.15	0.6
Naked Barley	-	-	-	-	-	-	0.07	0.6
Malt culms	-	4	1580	55	8.6	-	-	0.2
Brewer's dried grain	0.5	-	1550	33	0.9	-	-	9.7
Malt distillers dried solubles	-	-	2000	510	21.0	-	1.5	1.0
Dried distillery concentrate (Malt)	-	-	1000	270	15.0	-	-	-
Dried distinllery concentrate (grain)	-	-	1300	40	6.6	-	-	-
Dried dreg	-	-	400	34	2.7	-	-	-
Maize	5.0	4	1110	21	1.1	0.2	0.05	0.3
Maize germ meal	-	87	1550	31	3.3	-	3.00	0.2
Maize gluten feed	2.2	40	780	78	2.2	-	0.30	0.3
Maize gluten meal	26.6	24	1660	44	1.6	-	0.15	0.2
Millet	0.5	12	490	22	1.0	-	-	0.2
Oats	0.6	5	930	16	1.1	3.3	0.11	0.5

(Contd.)

Feed ingredients	Vitamin-A IU/g	Vitamin-E IU/kg	Choline mg/kg	Nicotinic acid mg/kg	Riboflavin mg/kg	Vitamin-B_{12} ug/kg	Biotin mg/kg	Folic acid mg/kg
Naked oats	-	-	1240	17	1.1	-	0.11	0.6
Rice rough	-	-	-	19	1.3	-	0.10	0.3
Rice brown	-	12	780	15	0.4	-	0.10	0.2
Rice Polishings	-	90	1000	660	2.2	-	0.62	-
Rice bran	-	60	990	275	2.6	-	0.42	-
Rye	0.2	17	-	16	1.6	-	0.06	0.7
Sorghum (Milo)	0.7	12	440	66	1.1	-	0.18	0.2
Wheat	0.4	16	730	58	1.1	-	0.11	0.4
Wheat Germ meal	0.4	130	2660	51	4.9	-	0.22	1.9
Wheat middlings	0.5	20	1110	100	2.2	-	0.37	1.1
Wheat fine middlings	0.4	57	1170	95	2.4	-	0.37	1.1
Wheat bran	0.4	1	1020	188	2.9	-	0.48	1.7
Bean meal, Viciafaba (Spring)	-	1	1110	29	3.1	-	0.11	1.3
Coconut meal	-	16	1110	27	3.3	-	0.06	1.3
Cotton seed meal, dec. Exp.	0.3	19	2610	33	4.9	-	0.10	3.7

(Contd.)

Feed ingredients	Vitamin-A IU/g	Vitamin-E IU/kg	Choline mg/kg	Nicotinic acid mg/kg	Riboflavin mg/kg	Vitamin-B_{12} ug/kg	Biotin mg/kg	Folic acid mg/kg
Pea meal	0.5	3	2210	24	1.8	-	0.11	0.3
Rapeseed meal	-	19	660	155	3.7	-	-	0.2
Safflower meal, dec. exp.	-	1	2570	22	4.0	-	1.40	0.4
Sesamemeal	-	1	1440	30	3.1	-	-	-
Soyabean meal, 50 percent	-	1	2900	38	4.2	-	0.32	3.6
Soyabean meal, 44 percent	-	1	2840	32	4.0	-	0.32	3.6
Sunflower meal, dec.	-	6	1200	250	4.0	-	-	-
Blood meal	-	0	1100	33	2.2	-	-	-
Feather meal	-	-	900	18	2.0	70.8	-	-
Fish meal (White)	-	21	3100	62	6.6	100.0	0.28	0.2
Fish meal (anchovy)	-	34	3700	64	6.6	100.0	0.28	0.2
Fish meal (Pilchard)	-	9	2200	55	9.5	100.0	0.26	0.2
Herring meal	-	27	4000	89	9.0	240.0	0.59	0.5
Fish solubles	4.0	-	2660	321	22.1	143.8	0.26	-
Liver and lung meal	49.6	-	7540	157	47.8	283.6	0.80	0.4

(Contd.)

Feed ingredients	Vita-min-A IU/g	Vita-min-E IU/kg	Chol-ine mg/kg	Nicoti-nic acid mg/kg	Ribof-lavin mg/kg	Vita min-B_{12} ug/kg	Biotin mg/kg	Folic acid mg/kg
Meat meal	-	5	2430	55	5.5	55.3	0.26	0.1
Meat and bone meal	-	5	2210	51	5.3	44.0	0.14	0.1
Milk, dried, Skim	0.3	1	1060	12	21.0	55.3	0.33	-
Poultry dressing plant by products meal	-	-	600	40	11.0	0.3	0.30	1.0
Whey, dresed	-	-	1550	11	26.6	22.1	0.25	0.6
Butter milk, dried	0.4	-	1000	11	28.8	88.5	0.30	0.40
Grass, dried	327.5	150	890	74	15.5	-	0.17	-
Lucern dried	267.0	200	1110	43	16.6	2.7	0.33	3.5
Mollasses	-	-	640	44	2.2	-	0.11	0.7
Potato meal	-	-	260	33	0.7	-	0.10	0.6
Yeast, brewers, dried	-	-	3260	487	45.2	1.3	12	
Yeast, Paraffin grown	-	-	6225	430	18.0	1.0	-	6.4
Ground nut meal dec. exp.	0.3	3	1880	166	2.2	-	0.39	0.4
Linseed meal, exp.	0.4	-	1660	40	3.5	-	-	-

Source : Poultry Nutrition by W. Botton and R. Blair, Published by Ministry of Agriculture, FIshers and Food, Bulletin No. 174. Her Majesty's stationary office, London, 1974.

Table 7.12. Elemental Composition of Salts used in mineral mixtures.

Salt	Formula	Element in salt (Percent)
Calcium		
Calcium carbonate	Ca Co_3	Ca : 40.05, Co_2 : 59.95
Dicalcium phosphate anhydrous	Ca H Po_4	Ca : 29.46, P : 22.77
Dicalcium Phosphate, dihydrate	Ca H Po_4, $2H_2O$	Ca : 23.29, P : 18.01
Tricalcium Phosphate	$Ca_3\ (Po_4)_2$	Ca : 38.76 P : 19.97
Calcium sulphate	Ca So_4	Ca : 29.43, So_4 : 70.57
Bone meal		Ca : 30.00, P : 15.00
Oyster shell grit		Ca : 38.00
Ground lime stone		Ca : 38.00
Chloride :		
Sodium chloride	NaCl	Cl : 60.65, Na. : 38.35
Potassium Chloride	KCl	Cl : 47.56,, K : 52.44
Chromium :		
Chrome alum	$Cr_2K_2.(So_4)_4.2H_2O$	Cr : 10.42, So_4 : 38.49
Chromic chloride	$CrCl_2$	Cr : 32.82, Cl : 67.18
Cobalt :		
Cobatlt chloride Pentahydrate	$CoCl_2$, $5H_2O$	Co : 26.80, Cl : 32.28
Cobaltous chloride, hexahydrate	$CoCl_2$, $6H_2O$	Co : 24.77, Cl : 29.84
Copper :		
Cupric sulphate	$CuSo_4$	Cu : 39.81, So_4 : 38.49
Cupric sulphate pentahydrate	$CuSo_4$, $5H_2O$	Cu : 25.46, So_4 : 38.49
Cupric chloride	$CuCl_2$	Cu : 47.27, Cl : 72.73
Fluorine :		
Potassium fluoride, dihydrate	KF $2H_2O$	F : 20.17, K : 41.54
Sodium floride	NaF	
Iodine :		
Potassium Iodide	KI	K : 23.55, I : 76.45

Salt	Formula	Element in salt (Percent)
Potassium Iodate	KIO_2	K : 18.27, I : 59.31
Calcium Iodate	$Ca\ (Io_3)_2$	Ca : 10.28, I : 65.09
Sodium Iodide	NaI	Na : 15.32, I : 84.68
Iron :		
Ferrous sulphate, Heptahydrate	$Fe\ So_4,\ 7H_2O$	Fe : 20.09, So_4 34.59
Ferrous acetate, tetrahydrate	$Fe\ (C_2H_2O_2)_2\ 4H_2O$	
Magnesium :		
Magnesium Carbonate	$Mg\ Co_3$	Mg : 28.84, Co_3 : 71.16
Magnesium Sulphate	$Mg\ So_4$	mg : 20.19, So_4 : 79.81
Magnesium sulphate, heptahydrate	$Mg\ So_4,\ 7H_2O$	Mg : 9.87, So_4 : 39.01
Manganese :		
Manganese dioxide	MnO_2	Mn : 63.19
Manganous carbonate	$Mn\ Co_3$	Mn : 47.79, Co_3 : 52.21
Manganous chloride, tetrahydrate	$MnCl_2,\ 4H_2O$	Mn : 27.76, Cl : 35.86
Manganous sulphate	$Mn\ So_4$	Mn : 36.36, So_4 : 63.64
Mangnous sulphate hydrate	$Mn\ So_4,\ H_2O$	Mn : 32.49, So_4 : 56.86
Manganous sulphate, tetrahydrate	$Mn\ So_4,\ 4H_2O$	Mn : 24. 63, So_4 : 43. 10
Molybdenum :		
Sodium molybdate, dihydrate	$Na_2MoO_4,\ 2H_2O$	Mo : 39.66, Na : 19.01
Sodium molybdate, pentahydrate	$NaMoO_4,\ 5H_2O$	Mo : 35.15, Na : 8.43
Nickel :		
Nickel chloride	$NiCl_2$	N : 45. 26, Cl : 54.74
Phosphorus :		
Orthophosphoric acid	H_3Po_4	P : 31.61
Potassium Orthophosphate	K_2HPo_4	P : 17.79, K : 44.90
Potassium dihydrogen orthophosphate	$K\ H_2\ Po_4$	P : 22.76, K : 28.73

Salt	Formula	Element in salt (Percent)
Sodium hydrogen orthophosphate	$Na_2H\ Po_4$	P : 21.82, Na : 32.40
Sodium dihydrogen orthophosphate, hydrate	NaH_2Po_4, H_2O	P : 22.45, Na : 16.67
Sodium dihydrogen orthophsophate dihydrate	$Na_3H_3Po_4, 2H_2O$	P : 19.86, Na : 14.74
Ammonium Phosphate	$(NH_4)_2\ HPo_4$	P : 23.86
Potassium :		
Potassium chloride	KCl	K : 52.44, Cl : 47.56
Potassium carbonate	K_2Co_3	K : 56.58, Co_3 : 43.42
Potassium bicarbonate	$K\ H\ Co_3$	K : 39.05, HCo : 60.95
Potassium orthophosphate	K_3Po_4	K : 55.25, P : 14.59
Potassium sulphate	K_2So_4	L : 44.87, So_4 : 55.13
Selenium :		
Sodium selenite	Na_2SeO_3	Se : 45.65, Na : 26.60
Sodium selenate	$NaSe\ O_4$	Se : 41.79, Na : 24.34
Sodium :		
Sodium chloride	Na Cl	Na : 39.35, Cl : 60.65
Sodium bicarbonate	$Na\ H\ Co_3$	Na : 27.38, HCo_3 : 72.62
Sodium sulphate	Na_2So_4	Na : 32.39, So_4 : 67.61
Tin :		
Stannic sulphate	$Sn(So_4)2, 2H_2O$	Sn : 34.22, So_4 : 55.36
Vanadium :		
Sodium orthovanadate	Na_3Vo_4	V : 27.69, Na : 37.51
Zinc :		
Zinc carbonate	$Zn\ Co_3$	Zn : 52.14, Co_3 : 47.86
Zinc Chloride	$Zn\ Cl_2$	Zn : 47.97, Cl : 52.03
Zinc oxide	Zno	Zn : 80.35
Zinc Sulphate	$Zn\ So_4$	Zn : 40.47, So_4 : 59.33
Zinc sulphate hydrate	$Zn\ Zo_4, H_2O$	Zn : 36.42, So_4 : 53.55

Source : Poultry Nutrition by W. Botton and R. Blair, Published by Ministry of Agriculture, Fisheries and Food, U.K. 1974. Bulletion No. 174.

8

POULTRY DISEASES

Disease may be defined as a condition deviated from normal stage of health. Disease is a greatest threat to the success of poultry enterprise. Severe outbreak of a contagious and infectious disease often result in heavy mortality. Whenever a number of birds are kept together, there is a danger of disease outbreaking amongst them.

The poultry diseases may be classified according to the type of disease causing organism. Such as

1. **Viral Diseases**

   Ranikhet disease (New Castle disease).
   Marek's disease
   Fowl Pox.
   Leucosis
   Infectious bronchitis (IB)
   Avian encephalomyelitis
   Avian monocytosis
   Infectious bursitis (IBD)
   Avian nephritis
   Avian influenza

2. **Bacterial Diseases**

   Pullorum disease
   Fowl cholera
   Fowl typhoid
   Avian pseudo-tuberculosis
   Chronic respiratory disease (CRD)
   Infectious coryza
   Botulism

3. **Fungal Disease**

   Aspergillosis (Brooder pneumonia)
   Aflatoxicosis
   Mycotoxicosis

4. **Protozoal Diseases**

   Coccidiosis

5. **Parasitic Disease**

   Ectoparasities : Lice, Mite, Flea and Ticks.
   Endoparasities : Round worm, Caecal worm, Tape worm and Gape worm.

6. **Nutritional Diseases**

   Nutritional Roup
   Rickets,
   Perosis
   Polyneuritis
   Chick dermatitis
   Curled toe-paralysis
   Haemorrhagic disease
   Encephalomalacia

7. **Miscellaneous Diseases in Poultry**

   Cannibalism
   Egg drop syndrome
   Egg bound
   Heat stroke
   Bumble foot

MODE OF TRANSMISSION OF CONTAGIOUS AND INFECTIOUS DISEASES

The contagious and infectious diseases may spread through various ways, as follows :

(i) The feed and water contaminated with saliva and droopings of disease affected birds may act as carrier of disease organism.

(ii) The virus can be transmitted through contaminated feed, water, droopings and litter.

(iii) Air borne transmission is the most common way of transmission of some diseases such as IB, Fowl pox etc.

(iv) The disease organism of some disease such as Pullorum, CRD etc maybe transmitted through infected eggs.

(v) The disease may be spread through the droopings of infected birds and contaminated soil of poultry house acts as vital carrier of disease organism.

(vi) Recovered adult birds act as a carrier and remains as a potential disease spreading agent.

(vii) Infected incubator may act as an agent for transmission of infection and the newly hatched birds get infected.

(viii) Some animals such as rodents, cats, rats, dogs, cockroaches and wild birds may act as mechanical carrier of infection.

(ix) Carcasses, if not disposed properly, will act as a potential sources of transmission of infection.

(x) Visitors or attendents may act as a carrier of infection through their feet, hands, clothes and shoes.

(xi) The disease organisms may be spread through direct contact with the infected birds

(xii) Poor hygenic and sanitary condition are the main causes of transmission of disease from flock to flock.

PREVENTION OF CONTAGIOUS DISEASES

(i) The poultry house must be kept dry. The houses and equipments should be throughly cleaned and disinfected before the arrival of chicks.

(ii) The birds of different age groups should be kept in separate room.

(iii) Chicks should be procured from a reliable breeder and disease free flock.

(iv) Overcrowding should be avoided and measures should be adopted to ensure good feeding and the maintenance of hygenic and sanitary condition in the farm.

(v) Cleanliness and disinfection of brooder house, brooder and incubator should be done regularly.

(vi) Birds suspected to be suffering from some infection should never be mixed up with those which are healthy.

(vii) The litter should be kept dry as far as possible and the litter should be changed before placing a new brood.

(viii) Feeders and waterer should be cleaned daily to avoid contamination.

(ix) Infected eggs should not be incubated for hatching. The incubators should be sterilised properly with fumigation.

(x) The infected house should not be used for rearing new birds at least for a fornight or a month.

(xiii) The droopings and excretion should be disposed with utmost care to check the spread of infection.

(xiv) All in and all out management will help to control the disease.

(xv) The house should be disinfected after the removal of disease birds. The dead birds should be carefully disposed and burried immediately.

(xvi) The contaminated food and water should be used for the healthy bird as they act as a carrier of infection.

(xvii) A proper prophylactic vaccination programme should be undertaken against the contagious diseases such as Ranikhet, Merek's disease, Fowl Pox etc.

(xviii) The new birds should not be given entry unless found free from illnes.

A. VIRAL DISEASES

1. RANIKHET DISEASE (NEW CASTLE DISEASE)

Ranikhet disease is a highly infectious and fatal Viral disease. *Tortor furens* is the causal organism of this disease. The outbreak of this occurs first at New-Castle in England and accordingly this is also known as New-Castle disease. This disease appears in our country n 1927 at Ranikhet in U.P. For this, it is also called as Ranikhet disease.

The disease spreads directly from birds to birds through the nasal mucosa and mouth discharge of the affectd birds, contaminted feed and litter and also by air. The birds recovered from this disease act as carriers of this disease. Mortality due to this disease may be as high as 100 percent in young flock. Laying is also affected by this disease where the mortality is less. It is widespread, highly contagious disease of respiratory and nervous system of poultry.

Symptoms

(i) Swelling of the face, eyes and throat.

(ii) Respiratory difficulty with pronounced gasping, coughing and rattling of the wind pipe.

(iii) Green diarrhoea with fowl ordour.

(iv) Pale comb and wattle which latter turn blue.

(v) The affected young bird walk in circle or stragger. This may consist of partial or complete paralysis of one or both legs and wings, tremor of head and body, incordination of movement and convulsion.

Table 8.1. vaccination scheduled for chicken.

Name of the disease	Names of the vaccine	Age at which vaccine is given	Dose	Route of administration	Remarks
Ranikhet disese	RD.F_1/Lasota vaccine	4-7 days.	1 drop.	Each into eyes and nostril	Can be given also at the old stage.
	R.D_1/Lasota	Fifth week	,,	- do -	To be given only in epidemic area
	RD R_2B (Mukteswar Strain vaccine)	8-10 weeks	0.5 ml	S/C or I/M	Limited reaction is usually noticed.
	RD oil adjuvant vaccine	17-18	0.5	I/M in neck muscles	To be given only in epidemic areas
Fowl pox	Chick embryofowl Vaccine	6-7 weeks	Few drops	By pricking of feather follicles	
	Pigeon-pox vaccine	3-4 weeks	,,	,,	To be given only in epidemic areas. This is to be followed by fowl pox vaccine at about 8-10th weeks.
Marek's Disease	HVT MD	Day old	0.2 ml	S/C cervical region or I/M into thigh musches.	-
Infectious brochitis	IB vaccine	15-16 weeks	0.5 ml.	S/C or I/M	Booster may be required. To be given in epidemic area.

As the commercial broilers are slaughtered by eight week they are to be given only RD. F_1 and MD Vaccine.
Source : Poultry Production (1989) by B. Panda and S.C. Mohapatra I.C.A.R. New-Delhi 110012.

(vi) The head may be twisted to one side, drawn back or down between the legs or straight back between the shoulders.

(vii) Egg production drops and egg quality deteriorates. The affected birds in many cases die without showing any visible symptoms.

Control Measures

There is no effective treatment of this disease. The birds should be vaccinated against Ranikhet disease. It is safe and effective for prevention of this disease. The chicks should be vaccinated with F_1 strain or Lasota strain on the first day or within five days after hatch and with booster dose R_2B Mukteswar strain at 8-10 weeks of age. The poultry birds affected with worm can not tolerate the vaccine. The birds should be given wormcidal medicine (i.e. Vermax : dose : 60 ml/100 birds, Piperzine : dose : 50 ml/100 birds, verman : dose 40 ml/100 birds) sevendays before vaccination.

2. FOWL POX

Fowl pox is a contagious viral disease. Birds of all ages are affected by this disease, resulting in high mortality rate. Chicken and turkeys are mainly affected by this disease. But some viral type may also affect pigeons, geese, pheasants and quails.

Spreads of the disease

The healthy birds may be affected with this disease by direct contact of the disease affected birds, contaminated water and feeds. Scales of diseased birds also transmit the disease. Mosquito and other biting insect often carry the virus.

Symptoms

There are three types of fowl pox as follows :

(i) **Skin or cutaneous type** : Wart like growths are seen on face, comb, wattles and featherless parts of the body. They grow readily and turn yellow and later turn blacks or brown lessions. After 2 or 3 weeks, the lesions dry up and become scabby. It is also called as dry pox which is more common than others.

(ii) **Buccal or mouth form** : White patches or slightly elevated nodules occur inside the mouth and tongue. The mucous membrane of the mouth and oesophagus are affected. The breathing may be difficult. This type of pox is known as diphtheritic type (wet type).

(iii) **Oculonasal form** : Eruption occurs on the opening of eye and nose. The ear and nose may swell and discharges from eye and nose may be seen. The affected birds do not eat and lie idley. Egg production drops in layers birds.

Control Measures

There is no satisfactory treatment of this disease. The birds should be vaccinated with pigeon-pox vaccine during first week followed by fowl-pox vaccine at 6-8 weeks of age as preventive measure. Control of mosquito is essential to check the spread of the disease. The disease affected birds should be given antibiotic and vitamin treatment for fast recovery.

3. MAREK'S DISEASE

Merek's disease is highly infectious viral disease of chicken. Chickens are affected by this disease at their early age and the infected birds remain viremia through their life. Chicken of 6 to 10 weeks of age are more susceptible.

Spread of the disease

The idsease spreads mainly through saliva, nasal washing, faeces and feather follicles of affected birds. Some birds of the flock suddenly affected by this disease. The disease may occurs at any time in the flocks.

Symptoms

(i) Unilateral or bilateral paralysis of legs, wings and neck due to enlargement of various nerves inside of the body. Birds are unable to stand. Legs and wings may be streched in either direction.

(ii) Laboured breathing is noticed.

(iii) The affected eyes become white and unilateral or bilateral blindness may occur.

(iv) Whistling and circulating movements.

(v) Young chicken may suffer from acute form which cause sudden death of the affected birds with the presence of viscerol tumours inside the body. Birds will show depression, droopiness, unthriftiness, dehydration, emaciation and anemia.

(vi) In many of the infected birds, the vent remains soil with green diarrhoea.

(vii) On posmortem examination whitish nodules in muscles of thigh, neck, kidney, testes and in ovaries are seen.

Control Measures

There is no satisfactory treatment of this disease. Administration of Macalvet injection (Dose : 2 ml/five birds) and Rovisol AD_3 EC with feeds proof beneficial for the affected birds. Vaccination with Merek's vaccine, made from Herpes virus of Turkey at day old age protect the birds lifelong from the manifestation of the disease. Merek's vaccine is most effective for the prevention of this disease.

4. AVIAN MONOCYTOSIS

This disease is also known as Blue Comb disease complex. It is an infectious disease of pullet caused by a virus. It is characteristic by uremia and kidney damage in 5-7 month old birds. There is a rapid onset of the disease and death rate is 5 to 50 percent.

Spread of the Disease

The mode of transmission of the disease is not known.

Symptoms

(i) Complete loss of appetite.
(ii) Whitish or watery diarrhoea.
(iii) High fewer, depression and emaciation.
(iv) Cyanosis of comb and wattles.
(v) Shunken and blue leg.
(vi) Pronounced fall of egg production of adult birds.

Control Measures

(i) Good management including sanitation is very effective in controlling the disease.
(ii) Treatment with antibiotic such as streptomycin, neomycin, tetracyclin, crythromycin, tylosin etc (@ 1 gm. per kg of feed coupled with vitamin for 5-7 days is effective in controlling the secondary infection.

5. AVIAN ENCEPHALOMYELITIS (EPIDEMIC TREMOR, ALAXIA)

This viral disease primarily affects the young chicks upto six week of age. But the birds of any age group may be affected by this disease.

Spread of Disease

Infected eggs, droppings of the infected birds containing large number of virus act as carrier of the disease.

Symptoms

(i) Affected young chicks show nervous signs which is characterised by dullness, depression, incoordination, ataxia, sitting on hatches and inabality to walk.

(ii) Partial or complete paralysis.

(iii) Diarrhoea

(iv) Trembling of head

(v) Birds usually remain drowsy but if any sound is made, they will get up and walk and finally go to tremor (Chakraborty 1991).

(vi) Drop of egg production upto 10-20 percent in adult birds.

Control Measures

(i) Infected egg should not be used for hatching.

(ii) The affected birds should be culled.

(iii) Hygenic and sanitation measures should be adopted.

6. INFECTIOUS BRONCHITIS (IB)

This disease is cauused by virus. It is highly contagious disease of chickens characterised by respiratory discomfort.

Spread of the Disease

Nasal discharge of the affected birds, contaminated feed and equipment act as a carrier of this disease.

Symptoms

(i) Gasping, coughing, distressed and open mounth breathing in chicks.

(ii) Discharges from eyes and nostril.

(iii) Chicks will huddle together.

(iv) The respiratory symptoms are mild and include gasping, coughing and nasal discharge in adult.

(v) Drop in egg production as high as 60-90 percent in laying birds. The eggs are of soft shelled, wrinkled, small in size and has poor albumen quality.

Control Measures

(i) Good management including sanitation can minimize the spread of the disease.

(ii) Birds of different age group should be raised separately.

(iii) Vaccination with inactvated or attenuated life viruus vaccine when day old with R.D. vaccine (F_1) is very effective in controlling this disease.

7. INFECTIOUS BURSITIS (GUMBORO DISEASE; INFECTIOUS BURSAL DISEASE)

It is a highly contagious viral disease of young chicks. The chicks from 2 to 6 weeks of age are usually affected by this disease. The mortality due to this disease is 5 to 15 percent.

Spread of the Disease

Contaminated feed, water, droppings and litter may act as carrier of this disease.

Symptoms

(i) Loss of appetite.

(ii) White watery mucoid drooping and soiled vent feathers.

(iii) Drowsiness, depresion listlessness, severe tremors and unsteady gait.

(iv) Ruffled feathers

Control Measuures

(i) Good management including santitation, disinfection and fumigation of poultry house before the introduction of new batch of chicks, disposal of dead bird by burning etc. can minimize the spread of this disease.

(ii) Broiler and layer should be raised separately.

(iii) Vaccination of day old chicks with virulent vaccine in combination with H.V.T. is very effective in controlling the disease.

B. BACTERIAL DISEASE

1. PULLORUM DISEASE (BACILLARY WHITE DIARRHOEA; B.W.D.)

Pullorum disease is a contagious bacterial disease of poultry birds. This disease affects both young and adults, though it is primarily a disease of young chicks. The disease is caused by gram-negative bacteria known as *Salmonella pullorum.* This organism can also affect the ducks, quinea fowl, guails, pigeon, turkeys, and phesants.

Speed of the Disease

The organism of this disease is found in ovaries, heart, liver etc. This disease is transmitted through infeected eggs. The chicks hatched from infected egg suffer from this disease. Adult birds recovered from this disease acts as a carrier of this disease. The feed, water and litter contaminated with droppings of infected birds are the important means of spreading of this disease. The healthy birds may be infected with this disease by direct contact with diseased birds.

Symptoms

(a) **Chicks :**

(i) Chicks may die immediately after hatching in incubator with peak mortality on seventh day which may range from 20 to 80 percent (usually 50 percent).

(ii) Chicks huddle together near the source of heat as if they are chilled.

(iii) Labour breathing, dropping of wings, ruffled feathers as if they are dipped in water, white chalky diarrhoea, pasted vent, great thirst, swelling of abdomen and emacication of a peqular continuous cripping sound are the characteristics symptom of this disease.

(iv) Chicks having 3 to 8 weeks of age may show lameness, swelling of hocks and foot joints.

(b) **Adults :** In adult the symptoms are not prominent. But the following symptom should be taken into consideration

(i) Some birds may show inappetance, weakness and ruffled feather

(ii) Greenish brown diarrhoea, dropping of wings and head, dull and depression along with paleness of comb are seen.

(iii) On postmortem examination, changes in ovari include dark shrunken and inactive follicles, dark and enlarged liver are seen.

Control Measures

(i) The birds showing the symptoms of pullorum disease should be culled and slaughtered.

(ii) The hygienic conditions in all farm operations including egg sanitation, fumigation, hatchery and brooder sanitation should be followed to keep the infection out of the flocks.

(iii) It is essential to purchase the birds from the farm free from pullorum disease.

(iv) The following drugs may be used for the treatment of this disease.

(a) *Furazolidine Prefix.*

Dose : Treatment : 100 gm. per 100 kg feed for a week.
Preventive : 50 per 100 kg feed for a week.

(b) *Sulphamezathin-16%*

Dose : 7.5 ml. per litre of water for 25 birds for 4 days.

(c) *Oriprim Tablet*

Dose : 1/2-1 tablet for 60 birds daily

(d) *Auromycin Powder*

Dose : Treatment : 8-16 gm. per 10 litre of water.
Preventive : 4-8.gm. per 10 litre of water.

(e) *Duaprim Powder*

Dose : 2.5 gm, 5 gm. and 10 gm daily for chicks, grower and layer respectively.

(f) *Chemozyme powder*

Dose 1 gm. per 8 kg body weight twice daily for 3-5 days

(h) *Amdon*

Dose : Treatment : 30 gms per 50 litres of water for 5-7 days. Preventive : 30 gm per 100 litres of water for 15 days. During the treatment, only medicated water should be administered to the birds and it should be consumed on the same day.

(i) *Doxyterin-D.S.*

Dose : Preventive : 1 gm per litre of water.
Treatment : 2 gm per litre of drinking water.

(j) *Zintrim-D.S.*

Dose : 0.5 to 1.0 gm per litres of water for 5 days.

2. CHRONIC RESPIRATORY DISEASE (C.R.D. Infectious Sinusitis, Air Sacculitis)

It is a chronic slow spreading contagious disease of poultry birds. *Mycoplasma gallisepticum* organism is directly associated with C.R.D. It is wide spread disease and large number of birds may suffer at a time. The young birds sustain mortality (30-40 percent during 6-8 weeks of age) and the old birds will suffer from reproductive failure. The disease appears with or without any secondary infection.

Spread of the Disease

The disease usually spreads through eggs, nasal discharge and dropping of infected birds. The attendants and visitors may act as carrier of the disease. The transmission is also possible through carrrier birds.

Symptoms

(i) C.R.D. without any secondary complication is frequentlyy sub-clinical.

(ii) The symptoms of this disease include coughing, sneezing and a nasal discharge, which are normally mild in nature.

(iii) In young birds, conjunctivitis and lacrymation are seen.

(iv) Adult birds lose their body weight considerably and egg production reduces about 40 percent. The eggs are not abnormal like other disease.

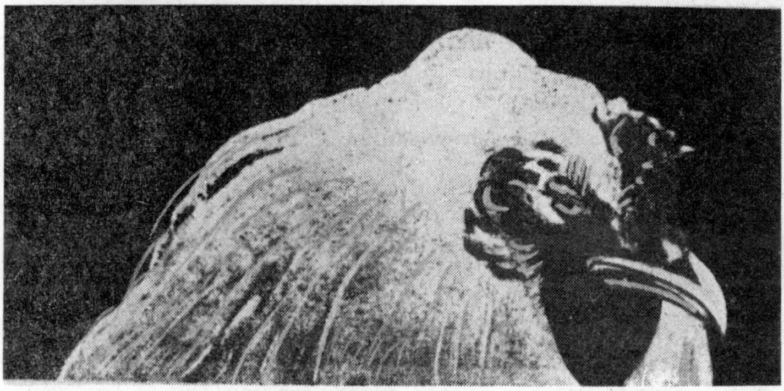

Fig. 8.1. CRD affectal birds

Control Measures

The following drugs are useful for the treatment of this disease :

A. (a) Tiamutin 45% soluble granules.
   (b) Rovamycin oral powder.
   (c) Tonet powder.
   (e) Taylan-50
   (f) Erystrim soluble powder.
   (g) Terramycin poultry formula with antigerm.
   (h) Aureomycin powder.

The medicines are to be mixed with water and administered to the poultry birds according to the direction of the manufacturer.

B. The following injection may be administered for the treatment of this disease :

(a) *Inj. Rovamycin*
Dose : 100 mg per Kg. body weight through subcutaneously.

(b) *Inj. Licomycin hydrochloride*
Dose : 1 ml. per bird through intramuscular route.

3. FOWL CHOLERA (AVIAN PASTEURELLOSIS)

Fowl cholera is highly fatal disease. It is caused by bacteria known as *Pasteurella multocida.*

Spread of the Disease

The feed and water contaminated with oral and nasal discharge, dropping of affected bird, flies and insect act as carrier of this disease organism. Recovered birds also act as carrier and continue to spread the infection.

Symptom

(i) **Acute form :** Sudden death is the first indication of this disease. The birds show the following symptoms prior to death : High fever, ruffled feathers and discharge from mouth and greenish yellow diarrhoea.

(ii) **Respiratory form :** Respiratory distress including sneezing, coughing and gasping. Cyanosis is noticed on unfeathered parts of head and face,

(iii) **Septicaemic form :** Wide spread haemorrhages in visceral organs, general dejection and diarrhoea having grey, yellow or green colour.

(iv) **Chronic infection :** It follows acute infection. The lessions are localised in sinuses, wing, leg. joints, foot and bursa. Lameness, walking in circle, incoordation etc. are the characteristics symptom.

Control Measures

(i) Good management including sanitation, isolation of infected birds, disinfection and fumigation of poultry houses and equiptment can minimize the spread of this disease.

(ii) The animal like dog, cat, pig etc should not be allowed in the close vicinity of the poultry farm.

(iii) The birds of different age group should be kept in separate house.

(iv) Vaccination with Fowl cholera vaccine @ 1 ml per birds at 8 weeks of age is very effective for prevention of this disease.

(v) The following drugs are effective for the treatment of this disease:

(a) *Sulphamezathin 16% solution*

Dose : 7.5 ml. per litre of water for 25 birds to be given for 4 days.

(b) *Chemozyme powder*

Dose : 1 gm per 8 kg body weight twice daily for 3-5 days.

(c) *Rosillin oral powder*
Dose : As per the direction of manufacturer.

(d) *Hostacycline powder*
Dose : Treatment : 5 gm. per 4.5 litre of water.
Preventive : 2.5 gm per 4.5 litre of water.

(e) *Auromycin powder*
Dose : Treatment : 8-12 gm per 10 litres of water.
Preventive : 4-8 gm per 10 litres of water.

(f) *Terramycin Inj.*
Dose : As per the direction of the manufacturer.

(g) *Teramycin Liquid*
Dose : 1 ml per litre of water.

(h) *Haustracyclin*
Dose : 2 gm per litre of water.

(i) *Duaprim powder*
Dose : Poultry for 100 birds, through drinking water.

Chicks	:	2.5 gm daily.
Grower/Broiler	:	5.0 gm daily.
Layer	:	10.0 gm daily.

(j) *Doxyterin - D.S.*
Dose : Preventive : 1 gm per litre of drinking water.
Treatment : 2 gm per litre of drinking water.

(k) *Gentim (Gentamicin sulphate : protent antibiotic injection)*
Dose : 0.2-0.4 mg/day old chicks.

4. FOWL TYPHOID

Salmonella gallinarum bacteria is the causal organism of fowl typhoid. It is highly septicaemic disease of poultry. The growers and adult birds are generally affected by this disease. But the birds of all age group may be affected.

Spread of the Disease

The feed and water contaminated with droppings of affected birds, carcases etc. act as carrier of this disease organism. The recovered birds will remain as carrier and will spread the infection through their dropings.

Symptoms

(i) Birds may die abruptly all of a sudden without showing any appreciable clinical symptom.

(ii) Head remains downward with the closure of both the eyelids.

(iii) White chalk like diarrhoea, pasted vent, general depression, huddling and weight loss.

(iv) The breathing is rapid with elevation of body temperature.

(v) Dejection of posture, dropping of wings and tails, ruffled feather and comb and wattle appear pale.

(vi) The affected birds die within three weeks. Mortality may vary from 20-80 percent.

Control Measures

(i) Good management and hygienic condition including sanitation, disinfection and fumigation of poultry houses and equipment is very essential for the control of this disease.

(ii) Vaccination with vaccine made from liver attenuated microorganism at 8 weeks of age @ 1 ml per bird is very effective for the prevention of this disease.

(iii) Followings drugs are effective for the treatment of this dsease :

(a) *Furazolidine 50% Powder*
Dose : 100 gm per ton feed for week.

(b) *Furazolidine Premix*
Dose : Preventive : 0.5 gm per kg feed for a week.
Treatment : 1.0 gm per kg feed for a week.

(c) *Sulphamezathin 16% Solution*
Dose : 7.5 ml per litre of water for 4 days for 25 birds.

(d) *Caprisol powder*
Dose : As per direction of manufacturer.

(e) *Neftrin-50*
Dose : 4 gm per kg feed.

(f) *Furazol*
Dose : 1 gm per litre of water.

(g) *Rosicillin oral powder*
Dose : As per direction of the manufacturer.

(h) *Inj. Enteromycelin*
Dose : one bolus for 20-30 brids.

(i) *Duaprim powder*
Dose : Poultry for 100 birds, through drinking water
Chicks : 2.5 gm daiily.

Grower/Broiler : 5.0 gm daily.
Layers : 10.0 gm daily.

(j) *Amdon*
Dose : Preventive : 30 gm per 100 litres of water for 15 days.
Treatment : 30 gm per 1000 litres of water for 5-7 days

(k) *Doxyterin D.S.*
Dose : Preventive : 1 gm per litre of drinking water.
Treatment : 2 gm per litre of drinkiing water.

C. FUNGAL DISEASES

1. ASPERGILLOSIS (BROODER PNEUMONIA)

Aspergillosis is commongly known as brooder pneumonia. This disease is caused by *Aspergillus fumigatus.* Birds of all age group may be affected, but birds upto 4-6 weeks of age are more susceptible to this disease, causing fairly high mortality (10-50 percent).

Spread of the Disease

The disease is generally transmitted through contaminated litter and feed stuffs and also by the inhalation of fungal spore from hatchery or from mouldy feed or litter.

Symptom

(i) Difficult breathing with some gasping and accelerated breathing through the open beak.
(ii) Loss of appetite, weakness, emaciation, blindness, encephalitis, more thirst and watery diarrhoea are clinical symptoms of this disease.
(iii) The disease affected birds huddle together and are reluctant to move.
(iv) Drooping of feather with slightly dark comb.
(v) The affected chicks die within 24 to 48 hours following appearing of the signs.

On postmortem examination, yellow to greenish P.M. lession are seen in the affected tissue. The postmortem lessions are mostly seen in eyes, liver, lungs, brain and air sacs.

Control Measures

The following drugs may be used for the treatment of this disease :

(i) Copper Sulphate : @ 1 : 2000 concentration for 7 days.

(ii) *Hamycin*
Dose : 10 ml/litre of water for 10-15 days.

(iii) *Propionic acid*
Dose : 500 gms per ton of feed.

(iv) Potassium Iodide ; 33 percent.
Dose : 2 ml per 100 birds.

The following measures should be taken for the prevention of this disease:

(i) Mamycin : Dose 5 ml per litre of water may be used in drinkinng water as a preventive measures.
(ii) The builtup, caked and mouldy litter should be removed to prevent the growth of the fungus.
(iii) The litter should always be dry. The litter of the brooder house should be stirred at regular interval.
(iv) Feeder and waterer should be cleaned regularly with detergent and wastage of feed in feeder should be avoided.
(v) The incubator should be fumigated with 40 percent formaldehyde and potassium permanganate.

2. FAVUS (WHITE COMB)

Favus is a skin disease of poultry. It is caused by *Trichophyto meganini.* It mostly affects the comb.

Symptoms

(i) The comb appears as dusted with flour.
(ii) Yellowish white scaly lesions on the comb.
(iii) Exhaustion and anaemia.
(iv) Mouldy odour.

Control Measures

(i) Local application of iodine or pentachlorophenol (0.5%) is effective.
(ii) It is better to kill the affected birds as the treatment is unsatisfactory.

3. THRUSH (MONILIASIS; SOUR CROP; CANDIASIS)

It is caused by *Monilia albicans,* Excessive feeding of antibiotic or sugar in feed and stress predispose the birds to thrush.

Symptoms

(i) Stunted growth, emaciation and listlessness.

(ii) Ruffled feathers
(iii) Foul smelling discharge from the mouth and anorexia.
(iv) Turkish towel appearance of the crop.
(v) Ulcerations are seen in crop, intestine and liver.

Control Measuures

(i) Good management is effective.
(ii) Stress and feeding of heavy doses of antibiotic should be avoided.
(iii) Followings drugs are effective for the treatment of this disease :

(a) *Nystanin*
Dose : 50 - 1000 mg per kg of feed.

(b) *Copper sulphate*
Dose : 1: 200 solution in drinking water every alternate day for 7-10 days.

D. PROTOZOAL DISEASE

1. COCCIDIOSIS

Coccidiosis is highly contagious disease and caused by microscopic unicellular protozoan parasites called coccidia, mainly infecting the intestinal tract of bird. The infection is severe in young chicks upto ten weeks of age. The following nine species of coccidia of genus Eimeria are important to poultry farmers :

Eimeria tenella, Eimeria necatrix, Eimeria acervulina, Eimeria precox, Eimeria hagani, Eimeri brunetti, Eimeria motitis, Eimeria maxima and Eimeria mivali. Out of these, *Eimeria tenella and Eimeria necatrix* is important which produces Caecal coccidiosis and intestinal coccidiosis respectively.

Spread of the Disease

The causal organism of the disease is transmitted through the feed, water or other materials contaminated with coccidia. The food and drinking water get contaminated with the droopings of infected birds. Rodents, cockroaches, pets, wild birds and attendents may also act as mechanical carrier of infection.

Symptoms

(a) **Caecal coccidiosis :** It is fatal disease and is caused by *E. tenella.*

(i) Face and shank becomes pale.
(ii) Bloody dropping from fifth day of infection, ruffled feathers,

depression, listlessness and droopiness are the clinical symptom of this disease.

(iii) The chicks huddle together, eyes remain closed.

(iv) The affected birds disincline to move due to weakness of legs.

(v) The affected chicks take less feed.

(vi) Sudden death of the chickens.

(b) **Intestinal coccidiosis :** Paleness is the significant symptom of intestinal coccidiosis. It is caused by *E. necatrix.*

(i) The beak, leg, comb and wattle become pale.

(ii) The intestine becomes swollen and remains with full of blood.

(iii) Loss of appetite and weight.

(iv) Bloody dropping in severe cases following six or seven days of infection.

(v) Partial paralysis and chick die at last.

Control Measures

The following drugs may be used for the treatment of this disese

(i) *Sulmet* (Dose : 30 ml per 4 litres of water). It may be given in 3-2-3 interrupted schedule (i.e. medicated water for 3 days, no drug for 2 days and again medicated water for 3 days).

(ii) *Sulphamezthine (16% sol.)*

Dose : 30 ml per litres of water for 4 days for 100 birds.

(iii) *Sulphadimidine (16% sol.)*

Dose : 30 ml in 4 litres of water for 4 days for 100 birds.

(iv) *Embazin - 10.32 % solution*

Dose : 4 ml per litre of water. It may be given in 3-2-3 interrupted schedule for caecal coccidiosis and 3-2-3-2-3 interrupted scheduled for intestinal coccidiosis.

(v) *Bifuran powder*

Dose : Treatmen : 1 gm per kg. feed.

Preventive : 0.5 gm per kg. feed.

(vi) *Bifuran Soluble Tablet*

Dose : Treatment : one tablet per litre of water for 7 days.

Preventive : one tablet per 4 litre of water for 7 days.

(vii) *Embazin Premix*

Dose : Treatment : 2 gm. per kg. of feed for 7 days.

Preventive : 0.5 gm per kg feed for 8 weeks.

(viii) *Furasol powder*

Dose : Chicks (below 2 weeks of age) :

0.5 gm per litre of water for 7 days.

Adults : 1 gm per litte of water for 7-10 days.

(ix) *Cordinal*

Dose : Treatment : 4 gm per litre of drinking water for 2-4 days.

Preventive : 1 gm per litre of drinking water for 2-4 days.

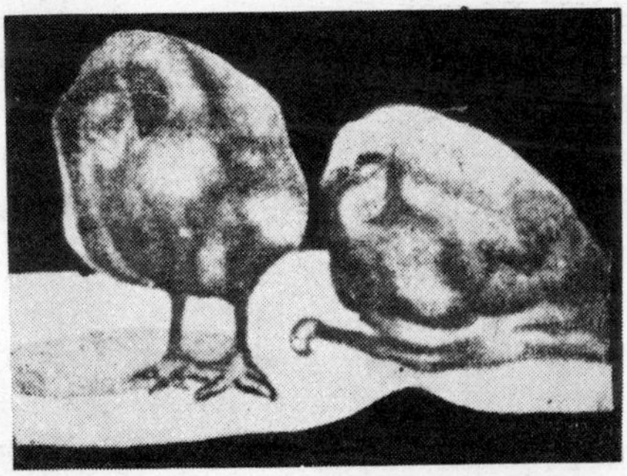

Fig. 8.2. Coccidiosis affected birds

(x) *Aprosol*

Dose : 30 gm in 25 litres of water for 5-7 days.

(xi) *Duaprim Powder*

Dose : Poultry for 100 birds, through drinking water :

Chicks	:	2.5 gms daily.
Grower/Broiler	:	5.0- gms daily.
Layer	:	10.0 gms daily.

(xii) *Amprolium and Ethopabate Premix B.P. (Vet.)*

It should be incorporated in feed @ 250 to 500 gms per ton of feed for prevention of coccidiosis in chickens and turkeys.

(xiii) *Femix-100*

Dose : 1 kg of Femix-100 per ton of feed as an aid in the prevention of coccidiosis in broilers, chickens reared for laying and turkeys upto 16 weeks of age.

(xiv) *Furalin*

Dose : 250-500 gms per ton of feed.

(xv) *Mericlose :*

Dose : 500 gm. per ton of feed as an aid in the prevention of coccidiosis in chickens.

E. PARASITIC DISEASES

The animal form that lives on or within the birds to its detriment is called parasite. Here the bird is the host. The parasites that live on or within the birds are called external parasites and internal parasites respectively. The parasites undergoes many adaptive structural changes such as claws on the feet of ectoparasite or development of hooks or sucker as in tapeworm for fixing to the host. Parasities come from different groups of animals attacking invertebrates and vertebrate. The parasites are evolved from the free living species.

A. EXTERNAL PARASITIES OR ECTOPARASITES

1. LICE

Lice is common external parasities of poultry birds. Lice is prolific in nature. They spend their life in host. There are different types of lice :

(i) Head louse : *(Cuctotagaster heterographa).*

(ii) Large chicken louse : *(Goniodes gigas)*

(iii) Wing louse : *(Lipeurus caponis)*

(iv) Shank louse : *(Menopon gallinae)*

They are small, wingless with flattened body, broad and with roundhead and yellow to greenish colour. They are transmitted by direct contact and abundant in summer.

Symptoms.

(i) Chicken becomes restlessness as they cause irritation.

(ii) Chicken pick their own fetather.

(iii) Loss of appetite, body weight and egg production.

(iv) Pale comb and wattle and anaemia.

(v) The birds affected severely may die.

Control Measures

Following chemicals may be used to control the lice infestation

(i) **Nicotin sulphate :** Perches should be treated with 40 percent nicotin sulphate just before night. The lice do not endure the fumes evolved from this and die due to suffocation.

(ii) **Sodium Flouride Solution :** Dipping the lice infected birds into the solution (45-60 gms per 10 litres of water) make the birds free from lice. This operation should be done on sunny day.

(iii) **The following insecticides may be used for controlling the lice:** Sevin (Carbaryl) - 5 percent, malathion 2-3 percent, and gammaxene-1 percent. These insecticides may be dusted on the affected bird or rubbed on the feather and skin. Lice on poultry can be controlled by dusting the infected bird with a dust mixture containing one part of tobacco powder, one part sulphur and ten parts of wood ash.

2. MITE

The mite that attach poultry birds is very small in size. Mites have four pairs of legs. They live in or near about cracks and crevices of the poultry house in the day time and attack the poultry birds at night coming from there. Mites have several species. Out of these followings are most common

(i) Red mites : *(Dermanyssius gallinae)*

(ii) Scaly leg mite : *(Cnemidocoptes mutans)*

(iii) Depluming mite : *(Cnemidocoptes gallinae)*.

The mites suck blood and tissue fluid through piercing type of mouth.

Symptoms

(i) Chicken becomes restlessness as the mites cause irritation.

(ii) The chicken pull out their feathers.

((iii) Loss of appetite, egg production and body weight.

(iv) Anaemia in severe cases and death.

(v) Thickening and wrinkling of the leg skin is seen in case of leg mite.

Control Measures

(i) Dusting the birds with Malathion 5 percent or Sevin-5 percent or Sulphur dust may be helpful for controlling the mite.

(ii) The surroundings and house should be sprayed with any one of the aforesaid insecticides.

(iii) The affected birds should be isolated and avoided overcrowding.

3. TICKS *(Argas persicus)*

Ticks are tenacious blood sucking parasites among the external parasites. They are noctural and are very tenacious., They can live upto three years without feeding.

Symptoms

(i) Sever itching due to bites.
(ii) Weakness, restlessness, ruffled feather, emaciation, and retarded growth.
(iii) Loss of body weight and egg production.
(iv) Anaemia in severe cases.

Ticks are responsible for the tick fever (Spirochactosis), which is a septicaemic disease of poultry. The organism of the tick fever is *Spirochaeto gallinarum or Borellia gallinarum* and the ticks act as vector for the transmission of this disease. Mortality is usually high upto 60 percent.

Symptoms

(i) Temperature rises to 43°C and above.
(ii) Comb and wattles becomes pale.
(iii) Hyperthemia, increased thirst, cyanosis of head and yellow green diarrhoea.
(iv) Birds become listlessness, disinclined to move and rapid emaciation.
(v) Anaemia in severe cases.
(vi) Some birds show paralysis of leg, wing or both.

Control Measures

(i) Dusting the birds with Sevin or D.D.T. or Malathion helps to control the ticks.
(ii) Spraying the surroundings with Malathion or other chemicals is very effective for controlling the ticks.
(iii) Vaccination and control of ticks, prevents the disease.

4. FLEA *(Echidnophage gallinaceea)*

Flea is small, active and dark brown to black colour parasities having piercing and sucking type mouth. Body is flattened from side to side.

Symptoms

(i) Flea is most abundant in comb, wattle and around the eye and cause damage to the affected parts.
(ii) Egg production is reduced due to irritation.
(iii) The growth is reduced and the young birds affected seriously may die.
(iv) Adult birds my have ulceration due to parasitis barrows.

Control Measures

Dusting with Malathion-5 percent or D.D.T-5 percent or spraying with Malathion on the surroundings and houses may be effective for controlling of the flea.

B. INTERNAL PARASITES OR ENDO PARASITES

1. ROUND WORM *(Ascaridia galli)*

Round worm is most prevalent internal parasites in poultry. They are 2.54 to 5.0 cm long. They transmitted through embryonated egg eaten through contaminated feed and water. The young birds under three months of age are most susceptible to round worm infestation.

Symptoms

(i) Unthriftiness, debility, poor growth, loss of weight and egg production.

(ii) There is diarrhoea due to irritation of the intestinal mucosa.

(iii) Emaciation and anaemia may result due to heavy worm burden.

Control Measures

Following wormicidals may be used for the treatment of round worm infected birds.

(i) *Piperzine hydrate (Liquid)* : A highly concentrate stable and safe aqueous solution of piperzine hexahydrate for oral adminsitration in the round worm infestation in poultry.

Dose : 50 ml per 100 birds per month for grower and layer.

(ii) *Piperzine Citrate*

Dose : 100 to 150 gms per kg body weight.

(iv) *Piperex*

Dose : 4 spoonful medicine dissolved in two litres of water is suitable for 100 birds.

(v) *Wopell*

Dose : 0.5 to 1% W/W with feed once a month. It should be administered orally to birds mixed with feed preferably on an empty stomach.

(vi) *Banif Powder*

Dose : Poultry for 100 birds through drinking water :

Grower/Broiler : 5.0 gms.

Layers : 10.0 gms.

(vii) *Vermex*

Dose : Birds upto 4 to 6 weeks of age : 2 table spoonful (30 ml) per 100 birds in 3.4 litres (3/4 gallon) of water. Birds over six weeks of age : 4 table spoonful (60 ml) per 100 birds in 4.5 to 9.0 litres (1-2 gallon) of water.

2. CAECAL WORM *(Heterakis gallinarium)*

Caecal worm remain in the caecum of poultry birds and produces a disease known as Heterakiasis. Caecal worm are small roundworm measuring 1.2 to 1.9 cm long. Young and debilitated birds are more susceptible to the infestation of this worm. These worm act as a carrier of black head disease producing organism, the *Histomonas meleagridis.*

Symptoms

(i) Weakness, drooping of wing and emaciation.
(ii) Drooping of wing and tail.
(iii) Soiled vent with sulphur coloured diarrhoea.

Control Measures

Same as round worm.

3. GAPE WORM

Gape worm remains in the trachea of the poultry bird. Young birds are more susceptible than the adults. The worm produces ulceration, obstruction and respiratory distress.

Symptoms

(i) Birds show weakness, emaciation, dyspnoea (respiratory distress) and anorexia.
(ii) There are signs of pneumonia, side shaking of head and coughing.
(iii) The birds keep their beak open and periodical extension of head.
(iv) The birds may die due to respiratory difficultry (asphyxia) and anaemia.

Control Measures

Following drugs are used for the treatment of grape worm infested birds

(i) Antimone
(ii) Barrium tartrate

This are used for inhaltion of affected birds and this aids in killing the worm.

4. TAPE WORM

Tape worm infestation causes problem in poultry production. They resemble tape and 5.0 to 12.5 cm long. They require intermediate host for completion of their life cycle. The poultry birds get infestation by eating the intermediate host (i.e. earthworm, bettle, ant, slugs etc.) of the tape worm. Young chicks suffer more due to tape worm infestation.

Symptoms

(i) Malnutrition is produced due to tape worm infestation and progressive weight loss.

(ii) Birds will huddle together in a solitary corner place and their feathers turn dry and ruffled.

(iii) Birds become unthrifty, emaciation and anaemia.

(iv) The laying birds stop laying and loss of meat and egg production.

Control Measures

Following wormicidal may be used for the treatment of tape worm infested bird :

(i) *Wormin Powder or Zodex Powder*

Dose : 5-10 gm per 100 birds through drinking waterr.

(ii) *Helminta-P-tablet*

Dose : 8 tablets per 100 birds.

(iii) *Nictex tablet (0.1 gm)*

Dose : 1-2 tablets per birds.

(iv) *Vermax*

Dose : 60 ml per 100 birds.

(v) *Vermax*

Dose : 60 ml per 100 birds.

(vi) *Taenil*

Dose : 2% W/W mixed with feed. It should be given once mixed with feed. The dose should be repeated after three weeks.

(vii) *Antipar Liquid*

Dose : 60 ml per 100 birds.

(viii) *Banif powder*

Dose : 25-50 gms for 100 birds through drinking water.

F. MISCELLANEOUS DISEASE IN POULTRY

1. CANNIBALISM

Cannibalism is a vice that can create a problem in poultry farming. It may occur in all age group of poultry birds, Toe picking, feather picking, vent picking, head picking, wing picking and breaking of egg are common observation in cannibalism. Many chicks die due to excessive wounds created by pecking.

Causes of the Vice

(i) Poor and faulty management
(ii) Over crowding of birds and bright light
(iii) Lack of feeding and watering space
(iv) Unbalanced feed and less green feeds.
(v) Irritation due to parasitic infestation may be an added factor in causing this ailment (Sing, 1985).

Control Measures

(i) Proper management should be adopted.
(ii) Over crowding should be avoided.
(iii) Balanced feed including green vegetables should be provided.
(iv) Adequate space should be provided.
(v) Appropriate measures should be adopted to control the parasites infestation.

2. EGG BOUND

This is a condition where an egg is blocked in the cloaca and hen fails to lay egg. Followings may be the causes resulting in egg bound cases :

(i) The pullets that starts laying in early ages.
(ii) The anatomical abnormality of oviduct and partial paralysis of oviduct.
(iii) Production of abnormally bigger size of egg.

Control

No medical treatment is fruitful. Physical help provided from outside may be helpful for the relieving of this case. It is done by inserting lubricated finger into the cloaca and exerting slight pressure on the abdomen with the other hand. Otherwise, there is every possibility of breaking of egg.

3. HEAT STROKE

Poultry keeps well at a normal temperature of 70°F to 80°F (21.1°C to 26.6°C). The temperature above the normal produces stress on the birds. Birds suffer more in the high temperature as they have no sweat gland. At high temperature there is gradual drop in feed consumption and production and birds suffer from weakness and respiratory distress;

Control

(i) The house should be reasonably cool in summer and free from drafts. For this, the roof of the house is covered with straw or any other suitable materials and water is sprinkled on the materials.

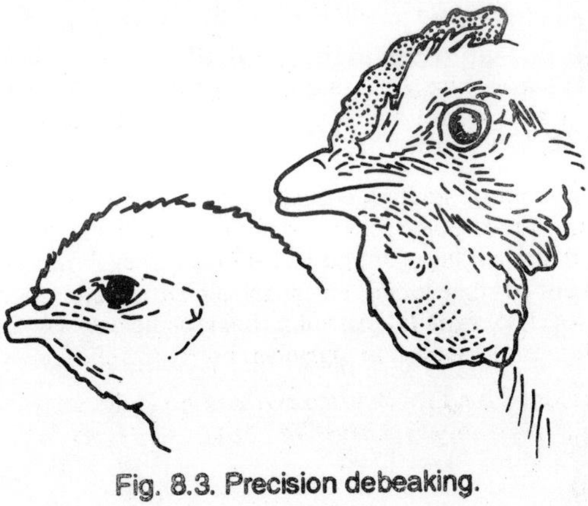

Fig. 8.3. Precision debeaking.

(ii) The birds should be provided with plenty of cold drinking water.

(iii) Electrolytes, glucose and vitamin-C may be added in drinking water to overcome heat stress (Chakraborti, 1991)

9

EGGS AND ITS PRESERVATION

Poultry egg is the largest cell of the world. It is a wounderful creation of the nature. It meets the entire nutritional requirement of the developing embryo from the time the egg is laid untill about 48 hours after the hatch.

STRUCTURE OF EGG

The egg consits of shell, shell membrane, albumin and yolk.

1. Shell

The shell is the hard outermost covering amounting about 8-10 percent of total egg. It is composed with the following substances

Calcium carbonate	: 95 percent.
Calcium Phosphate	: 1 percent
Magnesium Carbonate	: 1 percent
Organic matter (Chiefly protein)	: 4 percent

The shell provides protecting covering to the liquid protein having pores for exchange of air during embryo development. The shell is also covered with a thin mucous membrane known as cuticle which provides natural protection to shell pores. Cuticle is bacteriotatic in nature. Shell colour varies with the breed.

2. Shell Membrane

Next to shell, there are two membrane : outer and inner shell membrane. The outer membrane is slightly thicker than the inner one. The shell membrane remains attached to the shell throughout the egg except in the area where air cell is formed. Both the layer together are 0.01 to 0.02 mm thick.

3. Albumin

Albumin or egg white is not homogenous mass. Total egg white is 58 percent of total egg weight. It is composed with the following four layers :

(i) **Thin albumin or outer thin white :** This layer remains immediately beneath the inner shell membrane and constitues about 21 percent of total egg white.

(ii) **Outer thick white :** The outer thin white is followed by a firm or thick layer of albumin which is the major layer and constitutes about 55 percent of total egg white.

(iii) **Inner thick white :** The outer thick white is followed by thick layer known as inner thick white.

(iv) **Inner Thin White :** The inner thin white or inner thin albumin remains below the inner thick white or thick albumen which is about 17.5 percent of total egg white. The inner thin white is also known Chalaziferous layer which surrounds the yolk. The chalazae, a chord like structure, emerge from the chalaziferous layer towards both end of the egg and hold the yolk in position.

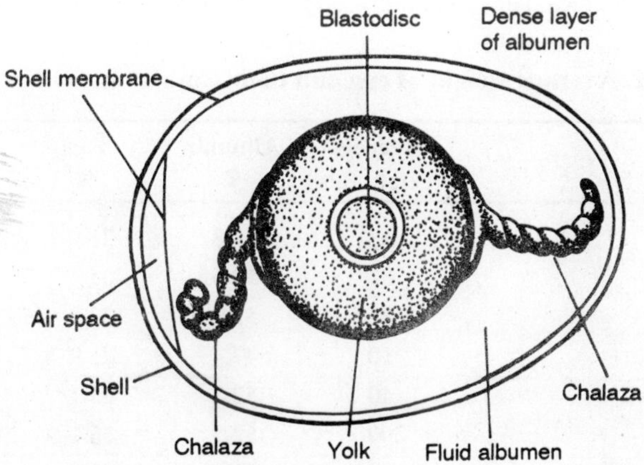

Fig. 9.1. Hen's egg (Viewed from above) Through a cut in the shell.

4. Yolk

Yolk is a yellowish ball like structure which is enclosed in a thin vitelline membrane. Under the vitelline membrane, there are 7 to 9 concentric rings of light and dark yolk materials which are formed due to diurnal eating behaviour of the hens. There is a neck like structure called Latebra which hold the germinal disc or bastoderm. The germinal disc is very clear in case of fertile egg. The yolk accounts for 27-32 percent of total egg.

NUUTRITIVE VALUE OF EGG

Egg is a rich source of high quality animal protein. Animal protein is more valuable than that of plant protein. Egg is a valuable and palatable food.

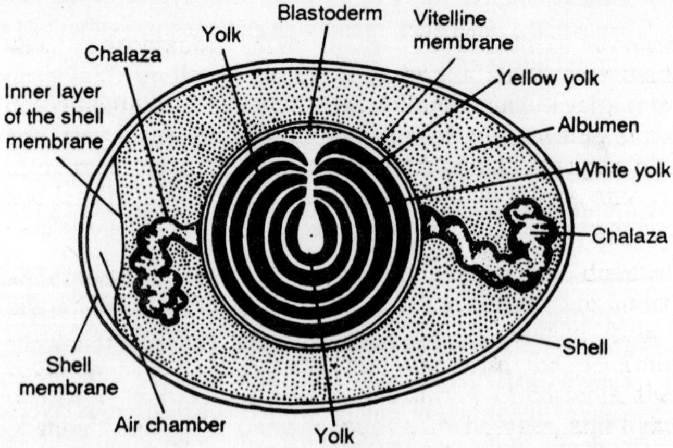

Fig. 9.2. Vertical section of hen's egg showing its internal organisation.

Table 9.1. Average weight of egg and their content in various species.

Species	Average Weight (gm)	Albumin %	Yolk %	Shell %
Chicken	58	55.8	31.9	12.3
Duck	80	52.6	35.4	12.0
Turkey	85	55.9	32.3	11.8
Quail	10	47.4	31.9	20.7
Guinea fowl	40	52.3	35.1	12.6
Goose	200	52.5	35.1	12.4
Pigeon	17	74.0	17.9	8.1

Table 9.2. Composition of egg of various species (Without shell per 100 gm basis)

Species	Moisture (gm)	Protein (gm)	Lipids (gm)	Carbohy-drates (gm)	Ash (gm)	Energy (K cal)
Chicken	73.7	12.9	11.5	0.9	1.0	163
Duck	70.4	13.3	14.5	0.7	1.1	191

(Contd.)

Species	Moisture (gm)	Protein (gm)	Lipids (gm)	Carbohy-drates (gm)	Ash (gm)	Energy (K cal)
Goose	70.4	13.9	13.3	1.5	1.1	185
Guinea fowl	72.8	13.5	12.00	0.8	0.9	170
Pigeon	72.8	13.8	12.00	0.8	0.9	170
Quails	73.7	13.1	11.1	1.0	1.1	161
Turkey	72.6	13.1	11.8	1.7	0.8	170

* Kcal/100 gm edible egg = gm protein x 4.63 + lipids x 9.02 + gm carbohydrate x 3.87.

Table. 9.3. Details composition of hen's egg (per 100 gm)

Protein	:	12.1 gm.	Riboflavin	:	0.26 mg
Amino acids	:		Choline	:	532 mg.
Arginine	:	0.76 gm.	Niacine	:	0.09 mg.
Histidine	:	0.31 gm.	Pyridoxine	:	111 mcg.
Isoleucine	:	0.80 gm.	Biotine	:	9.25 mcg.
Leucine	:	0.95 gm.	Vitamin B_{12}	:	0.93 mcg.
Lycine	:	0.78 gm.	Inositol	:	20.30 mg.
Methionine	:	0.38 gm.	Minerals	:	1.0 mg.
Phenylalanine	:	0.62 gm.	Calcium	:	48 mg.
Threonine	:	0.63 gm.	Phosphorus	:	187 mg.
Tryptophane	:	0.22 gm.	Sodium	:	122 mg.
Valine	:	0.93 gm.	Potassium	:	141 mg.
Lipids	:	11.5 gm.	Chlorine	:	137 mg.
Fatty acids	:		Sulphur	:	134 mg.
Linoleic acid	:	2.2 gm.	Magnesium	:	50 mg.
Archidionic acids	:	0.24 gm.	Iron	:	2.4 mg.
Linolenic acid	:	0.50 gm.	Iodine	:	3.8 mcg.
Vitamin A	:	1015 IU	Manganese	:	4.18 mcg.
Vitamin B	:	925 IU	Copper	:	277 mcg.
Vitamin E	:	1.8 mg.	Cobalt	:	Traces.
B-complex			Carbohydrate	:	0.9 gm.
Thiamine	:	0.09 mg	Water	:	74.5 gm.

Source : Poultry production (1985) by R.A. Singh, p : 191-192.

FACTORS AFFECTING EGG PRODUCTION

Egg production depends on the following factors

(i) **Age of the bird :** The hen starts laying egg at about 22 weeks of age (Five and half months) which rises early, reaching a peak at about 32-35 weeks of age. The egg production then gradually declines at the rate of half a week. The birds that mature early is a good layer. A pullet is sexually mature when she lays her first egg.

(ii) **Season :** The hen lays more eggs during winter. Egg production declines during summer and rainy season.

(iii) **Broodiness :** Broodiness is a condition of hen when she stops laying and show tendency for nesting. The hen ceases to lay eggs during this period. Prolonged period of broodiness are certain to lower the annual production. Broodiness is the external evidence of maternal instinct.

(iv) **Moulting :** Moulting is the act or process of sheeding and renewing of feathers, which occurs generally once a year. Moulting or shedding of feathers provides some indication about the laying capacity of a bird. Good layer starts moulting late during the first year of laying. They complete the moulting period quickly and sometimes continue to lay during moulting period. Poor layer on the other hand moults early and takes usually long time (24 weeks or so) to complete moulting. They do not lay during moulting period. The hen shed their feather in the following order : head, neck, breast, body, wings and tail.

Egg production is measured as number of eggs or rate of lay and is expressed as hen house, hen day or survivor's production.

PRINCIPLE OF STORING EGG

The hen lay more than 56 percent of their egg by 9-11 a.m. Egg should be collected at least three times daily. Delay in collection of egg causes of loss of egg. Egg starts deteriotating from the moment it is laid. The hen also may do damage to the egg. The following points are very important for storing eggs :

(i) **Production of infertile eggs :** The infertile eggs remain well for long time than that of fertile eggs. The hen lays egg without mating with cock and this type of eggs is known as infertile egg. It is possible to produce infertile eggs by segregating the male and female birds in a separate house. But on free range system, it is difficult to produce infertile egg.

(ii) **Defertilization :** Embryo remains dormant in the fertile egg. The embryo starts developing at high temperature and may die at uneven room temperature. As a result the egg starts to rot. Defertilization helps to keep the eggs longer time without spoiling of the same. Defertilization can be done by immersing the egg in hot water (135° - 145°F or 57.2° - 62.7°C) for 15 minutes. The egg may be kept well at least 15 days in extreme hot weather. The eggs having dipped in lime water or slight hot coconut oils may kept well for more than three months.

(iii) **Cooling of eggs :** The just laying eggs having a temperature of 104 °F (40°C). The eggs may undergo spoiling if collection is delayed specially in summer season. 68°F (21°C) temperature is favourable for embryo development. The egg kept at a temperature of less than 68°F (21°C) remains fresh for longer time. The embryo remains dormant during winter season due to low temperature. Refrigeration lessens the spoiling of eggs. But it is not possible for general poultry farmer to keep refrigerator. So eggs are stored by controlling the temperature as follows :

(a) **Cool room :** Eggs keep well for longer time in cool room. Sprinkling water on the curtain that covers the doors and windows keeps the room cool. Straws spread on the corrugated or asbestor roof help to lessen the room temperature.

(b) **Undeground room :** Underground cellar may also be useful to store eggs.

(iv) **Frozen eggs :** The egg contents separated from egg shell are taken in the polythene bag and this is kept in refrigerator. The egg contents remain well for longer time, This type of egg is generally used for ice scream and confectionary.

(v) **Dried eggs :** The whole egg powder is made by dehydration of liquid portion of egg. 450 gm egg powder is made from 40 eggs. This Method is not yet accepted in our country.

PROCESSING OF EGG

Assembly

Assembly refers to collection and gathering of egg at a place. Collection should be done at least 3-4 times a day to maintain egg quality. Delay in collection leads to the damage of eggs.

Cleaning

Dirty eggs are covered with bacteria that will cause spoilage if they enter inside the egg. Wet washing of egg is most effective. Slightly dirt eggs can be dry cleaned with the help of rough cloth or sand paper. The temperature of water used for washing eggs should be at least 10°C higher than the egg temperature. Central Food Research Techonological Research Institute, Mysore has designed a simple egg washing machine.

Grading

Grading is the sorting out of eggs into different categories according to their individual size, weight and interior quality. It aids in reducing wastage and facilitates uniform packing, pricing and quality assurance to the consumers. The mark on each egg should consit of the word 'Agmark' together with grade designation as per the Agricultural Produce (Grading and Marketing eggs) Rule, 1937. This is placed centrally in a circle of not less than half inch diameter by means of rubber stamp. Egg can be sorted out into various grades mechanically by means of egg grading mahine.

Table 9.4. Agmark standards for marketable eggs.

Gradw	Weight (gm)	Shell	Air	Shitte	Yolk
A-Extra large A-Large A-Medium A-small	60 and above 53-59 45-52 38-44	Clean unbroken and sound, shape normal	Upto 4 mm in depth practically regular and better	Clear resonably firm	Fairly well centred, pracically free from defects, outline indistinct
B-Extra large B-Large B-Medium B-Small	60 and above 53-59 45-52 38-44	Clear, moderately stained, sound and slightly abnormal	8 mm in depth, may be free and slightly bubbly	Clear, may be slightly weak.	May be slightly centered, outline slightly visible.

Table 9.5. Standards for weight classification of shell eggs.

Grade	Weight per egg (gm.)	Weight per dozen eggs (gm.)
A-Extra Large	60 and above	596 and above
A-Large	53 - 59	526 - 596
A-Medium	45 - 52	446 - 525
A-Small	38 - 44	380 - 445
B-Extra Large	60 and above	596 and above
B-Large	53 - 59	526 - 595
B-Medium	45 - 52	446 - 525
B-Small	38 - 44	380 - 445

Table 9.6. Summery of U.S. standards for quality of individual shell egg (specification of each quality factor)

Quantity	AA Quality	A Quality	B Quality	C Quality
Shell	Clear, unbrok-en, practically normal	Clear unbrok-en, practically normal	Clear to very slightly stai ned, unbroken. May be slightly abnormal	Clear to moderately strained, unbroken. May be slightly abnormal
Air cell	1/8" or less in depth, Practically regular	3/16" or less in depth. Protically regular	3/8" or less in depth. May be free or bubbly	May be over 3/8" in depth. May be free or bubbly.
White	Clear, firm. (H.U. 72 or more.)	Clear, may be resonably firm (H.U. : 60-72).	Clear. May be slightly weak (H.U. : 31-60).	May be week and watery Small blood clots or sports may be present* (H.U.: less than 31.
Yolk	Outline sligh-tly defined. Practically free from defects	Outline may be fairly defined, Practically free froom defects	Outline may be well defin-ed. May be sli-ghtly enlarged and flattened. May show de-finite, not ser-ious Defects.	Outline may plinly visib-le. May show clearly visible Germ deverlop-ment but no bl-ood May show otther Serious defects

* of they are Smaull (Agreegating not more than 1/8" in diameter).

Table 9.7. Characteristics of Layer and Non-layer

Character	Laying hen	Non-laying hen
1. Breed type	Wedge shape body according to breed characteristics.	Shallow body
2. Temperament.	Alert, active and friendly.	Shy, nervous and quacky.

(Contd.)

Character	Laying hen	Non-laying hen
3. Vigour	Strong and healthy	Weak and unthrifty
4. Head		
(i) Beak	Stocky, well curved, wornout and less yellow.	Very long, thin and sharp pointed and yellow.
(ii) Eyes	Bright and alert	Dull and sleepy.
(iii) Ear lobes	Full, waxy and velvety.	Shunken, wrinkled and coarse,
(iv) Comb and wattle	Large, red, waxy, warm and velvety	Small, dry, hard, pale, shrunken, scaly and cold.
5. Neck	Stocky, rather short	Long and thin
6. Leg	Wide apart and well set	Close together and knock Kneed
(i) Shank	Thin and soft in back	Full, hard and round in back.
(ii) Toenails	Stocky and well curved.	Long and thin.
7. Body.	Capacious	Limited capacity
(i) Feather	Warm and coiled	Clean and perfect.
(ii) Skin.	Soft, thin and oily	Thick, dry and rough
(iii) Back	Broad and straight	Narrow and crooked.
(iv) Abdomen	Large, soft, free from fat and spread 3 to 5 fingers	Small, hard, fatty and usually less than 2 fingers
(v) Pelvic bone	Wide apart, thin, Pliable and spread more than 2 fingers.	Close together, thick, stiff and shrunken.
(vi) Pubic bone	2 to 5 finger spread between keel and pubic bone	Less than two finger spread
(vii) Vent	Full, large and moist	Small, dry, round and contracted.
8. Moulting	Late (September-october) and rapid	Early (july-August) and slow.

PACKING AND TRANSPORT OF EGGS

The eggs are more liable to damage during transportation. The profits and losses in marketing of eggs depend on the proper transportation method. Egg should be despatched in suitable containers. Generally the eggs are transported in the following three methods :

(i) **Transportation of egg in basket :** Bamboo basket is generally used for the export of eggs in distant market. The bottom of the basket should be flat. Some suitable materials such as straw, rice bran or wood dust is put on the bottom to prevent breaking of eggs. The packing materials and eggs are placed alternately in the basket. The open end of the basket is closed with lids or gunny bag and tied this with rope to the basket.

(ii) **Transportation of eggs in wooden boxes :** Wooden box is probably the best type of container. Wooden boxes with fillers and flats prevent the egg from coming in direct conract with other egg. Losses in this type of the container is less and the container, if properly handle, may be used a number of times.

(iii) **Transportation of egg in pitch board tray :** Now-a-days, pitch board tray is extensively used for transportation of egg. Pitch board trays have a separate chamber for placing egg individually. These prevent the breaking of egg.

(iv) **Transportation of egg by collapsible card board boxes :** Collapsible card board boxes are widely used for commercial packing of eggs.

(v) **Transportation of egg by plastic egg trays :** Plastic egg trays are also widely used for commercial packing of egg. This container, if properly handled, may be used a number of times.

ABNORMAL EGGS

(i) **Double yolk eggs :** Double yolk eggs result from simultaneous ovulation and development of two over it. Such type of occurance is more common in pullets than older birds.

(ii) **Meat spot :** Meat spot is sometimes found either on yolk or in the albumen.

(iii) **Blood spot :** Blood spot is a characteristics of an individual hen and it may increase because of low level of Vitamin-A and some other nutritional and management faults. Blood spot may be found as a result of haemorrhages of small blood vessels in the ovary or oviduct. Presence of spot in the albumen indicates a haemorrhage in the wall of the oviduct.

(iv) **Soft shelled egg :** Soft shelled egg is due to the deficiency of calcium, phosphorus, manganese and Vitamin-D in the layer's diet. This type of egg is more liable to damage in transit and is also likely to become infected with organism.

(v) **Foreign matter in the egg :** Feather and other foreign matter sometimes find their way in the oviduct and become embodied in the egg during the egg formation stages.

(vi) **An egg within an egg :** It is due to faulty development of egg.

(viii) **Pale yolk :** Constitutional anaemia may be the causes of production of pale yolk. But it is more likely due to the lack of carotene and other colouring substances. This defect can be rectified by providing maize or maize meal in poultry ration.

(ix) **Off-flavour in the egg :** It can result from poor quality fish meal or high level of fish meal in poultry ration, and excessive consumption of grasses.

(x) **Rotten new laid egg :** The over fat hen or a bird with oviduct disease or vent gleet has laid such type of egg. The egg that is completly formed fails to pass out of oviduct on account of one of those reason and remains bad.

PRESERVATION OF SURPLUS EGGS

Eggs are highly persishable commodity. It needs fast movement from the point of production to the point of consumption particularly during summer months. Eggs start deteriorating from the movement it is laid.

1. Home Preservation

Home preservation is generally adopted at farm level in absence of much equipments for preserving surplus egg. Following are the important methods of preservation of egg under this category :

(i) **Oil coating method :** The eggs are dipped in warm oil generally in coconut oil or groundnut oil. The oil used must be colourless, odourless, less viscous and free from fluorescent materials. The oil sealed the pores of the shell which prevent the evaporation of moisture and escape of gases. This prevents the weight loss of the egg and maintains the good internal quality, because of some of the physico-chemical change in the egg contents is being retarted for a resonable length of time. Oil treatment should be made as early as possible after the egg are collected from the farm. Because the egg quality starts deteriorating soon after it is laid.

Egg can be preserved without damaging their quality for a period of three weeks at a room temperature by cooling them with a mixture of liquid parafin and liseed oil. The coating mixture is prepared by mixing 75 parts of paraffin with 25 parts linseed oil in a bowl. The eggs are dipped in the mixture and taken out one after another and stored.

(ii) **Lime water method** : Lime water is very useful for preserving eggs under village condition. Lime water is prepared by mixing one kilogram of quick lime in one litre of boiling water in an enamelled or glazed earthen vessel. The fluid is brought to room temperature and 4 to 5 litres of cold water and 225 grams of table salt are added to it. The clear solution is decanted and is used for preservation of egg. The eggs are immersed in the clear fluid for 16 to 18 hours. Then the eggs are taken out from the liquid and dried at room temperature. The dried eggs can then be stored for 3 to 4 weeks at room temperature.

(iii) **Water glass method** : Water glass is prepared by mixing one kilogram Sodium silicate in 10 litres of water. The eggs are left immersed in water glass in a container of galvanised or earthen or cemented or made of wood. A thin coating of silica is formed on surface of egg shell and their pores are completely closed. By this method eggs may be stored safely for as long as six months.

(iv) **Thermostabilization** : This applies to the stabilisation of egg quality by heat. The eggs are immersed in water at 54°C for 15 minutes or 56°C for 10 minutes or 60°C for 5 minutes in order to stabilize the thick albumen. There are some advantages of this method as follows :

(a) Killing of bacteria on egg shell (Pasteurization of egg).

(b) Improves the keeping quality.

(c) Kills the embryo (defertilises the egg).

2. Commercial Method of Preservation

(i) **Cold storage :** Egg preserved in cold storage remain fresh for long time. The eggs are stored in cold storage at +0.5°C to -0.5°C (31-35°F) and 75-85% relative humidity. At this relative humidity, the evaporation is retarded and the moulds growth would be extremely low.

(ii) **Dehydration** : The egg contents are dried at a temperature of 31.1°C(50°F) to convert the white, yolk or whole egg into a fine powder. The method is very expensive. But there is a considerable saving in transport and less need for cold storage.

(iii) **Freezing :** The egg contents are freezed at a low temperature range of 10°F to 30°F below zero. It is a best method of preserving egg for longer time. Freezing of whole egg or yolk results in gelation.

10

DUCKS

Duck is a water bird in nature. Men has domesticated the wild bird for the production of eggs and meats. The duck first domesticated in Asia. The ducks that we see to-day are decendent of wild ducks that migrate in thousands from one country to other in different season. The domesticated ducks have been derived from wild Mullard ducks *(Anas boschas)* with the exception of Muscovy whose progenitor is American tree duck *(Cairna moschata)*. The domesticated duck belongs to the genus Anas and species Platyrhynchos and family Anatidae. The nomenclature of duck is follows :

1. Male duck : Drake
2. Female duck : Duck
3. Young duck : Ducklings.

Ducks are considered helpful, valuable domestic birds and occupy the unique position in Indian poultry industry by virtue of the fact that they produce about of 400 million of eggs every year constituting six percent of total egg production and seven percent of total poultry production.

There are some advantages of rearing ducks :

(i) Duck rearing needs small initial investment to start with. Duck rearing is a profitable business.

(ii) Duck rearing is profitable to get protein rich food with low cost.

(iii) Most of the villagers reared one or two ducks for meeting their requirement of egg. But there are prejudices amongst a large section of the Indian people against the consumption of hen egg and poultry meat.

(iv) Ducks by virtue of their feeding habits supplement a part of their feed by foraging. They can make use of various kinds of by-product and other foodstuff unift for human consumption

(v) Duck rearing needs less care and management.

(vi) Ducks are quite hardy, more easily brooded and are resistant to many avian diseases.

(vii) Ducks eggs provide more nutrient as they are big in size (15-20 gm larger than hen egg).

(viii) Marshy river side and wet land where chicken or other type of live stock will not flourish, are excellent quater for the duck farming as they prefere moist and muddy condition.

(ix) Duck can easily be trained to go to the ponds and come back to their own residence in the evening.

(x) Ducks are suitable for mixed farming system such as duck cum fish farming.

(xi) Ducks have considerable longer laying period and lay satisfactorily in the second as well as third year. They lay about 40-50 more eggs than hen.

(xii) Ducks can be reared at any place provied water is available for them.

(xiii) Ducks can easily be reared under primitive condition of housing, feeding and management.

(xiv) Duck keeping in India is predominately a village occupation.

(xv) They have less problem with cannibalism and agnostic behaviour.

(xvi) Ducks do not require elaborated housing and good management.

(xvii) Duck meat and egg are widely accepted among the nonvegetarians. Duck meat contain 14.5 percent protein.

The duck population in India is mainly concentrated in West-Bengal followed by Assam, Tamil Nadu, A.P., Kerala, Bihar and Orissa.

BREEDS OF DUCKS

The breeds of ducks may be divided according to the purpose for which they are raised, as follows :

1. **Meat type :** This type of breeds are raised for production of meat. The important breads of this type are Muscovy, Aylesbury, White Pekin, Rouen etc.
2. **Egg type :** This type of breeds are raised mainly for production of egg. The important breeds of this type are Khaki Campbell, and Indian Runner. Most of the ducks normally begin to lay at about six months of age.
3. **Ornamental type :** This type of breeds are raised mainly for ornamental purposes. Creasted white, Call and Black, East India are the most important breed of this type.

MEAT TYPE DUCKS

1. **White Pekin :** The breed is originated from China at about 1873.

Characteristics : The body of this breed is long and broad and covered with large white feather. They have orange yellow bills, yellow skin and reddish yellow feet and shank. The egg of this breed is tinned white. This breed produces excellent quality meat. They are nervous in temperament and bad sitters. The live weight of this breed at maturity is as follows :

Drake : 4.0 mg.
Duck : 3.5 kg.

The ducks lay about 160 eggs during the first year of lay.

2. **Muscovy :** The breed is a native to Brazil and very popular in Australia

   Characteristics : The breed has big, long and broad body with greater breadth. The head and face of this breed are partly bare, with red, rough and carunculated skin. Unlike the drake of other breeds, the Muscovy male has no curl feather in his tail. There are two standard variety of Muscovy ducks, such as dark and white. The dark variety has a lustrous blue black, broken with some white in breast,body and back. The white variety has pure white plumage, pale orange or yellow legs and pinkish flesh coloured beak. The incubation period of this breed is 36 days and the duckling are not in first full feather untill 16 weeks of age. But the ordinary duckling is in full feather at about 12 weeks of age. The breed produces meat of excellent quality, and tasty and for this they should be marketed before 17 weeks of age. The duck of this breed are good sitters. Muscovy ducks require 32-35 days for incubation. They have long and sharp claws. The live weight of this breed at maturity is as follows :

   Drake : 4.5 kg.
   Duck : 3.25 kg.

   When crossed with other breeds, it produces sterile duck, known as Mule duck, which produces satisfactory meat yield.

3. **Aylesbury :** Aylesbury breed is a foreign breed and has originated from Buckingham in U.K. It has grained popularity for meat producing breed. The body of this breed is broad and deep. The plumages of this breed are white and the legs are short but sturdy and orange in colour and the eye and ear is orange colour. The bill is reddish colour. The meat of this breed is pliable, soft and tastful. The eggs are tinted white. They reaches market weight in eight weeks. The live weight of this breed at maturity is as follows :

   Drake : 4.5 kg.
   Duck : 3.5 kg.

4.. **Rouen** : Rouen breed has originated in Rouen town of French. It is reared largely in England. They are big in size. They have long, broad and deep body. The keel is long and straight. The head and tail is bright green, breast is light red, leg is orange colour and the bill is yellow but lower portion is brown colour. They have a white ring in the neck. Through they are meat type breed, yet they produces good egg. Eggs are blue although white shelled eggs are not uncommon. They need much time to become adult as they grow slowly :

The live weight of this breed at maturity is as follows :

Drake : 4.5 kg.
Duck : 3.5 kg.

EGG TYPE DUCKS

1. Khaki Campbell

Khaki Campbell is a cross breed and has been developed in England in 1901 from a cross of Fawn, White Runner, Rouen and Mullard ducks. As its name indicates, it has khaki colour. The draks have brownish bronze lower back, tail coverts, head and neck and green bills and dark orange legs and toes. The body is heavy and strong, neck is long, back is flat and broad, breast is full and

Fig. 10.1 Khaki Campbell

sloppy, legs are of medium size. Ducks have seal brown heads and necks and they have greenish black bills and brown legs and toes. The duck possess superior laying capacity. The egg production resembles that of Runner (i.e. 300 eggs a year) but the size is somewhat greater. They are hard and can survive some days without water. Khaki Campbell can be specially and strongly recommended where free range is available. Khaki Campbell is most popular for egg production. They lays on an average 300 eggs per annum.

The live weight of this breed at maturity is as follows :

Drake	: 2.5 kg.
Duck	: 2.0 - 2.2 kg.

2. Indian Runner

Indian Runner is supposed to be of Indian origin. There are three standard varieties of Runner ducks, such as the Fawn and white, the White and the Pencilled. All the varieties have the same shape but differ in plumage colour. The body is long and narrow, slopping gradually into the neck and carried errect with no indication of keel. The general shape of this breed resembles somewhat to penguin.

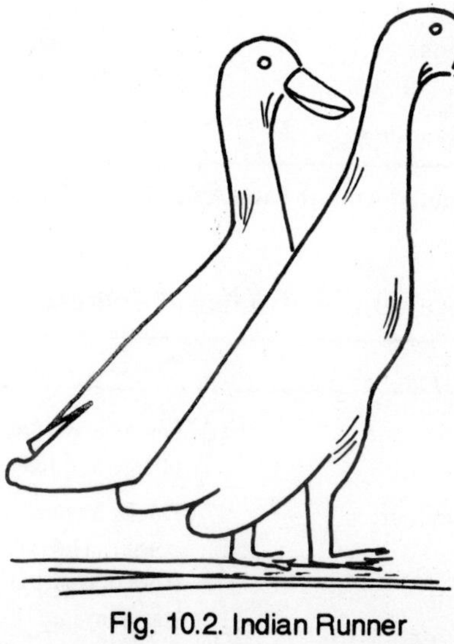

Fig. 10.2. Indian Runner

(i) **The Fawn and White :** The breed is fawn or grey and white. The colour of neck is white and a white line is running upto eyes and is extended around the bills. The shanks and toes are orange red. The young duck has yellow bill spotted with green which later becomes a dull green. But the bill of young drake is yellow which later becomes greenish yellow.

(ii) **The White Runner :** The white runner is pure white in all sections. The shanks and toes are orange in colour and the bill is yellow in colour.

(iii) **The Pencilled Variety :** The head of drake and duck is dull brown green and white and medium fawn and white respectively.

The ducks are wounderfull layer. They lay over 250 eggs in a year. They are hardy and capable of adopting in any a situation. They produced meat of excellent quality and taste. They walk very fast with their neck carried high. The ducks are not good sitter. The live weight of the breed at maturity is as follows :

Drake : 2.2 - 2.5 kg.
Duck : 1.5 - 2.2 kg.

Table 10.1. Comparative Reproduction.

	Duck	Hen
1. Incubation period (in days)	27 - 28	21
2. Age at sexual maturity (in months)	6 - 7	5 - 6
3. No. of eggs per year	120 - 180	230
4. Egg weight (gramma)	60	58
5. Fertility (%)	70	80
6. Hatchability of fertile eggs (%)	70	80

Source : Hafer, E.S.E., Reproduction in Farm Animals, 2nd. Edition, Lee and Febiger (1968).

Table 10.2. Key of identification of drakes and ducks

Drakes	Ducks
(i) Drakes are big in size and healthy.	(i) Ducks are comparatively small in size and lean.
(ii) Drakes have dark colour.	(ii) Ducks have comparatively lighter colour. The colour of bill changes from orange to light yellow as they starts laying.
(iii) Drakes have curled tail Feathers.	(iii) Ducks do not have curled tail feather.
(iv) Drake have softer voice	(iv) Ducks do the loud quacking. Voice differecne appear when ducks are 6-9 weeks old.

CHARACTERISTICS OF LAYING DUCKS

Ducks are prolific layer. They lays more eggs than hen. Laying duck is recognised by the following characteristics :

(i) Laying duck have upright carriage and considerably light weight.

(ii) The head and neck of laying duck is noticeably refined and leaner.

(iii) The breast of laying duck is full and broad.

(iv) The legs are wide apart.

TYPES OF COMMERCIAL DUCKERRY

The commercial duckery are of two types according to the purposes they are reared :

(a) **Laying type or egg type :** As mentioned earlier, this type of breed are raised mainly for production of egg. Khaki Campbell and Indian Runer are considered to be the best layer. Commercial birds can lay over 300 eggs per annum, if properly feed and maintained.

(b) **Table type or meat type :** As mentioned earlier, this type of breed are raised mainly for production of meat. Rouen and Ayelsbury are the best commercial broiler. Duckling of this type grow very fast. The table type bird must be tender meated with soft, pliable, smooth textured and flexible breast bone. There is much prospect of meat type breed in India. But the meat of the duck is of fine quality, juicy and well flavoured. It is more easier to keep meat type birds in complete intensive system.

SYSTEM OF DUCK FARMING

(i) **Free range system :** The poor farmers keep small number of ducks in this system. This method is oldest of all. Ducks by virtue of their feeding habits, supplement a part of their feed requirement by foraging. Accordingly, they are economical and inexpensive to maintain them in this system. Khaki Campbell and Indian Runner are the best breed for this system. Free range system saves feed cost. But this system of rearing ducks need large area of land. Duckling of three weeks of age can be allowed for free range.

(ii) **Intensive system :** This system of rearing duck is practised in the foreign country such as U.K. and Indonesia. In this system the breeding ducks are confined in a range of small pen. The ducks are provided with artificial small pond or shallow gumlas (earthen pot) with fresh water throughout the day. Six ducks and two drakes are kept in each pen. Ducks can also be rared in cages like fowls. The duck should never be off from waterer. The individual bird needs three square feet floor space till it attains the age of 16 weeks.

HOUSING

Ducks do not require elaborate housing. So housing is not a problem for ducks. Ducks, in general, prefer to stay outside at day and night throughout the year. But shelter during night is essential to save them from predators. They need only fresh airy shelter at night. Ducks can also be reared in deep litter system. The house made with bricks comprising pillars and strong netting in between the two pillars is good for protection against thieves. The house having earthen floor is generally better than wood or concrete.

Table 10.3. Floor space, feeder space and water space requirement of duck (under intensive system)

	Floor space Sq. ft)		Feeder space (Linear inches)		Water space (Linear inches)	
	Meat type	Egg type	Meat type	Egg trype	Meat type	Egg type
Upto 3 weeks	1.0	0.85	2	2	1	1
Upto 8 weeks	2.5	1.75	4	3	2	1.5
Upto 20 weeks	4.0	3.00	5	3.5	2.5	1.75
Adult	5.0	4.00	6	4	3	2

Source : Srivastava and Panda, Farmer's Jourrnal, September, 1982.

The waterer containing sufficient amount of water should be provided in the house. Though the duck is a water fowl, water for swiming is not at all necessary. But a pool provides exercise, promotes health, keep the eyes, bills and vent clean and give luster to the plumage. The water level in the waterer must be sufficiently deep to allow the emersion of their head and not themselves. Otherwise their eyes become scale and in extreme cases, blindness may follow.

Ducks lay more than 95 percent of their eggs before 9 a.m. So they should be confined in the house until at least 9 a.m. One nest has to be provided for every three ducks.

Good ventilation and sanitation is a must. The house should be washed and disinfected at least once a week. In deep litter system, dry litter should be added frequently and the litter should be kept dry by providing plenty of sunsine and fresh air. The built up litter should be changed and new litter should be placed after disinfecting the floor. Duck manure is a good compost, rich in nitrogen.

FEEDING

Ducks are voracious eater and are also very good foragers. Ducks are most efficient type of poultry to convert fallen grains of the field, vegetables, worm, insects and pond materials (i.e. fish, snails, fingerlings, earthworm, insects etc.) into edible meat and eggs. Ducks make better use of feed in compare of chicks, if water is available nearby at the time of feeding.

Three types of feeds can be used for duck as follows

(i) **Dry mash :** Dry mash is not suitable for ducks. Because the ducks have difficulty in swallowing dry feed. As a result, they waste a part of the feed.

(ii) **Wet mash :** Ducks prefer wet mash due to difficulties in swallowing. Water is added to make the dry feed a crumbly substances. Wastage of this mash is minimum. Wet mash is practical type of feed Products. Duckling need wet mash to start with.

(iii) **Pellets :** Pellets is the best out of the three types of feed. Pellet feeding is comparatively expensive. A pellet of 3 to 5 mm size is used. Pellet feeding has distinct advantage of saving little amount of feed and improvement in sanitary condition.

Duck consumes about 50 to 60 kg feed per annum. It requires about 3 kg. feed to produce a dozen of eggs as against 2 kg. required by hen and 3.22 kg. feed to produce 1 kg. of broiler duck. The feed should be provided *at libitum* at least for first eight week and later on twice a day. Ducklings should be feed as soon as they are removed from the incubator to brooder. The ducklings are hand feed for the first day or two as they do not readily learn to eat. Indian Runner and Khaki Campbell need 150 gm and 170 gm of mash and grain per bird per day respectively.

Table 10.4. Ration composition for ducks

Ingredients	Starter	Grower	Layer
Yellow maize	30.0 parts	30.0 parts	30.0 parts
Rice polish	20.0 parts	22.5 parts	25.0 parts
Oil cakes	27.5 parts	20.0 parts	20.5 parts
Fish meal	10.0 parts	8.0 parts	10.0 parts
Rish kani	10.0 parts	17.0 parts	10.0 parts
Shell grit	-	-	2.0 parts
Vit. B_2, D_3	0.025	0.025	0.025
Mineral Mixture	2.5	2.5	2.5

Table 10.5. Mineral and Vitamin supplement/kg of diet.

Supplement	Breeder	Grower
Vitamin A (I.U./kg.)	8000	6000
Vitamin D_3 (I.C.U./kg.)	2000	1500
Vitamin E (mg./kg.)	5	5
Vitaminn K (mg./kg.)	1	1
Vitamin B_2 (mg./kg.)	5	5
Vitamin B_{12} (mg./kg.)	0.005	0.006
Pantothenic acid (mg./kg.)	10	50
Niacin (mg./kg.)	25	25
Folic acid (mg./kg.)	-	0.5
Cho line (mg./kg.)	250	250
Zinc (mg./kg.)	7	7
Masnganese (mg./kg.)	75	75
Copper (mg./kg.)	2	2
Iodine (mg./kg.)	65	70
Methionine (mg./kg.)	-	500

Tble 10.6. Nutrient requirement of ducks

	NRC (1971) Starting and growing	(ARC (1973) Starting and growing	Level adopted at PRC Starting and growing	Breeding
M.E. (Kcal/kg)		3,100.00	3,000.00	2,050.00
Crude protein	17.00	23.00	22.00	18.00
Amino acid (gm/kg)	-	8.4	11.8	5.5
Arginine				
Glycine + Serine	-	11.3	11.3	-
Histidine	-	3.9	2.7	1.8
Isoleucine	-	6.9	6.4	6.0
Leucine	-	11.8	12.7	7.4
Lysine	-	8.9	8.9	8.2
Methionine	-	3.9	4.0	-
Methionine + Cystine	-	7.4	7.4	5.2
Phenylalanine	-	6.9	-	-
Phenylalanine + Tyrosine	12.8	12.8	9.0	

(Contd.)

	NRC (1971) Starting and growing	(ARC (1973) Starting and growing	Level adopted at PRC Starting and growing	Breeding
Threonine	-	5.9	6.4	3.9
Tryptophane	-	1.7	2.0	1.8
Valine	-	7.9	8.2	6.0
Major minerals (%)				
Calcium	-	0.56	0.9	2.75
Available Phosphorus	-	-	0.45	0.50
Total phosphorus	-	-	-	-
Minor minerals (mg/kg)				
Magnesium	-	500.00	500.00	300.00
Sodium	-	-	1500.00	1500.00
Chloride	-	-	-	-
Potassium	-	-	3000.00	-
Copper	-	-	3.5	3.5
Iodine	-	-	0.4	0.4
Iron	-	-	80.00	80.00
Manganese	-	-	100.00	100.00
Zinc	-	-	50.00	50.00
Selenium	-	-	-	-
Vitamin (IU/kg)				
Vitamin-A	-	-	2000.00	6000.00
Vitamin-D_3	220.00	300.00	600.00	800.00
Vitamin-E	-	-	25.00	25.00
Vitamin (mg/kg)				
Vitamin-K	-	-	1.3	1.3
Thiamin	-	-	3.00	2.00
Riboflavin	4.00	4.00	4.00	4.00
Nicotinic acid	55.00	25.00	28.00	28.00
Pantothenic acid	11.00	11.00	10.00	10.00
Pyridoxine	2.6	2.5	2.5	5.00
Biotine	-	-	-	0.2
Folic acid	-	-	-	0.5
Vitamin B_{12}	-	-	-	0.01
Choline	-	-	1800.00	1100.00

Source : Srivastava and Panda, Farmers' Journal, September, 1982, ARC : Agricultural Research Council, PRC : Poultry Research Centre, Edinburgh, NRC : National Research Council.

Table 10.7. Duck starter and grower rations.

Ingredients (Kg/100 Kg)	Starter (0-2 Weeks)			Grower (3-8 weeks)		
	1	2	3	1	2	3
Maize	32.00	43.00	32.34	31.70	45.00	30.32
Sorghum	11.00	-	15.00	17.00	-	25.00
Rice Polish	16.90	20.00	20.00	17.00	20.00	20.00
Rice bran	-	-	-	-	-	-
Wheat bran	-	5.00	-	-	9.00	-
Salseed meal (deoiled)	5.00	-	-	5.00	-	-
Groundnut cake (40% Pro)	11.00	-	10.00	9.00	-	6.00
Sunflower cake (40% Pro)	11.00	7.00	-	9.00	5.00	-
Mustard cake (40% pro) (Solvent extracted)	-	7.00	-	-	5.00	-
Maize glutenmeal (50% pro)	-	7.00	-	-	5.00	-
Sesame Cake (40% pro)	-	-	10.00	-	-	6.00
Fish meal (43% Pro.)	12.00	10.00	7.00	10.00	10.00	6.00
Meat meal (56% Pro)	-	-	5.00	-	-	6.00
Bone meal	0.70	0.50	0.40	0.90	0.60	0.50
Salt	0.24	0.25	-	0.24	0.24	-
Choline Chloride	0.50	0.02	0.50	0.05	0.05	0.007
Minerals + Vitamins	0.11	0.11	0.11	0.11	0.11	0.11
Total	**100.00**	**100.00**	**100.00**	**100.00**	**100.00**	**100.00**

NB. : If good quality fish meal is available, the quantity of fish meal can be reduced. Mineral mixture (Per 100 Kg diet) : Ferrous Sulphate : 20 gm. Manganese sulphate : 50 gm, Zinc sulphate : 25 gm, Copper sulphate : 1.5 gm and Potassium iodate : 100 mg., Vitamin mixture (per 100 kg diet) : Vitamin A: 800,000 IU, Vitamin D_3 : 1000,000 ICU, Riboflavin : 400 mg, Folic acid : 100 mg and Niacin : 5 gm. Pro : Protein.

Source : Srivastava and Panda, Farmers 'Journal, September, 1982.

Table 10.8. Suggested Practical level of nutrients in feed for ducks

	Starter (0-2 week)	Grower (3-8 week)	Grower (9-20 week)	Layer	Breeder
Metabolizable :					
energy (K cal/kg)	2750.00	2750.00	2700.00	2650.00	2650.00
Protein (%)	20.00	18.00	15.00	18.00	18.00
Mineals :					
Calcium (%)	0.80	0.80	0.80	2.5	2.5
Phosphorus (%)	0.45	0.45	0.45	0.45	0.45
Sodium (%)	0.15	0.15	0.15	0.15	0.15
Copper (mg/kg)	100.00	100.00	100.00	100.00	100.00
Zinc (mg./kg.)	60.00	60.00	60.00	60.00	60.00
Vitamins :					
Biotiin (mg./kg.)	0.1	0.1	0.1	0.1	0.1
Choline (mg./kg.)	1800.00	1800.00	1100.00	1100.00	1100.00
Folic acid (mg./kg.)	1.00	1.00	1.00	1.00	1.00
Niacin (mg./kg.)	60.00	60.00	60.00	60.00	60.00
Pantothenic acid mg./kg.)	15.00	15.00	15.00	15.00	15.00
Pyridoxine (mg./kg.)	6.00	6.00	6.00	6.00	9.00
Riboflavin (mg./kg.)	5.00	5.00	5.00	5.00	8.00
Thiamine (mg./kg.)	4.00	4.00	4.00	2.00	2.00
Vitamin-A (IU/kg)	4000.00	4000.00	4000.00	6000.00	8000.00
Vitamin-B_{12} (mg./kg.)	0.01	0.01	0.01	0.01	0.01
Vitamin-D_3 (mg./kg.)	600.00	600.00	600.00	1000.00	1000.00
Vitamin-E (mg./kg.)	20.00	20.00	20.00	20.00	20.00
Vitamin-K (mg./kg.)	2.00	2.00	2.00	2.00	2.00

Source : Srivastava and panda, Farmers' Journal, Sepember, 1832.

Table 10.9. Duck grower and layer rations

Ingredients	Grower (9-20 weeks or upto point of lay)			Layer and breeder (From point of lay)		
	1	2	3	1	2	3
Maize	33.69	-	62.00	31.89	47.00	35.82
Sorghum	-	44.70	-	-	10.40	-
Rice polish	40.00	40.00	-	35.00	-	30.00
Wheat bran	10.00	-	9.60	-	-	5.00
Rice bran	-	-	10.00	-	8.00	-
Groundnut Cake (40% Pro)	-	8.00	-	-	11.00	-
Sunflower cake (37% Pro)	5.00	-	-	11.50	11.00	
Mustard oil cake (40% Pro.) (Solvent extracted)	5.00	-	-	11.50	-	-
Maize gluten meal (50% Pro)	-	-	-	-	-	8.00
Sesame cake (40%)	-	-	9.00	-	-	8.00
Fish meal (43% Pro)	5.00	6.00	8.00	4.00	-	8.00
Meat meal	-	-	-	-	6.00	-
Bone meal	0.70	1.00	1.00	0.75	1.30	0.75
Salt	0.20	0.19	0.29	0.29	0.05	0.22
Limestone	0.30	-	-	5.00	5.10	4.10
Minerals + Vitamins	0.11	0.11	0.11	0.11	0.11	0.11
Total :	**100.00**	**100.00**	**100.00**	**100.00**	**100.00**	**100.00**

NB : If good quality fish meat is available, the quantity of fish meal be reduced.

Minerals mixture (per 100 kg diet) : Ferrous sulphate 20 gm. Manganese sulphate : 40 gm, Copper sulphate 1.50 gm and Potassium iodate : 100 mg. Pro : Protein.

Vitamin mixture (per 100 kg diet) : Vitamin-A , 800,000 IU, Vitamin D_3 : 100,000 ICU, Riboflavin : 400 mg, Folic acid : 100 mg and Niacin : 5 gm.

Source : Srivastava and Panda, Farmers; Journal September, 1982.

INCUBATION AND HATCHING

The ducks, in general, lay eggs early in the morning. As stated earlier, duck lay more than 95 percent of their egg before 9 a.m. They lays their eggs here and there. So the loss of eggs is possible. They should be kept confined in the house until at least 9 a.m. to avoid the loss of eggs. The eggs production depend on the weather, breed and management practices.

Ducks sometimes stop laying eggs for a certain period for some reasons. The duck do not lay eggs regularly due to any kind of illness, Ducks that lay egg are naturally nervous. They become nervous as a result of a little exicitement and disgust and for that reasons they stop laying eggs. So such ducks should be kept in such a place where there is not the slightest possibility of being affraid of any thing. If their shelters are equipped with straw and grasses, and if they like such shelter, that is to say, if they are kept with comfort and care, they lay eggs daily in the same place. They should be handled in such a calm and cautious manner so that they are never to be afraid. They should not be driven away by showing fear. If it is necesary to catch them at a certain time, they should be driven in the shelter very slowly and cautiously and there they ought to be caught in the aforesaid manner.

HATCHING EGGS

Hatching eggs should be fresh, clean and not more than six days of their being laid. The hatching eggs should be stored for longer time before setting them in the incubatior. The duck's egg tend to dry out more quickly as the shell of duck egg have much larger pores than the hen's egg. The duck should be provided nest boxes at about one month before the ducks are expected to start laying. They become habituated to lay their eggs in the nest boxes. The hatching eggs stored above 20°C, the little embryo starts to develop and the eggs are subjected to spoiling. The male (drake) and female (duck) ratio at 1 : 7 is good for producing fertile egg. The duck may lay egg without mating with the drake. But in this case, the eggs laid by the ducks are infertile.

METHOD OF HATCHING

(a) **Natural hatching :** The birds generally hatch their eggs by providing their body temperature. But most of duck breed are not broody. Muscovy duck can be employed for hatching egg as they are broody. The broody hens are generally used for hatching duck eggs. The broody hen can hatch 6-7 duck's egg. Like hen's egg, the duck egg should be placed in a nest.

(b) **Artifical hatching :** Like hen eggs, artifical hatching of duck eggs is done in the incubator. The flat type and cabinet type incubator are generally employed for hatching duk eggs. The duck eggs are placed in the incubator with round end uppermost and they need cooling daily for a short period with exception of first three days.

This can be done by either taking the tray outside the incubator or spraying the eggs with luke warm water. Out of these, the latter method is preferable. A dutchman scientist, Dr. R.S. Kaltofen, observed that the duck eggs which were sprayed daily from the third day onward produced on an average six percent more duckling than eggs which were sprayed only once per week.

BROODING

(a) **Natural brooding :** Natural brooding is done with the help of a broody hen or duck. A large hen can brood 12-18 ducklings. The duckling should be protected from wild birds. After two to three weeks, no further mothering is necessary.

(b) **Artifical brooding :** Like chicks, the ducklings are also brood in the brooder at the age of 3-4 weeks in case of Khaki campbell and 2-3 week in case of Peckin. The temperature of the brooder is maintained at 29°C to 32°C during the first week and thereafter it is rreduced by about 3°C per week till it reaches 24°C during the fourth week. The space required for first to eight weeks of age is given below :

Age in weeks.	Floor space (sq. ft/bird)	Sq.m/bird.
1 - 2	1.0	0.09
2 - 3	1.5	0.13
3 - 4	2.0	0.19
4 - 5	2.5	0.23
6 - 6	4.0	0.37

COMMON DUCK DISEASES

Duck Plague

Duck plague is a virus disease and is caused by herpes virus. It is also known as duck virus enteritis. Duck of all ages are affected by this disease and it can cause 80-90 percent mortality. The disease affected birds may die without showing any symptom.

Symptoms

(i) Listless with drooping wings, ruffled and dull feathers.

(ii) Laboured breathing, nasal discharge with dry nostrils.
(iii) Loss of appetite but increase thirst.
(iv) Swollen and moist eyes with sticky discharge.
(v) Watery greenish yellow diarrhoea, sometimes mixed with blood.
(vi) Swollen and protruting penis in males.
(vii) Drop in egg production in females.

Control Measures

(i) The birds are vaccinated with duck plague vaccine at 2 weeks, 10 weeks and 24 weeks of age as a preventive measures. The birds are to be vaccinated thereafter every six months
(ii) The affected birds should be isolated from healthy birds.

DUCK CHOLERA

Duck cholera is a bacterial disease and is caused by *Pasterella multocida*. The ducks over four weeks of age are generally affected by this disease. The affected birds may die without showing any symptom.

Symptoms

(i) Loss of appetite along with increased thirst.
(ii) High body temperature, ruffled feathers and mucous discharge from mouth.
(iii) Diarrhoea with muscoid droppings followed by light greenish droopings.

Control Measures

(i) Sulphonamides and antibiotics are effective in controlling the disease and reducing mortality. They can be used either in feed or in water.
(ii) The birds should be vaccinated with duck cholera vaccine at least twice, fiirst at the age of two to three months and second in one to two months later as preventive measures.
(iii) The carcas should be destroyed carefuly.

PARATYPHOID

The ducks in big farms are affected by this disease which is caused by *Salmonella sp.* Infected feed and direct contact etc. is the main agent of transmission of this disease.

Symptom

(i) Duckling huddle together under the source of heat.

(ii) Drooping of wings and ruffled feathers.

(iii) Watery diarrhoea along with increased thirst.

(iv) The affected birds loss body weight rapidly.

Control Measures

(i) Furazolidone is used for controlling this disease.

(ii) Hygenic management is very effective for the prevention of this disease.

BOTULISM (LIMBER NECK OR WESTERN DUCK SICKNESS)

It is a intoxication problem of ducks and young and adult ducks suffer from this problem. Fowl may also suffer in this problem. It is caused by the toxin liberated by the bacteria, *Clostridium botulinum*. This bacteria grows in decaying plants and animal materials.

Symptoms

(i) The manifestation of illness depends on the amount of toxin absorbed by birds.

(ii) Dullnes, weakness and incoordination of movement.

(iii) Birds lose control of their neck and head muscles and usually drooping of head downward may occur.

(iv) Drooping wings, ruffled feathers and lameness due to motor paralysis.

(v) Laboured breathing, coma and death.

Control Measures

(i) The birds can be saved by providing fresh and clean water, if the dose of toxin is low.

(ii) Hygienic management is beneficial for controlling the outbreak of this problem.

(iii) C-type antitoxin, if available, may be used for the treatment of sick birds.

VIRUS HEPATITIS

It is a virus disease. Ducklings under five weeks of age are only affected by this disease. The feeds contaminated with droopings of infected birds act as a carrier of this disease.

Symptoms

(i) Dullness, depression and ruffled feathers.

(ii) The affected birds stop eating.

(iii) The affected birds sometimes fall on the sides with head drawn back and paddle spasmodically with their feet.

Control Measures

(i) Administration of Duck virus antiserum intermuscularly @ 0.5 ml per affected bird is helpful for reducing the mortality in the birds.

(ii) Sanitation of the house and premises is beneficial to control of this disease.

11

QUAILS

Quails are the newly introduced species in poultry industry. Japanese quails *(Corturnix corturnix japonica)* are widely distributed in Europe, Africa and Asia where they are regarded as migratory species. They were first raised as pets or singing birds, but they are widely used for meat and egg production, in Japan by 1900.

The quails are classified as follows :

Phylum	:	Chordata
Sub-Phylum	:	Vertebra
Class	:	Aves
Order	:	Calliformes
Family	:	Phasianidae
Genus	:	Corturnix
Species	:	Cortunix
Sub-Species	:	Japonica

CHARACTERISTICS OF QUAILS

(i) Quails are hardy and it can adopt varied environments with reasonable limits.

(ii) They are fast growing birds and mature in about six weeks. The live weight of mature bird is as follows :

Male quail : 120 - 150 gms.

Female quail : 150 - 180 gms.

(iii) They produces high rate of egg. The quail hens lay 260 eggs in their first year of lay. They are prolific layers.

(iv) They are very early in sexual maturity and they are able to produce three to four generation per year.

(v) Quails are fairly resistant to common avian diseases.

(vi) Quails need comparatively less floor, feeder and waterer space in comparision to chickens and ducks.

(vii) The quail hens are usually in full egg production by about 50 days of age. They lay 75 percent of their egg between 3 p.m. and 5 p.m. and 25 percent at night.

(viii) The incubation period is only 17-18 days.

Followings are the important varieties of quails :

(i) Briitish range
(ii) Pharach (Wild type)
(iii) English white
(iv) Tuxedo
(v) Manchurian golden

REPRODUCTION

Domesticated quails reproduce throughout the year when they attain their age between 10 to 20 weeks. One male should mate one to three females for production of fertile eggs. The eggs should be collected for hatching four days after the introduction of males to females. The quail egg are thin shelled and break easily. So special care should be taken during collection and handling of hatching eggs. The average weight of quails egg is about 10 grams. The hatching egg should be stored at a temperature of 15.5°C at 80 percent relative humidity after fumigation them with formaldehyde gas for about 20 minutes. The eggs are hatched naturally under hen or artifically in incubator. The incubator used for chicken may also be used for the incubation of quails egg. But the setting trays need to be modified for holding the small sized egg of quail. The egg should be placed with larger ends up in setting trays. The temperature should be maintained at 37°C along with 60 percent relative humadity upto 14th days of incubation. The eggs should be turned once for every 2-4 hours. Egg can be transfered to hatching trays on the 14th day or earlier. The chicks are removed from incubator to brooder on the 18th days of incubation.

Quails are comparatively more delicate than chickens and need better care during the first two weeks of their life. Thereafter they become hardier. Both battery and floor system of broodig and rearing can be employed with satisfactory result. But the battery brooding upto three weeks of age gives better result than floor brooding due to small size of the chickens. The brooding temperature should be adjusted as per the behaviour of the chicks.

HOUSING AND EQUIPMENT

A small pair cage measuring 12.5 x 20.0 cm is suitable for commercial egg and meat production. 1.25 cm welded wire mesh is recommended for the construction of cage or pen.

The cage should be provided with feeder and waterer. The feeder and water space requirement during the brooding period are 2-3 cm and 1-1.5 cm respectively. The adult quail will need 2.5 cm of feeder space.

Males and females should be separated as soon as possible and grown separately. The female should be housed in laying quarters around six weeks of age. Continuous lighting is necessary for first 48 hours.

Feeding

Quails need sufficient amount of balanced food. The diet should have higher nutrient level. Quails can be classified as starter (0-3 weeks), grower (4-5 weeks) and layer or breeder (6 weeks onwards) depending upon their growth rate and reproduction and accordingly they should be provided food. The starter period is the most crucial period and needs special management and feeding care.

Table 11.1. Ration for japanese quail

Ingredients	Starting and growing quails			Breeding quails		
	1	2	3	1	2	3
Maize	34.00	34.80	45.70	30.00	47.90	46.25
Rice polishing	10.00	10.00	-	20.00	-	-
Rice bran	-	-	-	-	-	8.00
Wheat bran	-	-	-	-	5.00	-
Groundnut cake (43% protein)	32.00	27.00	20.00	26.00	23.00	21.00
Mustard oil cake (40 % protein)	10.00	-	10.00	10.00	-	-
Solvent extracted Maize gluten meal 950% protein)	-	-	10.00	-	10.100	10.00
Sunflower cake (37 % protein)	-	15.00	-	-	-	-
Fish meal	13.00	6.00	13.00	6.00	6.00	-
Meat meal (56% protein)	-	6.00	-	-	-	6.00
Bone meal	0.30	0.38	0.60	1.00	1.90	1.50

(Contd.)

Ingredients	Starting and growing quails			Breeding quails		
	1	2	3	1	2	3
Lime stone	-	0.40	-	6.30	5.50	6.70
Salt	0.40	0.12	0.40	0.40	0.40	0.25
Minerals + Vitamins	0.20	0.30	0.30	0.30	0.30	0.30
Total	**100.00**	**100.00**	**100.00**	**100.00**	**100.00**	**100.00**

Table 11.2. Suggested practical level of nutrients in feed for Japanese quail.

Ingredients	Starter (0-3 weeks)	Grower (4-5 weeks)	Layer/ breeder/adult
Metabolizable energy (K cal/kg)	2,750	2,750	2,650
Protein (% diet)	27	24	22
Minerals :			
Calcium (% diet)	1	0.8	3
Phosphorus (% diet)	0.45	0.45	0.45
Sodium (% diet)	0.2	0.2	0.2
Copper (mg/kg diet)	8.0	8.0	8.0
Iodine (mg/kg diet)	0.6	0.6	0.6
Iron (mg/kg diet)	100	100	100
Manganese (mg/kg diet)	120	120	120
Zinc (mg/kg diet)	80	80	80
Vitamins :			
Vitamin-A (IU/kg diet)	10,000	10,000	10,000
Vitamin-D_3 (ICU/kg diet)	1,250	1,250	1,250
Vitamin-E (IU/kg diet)	50	50	50
Vitamin-K (mg/kg diet)	3	3	3
Vitamin-B_{12} (mg/kg diet)	0.005	0.005	0.005
Thiamiine (mg/kg diet)	4	4	4
Niacin (mg/kg diet)	6	6	6

(Contd.)

Ingredients	Starter (0-3 weeks)	Grower (4-5 weeks)	Layer/ breeder/adult
Pantothenic acid (mg/kg diet)	60	60	60
Pyridoxine (mg/kg diet)	6	6	6
Biotin (mg/kg diet)	0.2	0.2	0.2
Folic acid (mg/kg diet)	3,000	3,000	3,000
Amino acids :			
Arginine (% diet)	1.57	1.39	0.99
Glysine (% diet)	1.44	1.28	-
Histidine (% diet)	0.55	0.48	0.37
Isoleucine (% diet)	1.08	0.96	0.88
Leucine (% diet)	1.89	1.68	1.43
Lysine (% diet)	1.40	1.24	0.74
Methioninee + Cystine (% diet)	0.76	0.67	0.62
Phenylalanine + Tyrosine (% diet)	1.81	1.61	1.17
Threonine (% diet)	1.0	0.89	0.64
Trytophan (% diet)	0.27	0.24	0.18
Valine (% diet)	1.19	1.06	0.88

Source : Poultry Production (1989), by B. Panda and S.C. Mahapatra, Published by Indian Council of Agricultural research, New-Delhi-110012.

INDEX